The One Open Door

Adventures of a Zen Buddhist Monk

By D.J. McKay

Published by One Open Door Books
May, 2016
Djmckay429@gmail.com

ISBN: 978-0-9973644-1-5

Cover design by Philip McKay
Editing by Lisa Thompson and Anna Switzer

Contents

A NOTE TO THE READER

At the age of twenty-nine, on a glorious spring morning full of frogs and daffodils, I abandoned the life I had known up to that point, with all of its drama and suffering, and entered a Zen Buddhist monastery in California. Today I sit in a lawn chair beside an old pick-up truck, my temporary home and zendo, and gaze up at the snow-covered Colorado Rockies as I write. Eighteen years of silence lie in between.

For a long while I assumed I would never leave the monastery. It seemed that my destiny lay in the simple but profound life offered there, practicing peace and presence as over time I had learned to do. I wanted to remain, but a number of years ago a rumble began in my heart and mind that erupted finally last September, calling me to a new life back in the world. Now, to my astonishment, I find myself to be a middle-aged man with almost no worldly history and an opportunity to create myself anew against the frenetic backdrop of modern society. My hair, which was a rich brown when I began my life as a monk, is now grey, as is my beard. My body remains strong, but I feel its age. My heart is strong also, and I count this as my greatest gift: something happened to me during those years as a monk, something profound and beautiful, that I carry with me into my new life. I have nothing else to show than a sometimes clarity and compassion for all those years of practice, and yet this is everything to me. I spent my youth for it, and gladly. I learned how to live, and nothing could be more precious to me than that.

A number of years after I entered the monastery I began to write about my experiences there, partly as a way of processing them for myself and partly because of a desire to share the deep changes I witnessed as they were wrought upon my heart and mind. I wished to offer others the opportunity to make the same choice I had: to retreat from the world of ambition and power, greed and despair, and follow the practice of liberation that the Buddha taught so long ago. Few are called to be monks, to be sure, but all are called to relinquish suffering in whatever way is appropriate for them, it seems to me. It is possible to set aside the egocentric orientation to life that we are all trained to pursue and, through this labor, to join with the invisible author of all that we experience in a life of magic and joy--this was what I learned and what I wished to share. What follows is the result of my efforts. I wrote early in the morning for the most part, before daylight. Time and again I set the work aside and then picked it up months or even years later. I discarded mountains of words along the way. Finally the day came, some two years ago, as I prepared to leave the monastery, when I felt that it was finished.

I had hoped the book would receive the approval of my teacher, that it would be published by the monastery, and that it would serve the practice that I learned there. This was not to be. My transition away from the monastery was too full of angst and struggle to allow for the collaboration needed to make this happen—there just wasn't room for it—and so I departed in possession of the book but without the guidance I wished for in relation to its contents. This puts me in a delicate position. The book is undoubtedly full of misunderstandings that I am not aware of, statements and implications that do not accurately reflect the teachings I received or the teacher who passed them down to me. In addition, in numerous places I have put words into my teacher's mouth that are not her own. Without her approval I do not feel that I can ascribe those words to her or offer myself as an interpreter of her teachings. For some time I have waffled in the midst of this dilemma, and I've been often tempted to just put the thing away and leave it unpublished. Finally, though, I have decided that it needs to have its own life in the world. Whatever confusion this book contains, I still believe it may be helpful to those who are in need, like I once was, of deeper choices than the ones society typically prescribes. I have resolved, therefore, to accept the consequences of setting this book loose in the world, in the hopes that it will do at least some little good.

Much has happened since the day I finished the work in my little hermitage at the monastery. I am no longer a monk, and my short experience in the world since I departed has given me a new perspective on the ways monastic training has served my unfolding life. Even so, I have decided to publish these pages unchanged and undiluted, with one exception. In an effort to take full responsibility for the contents of this work and to remove that responsibility from my teacher, I have decided to refer to her in this book as "the Roshi" instead of using her name. "Roshi" is a title used in Zen monasteries in Japan to honor venerated masters. My teacher does not use this title herself, but it fits, and I hope it will capture the deep respect and admiration that I felt for her during our years together. This change is difficult for me because I owe her such a tremendous debt of gratitude. I love my teacher still and will always cherish the profound impact she has had upon my heart and mind. I wish for her to have credit for the life-altering gift she gave to me, and yet this step feels correct. I hope both she and the reader will understand.

The best way to approach this book, I believe, is as a work of fiction. The story it contains is based upon real events as I remember them, and I have done my best to portray them accurately, but it remains, at least in outward form, a mere story, recorded in solitude months or even years after the events occurred. There is nothing real in the detail, in other words, but I hope that this work, as with any good piece of fiction, will point to truths that are often hard to get at in a more direct way. It might be said that the characters who inhabit the following pages are creatures of my imagination. This includes the hero: that sometimes troubled, often confused, regularly ecstatic young man named "Dave". He possesses no reality of his own, as I have learned through much anguish over time, and yet there is something universal about his story that mirrors both the deep human longing for a true life that we all feel and the way open to each of us to find it. The story is also full of adventures, scrapes, and assorted pitfalls that I hope will entertain the reader along the way.

My wish as I sit here today is that this book will bring the reader even a tiny fraction of the joy, fun, and insight that it brought to me as I wrote it. Enjoy.

Glenwood Springs, Colorado.

April 11, 2015

Preface

First I heard the clicks and chirps of birds. Then I felt the cold air as it passed over my nostrils and the unfamiliar scratch of wool blankets against my face. I wondered sleepily as some strange creature howled in the distance. An insect crawled along my neck above the collar-bone.

Startled, I opened my eyes to the dawn as it cast shadows through the primitive structure that sheltered me. For a few groggy moments I could not recall how I had come to be there. I rolled over and stared in bewilderment at the bed beneath me, constructed of old, mismatched boards and a piece of foam; at the several pieces of old carpet, each one a different color, that made a patchwork on the floor; and at the wood-burning stove in the corner. I marveled at the unpainted plywood walls and the bare skeleton of the framing that held them up. Makeshift shelves were tacked here and there between the studs, holding dusty trinkets: a fragment of a mirror, a small basket full of paper cut into precise squares, an oil lamp, a tiny stone Buddha. Each one seemed a piece of some mystery I did not understand. Peering through the windows I saw, to my alarm, not the lush eastern forest I was accustomed to, but a desert picture of thirst and want.

Then I recalled the dark walk to this same cabin the evening before, the few simple words with which it was shown to me, and my gratitude at finding a place to rest at last. I recalled the life of turmoil and desperation I had left behind to travel to this place and the sweet eruption in my heart that had given me the courage to take that step. My life as I had known it now was gone, perhaps forever. I had just spent my first night on the grounds of a Zen Buddhist monastery. The day before, I remembered, I had become a monk.

For a long while I lay there as still as I could, attempting to absorb that news. "I'm a what?" I asked myself. Nothing could have seemed more strange or improbable. I had never wanted to become a monk or even imagined such a thing was possible before that fateful day just two months past when, filled with ecstasy and horror, I had renounced the life I was brought up to live and had committed myself to monastic training, come what may. "What in the world have I done?" I wondered.

I entered the monastery because my life stopped working—that's the bottom line. At some point, I think, it did work. Photos of the boy I once was suggest this, at any rate. I had freckles, a gigantic pile of curly hair, and no self-consciousness. I smiled in those old pictures with delight and enjoyment, perfectly engaged with the world I was born into. Even in the rare places where I frowned or cried a delightful innocence remained, promising that I would smile again as soon as whatever troubled me had passed. But as time went by and my body grew up, my mind and emotions did not, and somewhere along the way I lost my smile. How tragic that the happy adventurer I once was should have forgotten joy! Yet this is what occurred: I arrived at adulthood wearing a scowl, expecting little more from life than to survive it until death.

I always figured that I would live as others do, but somehow I never could. I tried with great determination to embrace the life my family and society offered me. I worked to learn what it seemed I must and to forget what I knew before; I cheered mightily for the passing show and flattered those who constructed it; I chased girls to the best of my ability; I dreamed about becoming something great and important—I followed every precept I was taught, in fact, in order to live a life that was not mine, but I could not do it. There has always been a stubborn faith within me that will not settle for less than my true life. This faith finally destroyed the false life I tried to live and left me with little more than the hope that there existed some alternative.

Now, outwardly you could not have perceived this of me because I hid my unhappiness from the world. Even I did not see it, as I concealed it just as effectively from myself. Under the pretense, however, I despaired. The spark of life that had animated that freckled boy never completely perished—if it had, then I would not have this story to tell—but most of the hope I once enjoyed had evaporated by the time I became, in the world's estimation, though not in actuality, a man.

If things had continued along this same course, disappointment would have eventually extinguished all hope. I would have yielded to the deception that said I could never be happy, and I would have settled for a living death. At some point I would have given up, but a miracle happened instead. Before my heart closed, my true life found me in a form I never would have anticipated. It came in the practice of awareness and self-acceptance as first taught by the Buddha ages ago. This practice completely swept me off my feet from the first moment I encountered it and carried me towards a way of life I could never have imagined before.

This world we live in must be just about the most beautiful and interesting place around. Everywhere else but in our little corner of it, as far as we can tell, the universe frowns upon life with spectacular hostility, but here life bursts forth from nearly every inch of ground. Even where it does not the potential exists, needing only a bit of water to call it up. No matter where you turn your eyes, to the widest mountain expanses or the tiniest patch of earth, the view will take your breath away.

All of the critters and all of the plants that inhabit this world with us seem to get that on some level. They all seem to cooperate with great enthusiasm no matter their part in the amazing scheme of things. They run and fly and swim and crawl with astounding energy, and they eat their food with gusto no matter how disgusting it may be. All of the critters and all of the plants participate in life with an identical willingness to fully live—all of them, that is, except for us. What an astonishing fact! We seem to have a special arrangement as human beings that, along with our intelligence, we possess the unique capacity to feel misery amid the splendor that exists all around us.

How do we do that? How do we suffer in a world of such abundant grace? How do we manage to separate ourselves from our intrinsic contented nature and experience misery and dissatisfaction instead?

This is the riddle the Buddha solved more than two thousand years ago. Since his day innumerable people have devoted their lives to the understanding that the Buddha realized and taught: through the practice of awareness, presence, and compassion, we may live in each moment with the peace and joy we were born with. The dedication of these people is the inheritance of anyone who wishes to take the same journey.

First thing every morning the monks gather to practice formal sitting meditation. In the winter two oil lamps, one at each end of the meditation hall, guide us to our places; in the summer we find our way by the faint light of dawn. As we enter the hall we bow to express our willingness to end suffering; likewise, we bow as we choose our places, and then once more as we sit down on our cushions and spin to face the wall. When the time comes to begin the room is silent and still. It is a wonderful thing to see the monks as they sit, facing the blank wall, facing the deep mystery of their lives, by the first light of day. The rattling of beads can be heard as the monks finger their rosaries. A bell rings, we all bow once more, and then the guide for the day leads us in our morning recitation.

In unison the voices of the monks rise as we vow to end suffering and to travel along the spiritual pathway that the Buddha established to accomplish this. At its most basic level, the life of a monk consists of the commitment to follow this vow in every moment of every day. This is what we are all here to practice.

I do not often leave the monastery grounds, but when I do I notice that frequently people have never met someone who calls himself a monk. They wonder what that means. It's a lot like eating an artichoke, I tell them: if you have never had one (as I had not, myself, until I came to California), words will not assist you much. If people persist, as they rarely do, I tell them this: monks are men and women who have seen that it is possible to awaken to their natural joy and who have the willingness and courage to give themselves completely to that opportunity. A monk has glimpsed the treasure that lies in the shifting sands of every human life, beneath the ocean of illusion and self-deception that covers it over, and has traded wandering here and there upon the surface to dive beneath the waves in search of it.

A monk pays attention. That is our sole intention: to attend in every moment to the life that moves in and around us. Everything about the structure of the monastery is designed to assist with this. We live in silence, speaking only when it is essential, and we avoid making eye contact with each other. We do not read or listen to music or talk on the phone or shop or anything else that would draw our attention away from the process of life occurring within us. In addition, we make almost no decisions for ourselves: in choosing to train monastically all of us have committed to accept the authority of the monastery in all aspects of our lives. We eat what is set before us, we do what we are asked to do, and we open our minds as we are able in every moment to the guidance of our teacher and to the practice of spiritual awakening that she offers. We enjoy little of what the world calls "freedom." For example, I never leave the property past where my legs will carry me unless I am asked to do so. Now, I will admit that on many a Sunday afternoon, when there are some few hours given to us for leisure, those legs have taken me many, many miles away before I have been forced by darkness to turn back—but I always do turn back. As monks we eat, we sleep, we work, we meditate—and we receive life, we let go of unhappiness and sorrow, and we accept ourselves with unconditional love and compassion to the best of our ability in every moment.

Why would someone choose such a bizarre and difficult life? This is what most people do not understand. Is life as bad as

13

that? How does one go, as all of the monks have done, from being a regular person, basing one's choices upon the thoughts and feelings one was socialized to have, to being someone who vows to go beyond those same thoughts and feelings? How does one make that choice?

I became a monk when at last my sorrow grew too painful to ignore. I was fortunate in this, because without that pain I never would have done it. All of us who train as monks have made the same discovery, that somehow along our human way we forfeited the lives that we were born to live. We have seen that joy is denied us by something which most of the time we cannot see or understand; we have glimpsed the possibility that we may see through that something, and may reclaim and enjoy the beautiful and perfect life that we have lost.

When I first entered the monastery this explanation satisfied everyone except those who loved me most. "But why you?" they wanted to know, even those who could sympathize with the draw to an examined life. How could I explain to them the awesome necessity of that choice, when I understood it so little myself? All I knew was that somewhere between my heart and my belly there was an awful, aching cavity where once my youthful joy had been. I had attempted to fill that hole with everything within my famished reach—with food, with sex and other sorts of pleasure, with ambition, with human love—but nothing worked. I can see now that I might have swallowed the entire world and still that hole would have remained empty, longing to be filled. What I sensed instinctively but could never have expressed is that the only power large enough to heal that ache was my own love for myself. And, somehow, I knew that I must abandon the empty life that I had wearily pursued to find that love.

"Because I'm not happy...." I tried to explain.

"So what?" they objected. "But why go to a monastery? Why not just go to the movies?"

I could only shrug in reply. There was something much larger than the dread of my own misery that called me to monastic practice—after all, I could easily (though painfully) have simply avoided the experience of my unhappiness, surviving my life until I died, like many do—but I could not name what it was. Something within me called me to be awake, and when that something spoke, I knew I had no choice.

I did not know that I was setting out upon the most breath-taking adventure possible for a human being. I had always been a gutsy sort of fellow, and my days had been filled with thrills and spills of every kind, but there was no real adventure in it. I had experienced only the mock intensity of an outwardly focused life. Just at the time when I exhausted the power of external things to stir my heart, even the mountain creeks and serene desert canyons that had consoled me in my discontent, I discovered spiritual practice and began to experience the much more profound adventure that awaited me within myself. Slowly, I began to turn inward. Over time I began to sense the tremendous freedom existing within my own heart and mind and the tender invitation that accompanies it. This growing awareness carried me ultimately from the life in the world that I endured to this little cabin so far away from all I had known before.

As I wondered at all this that first morning, the deep bell rang that summons the monks to meditation. It was the first time I heard it, and its solemnity both thrilled and appalled me, as it does even now. Having no other option but to obey, I got up, dressed, and found my way to the meditation hall. Then, in perfect silence with the other monks, and all alone with myself, I sat down cross-legged on a black cushion. When a softer bell rang to begin meditation, I bowed with the others, folded my hands in my lap and sat perfectly still, filled my lungs with air and emptied them again, and attempted to embrace the strange twist in the plot of my life that had placed me there in that moment, far from everything I had known before.

For a long time afterwards the wonderful and bizarre circumstances of my new life continued to astound me. I traveled through each day of monastic training as if it were a dream, working and meditating and receiving the teachings as if I lived by accident someone else's life and might at any moment wake up and resume the life my early training had prescribed for me. So far this has yet to happen. In fact, I have grown so accustomed to the life of a monk that the life I led before, with all of my expectations from that time, now appears to be the dream. Though that former life seemed to be without sense or significance as I passed through it, looking back now over all that has occurred, and understanding the opportunity I might have missed, I see the thread of intelligence and necessity that has carried me on from the very beginning towards my peculiar destiny. There is a kindliness in all that has come before this moment that moves a spirit of awe within me. This is my life.

The days became weeks, then months, then finally years, and now I find myself, with perhaps as much astonishment as I felt on that first morning, having sat down to write about the sometimes strange, sometimes wonderful adventure that my life has been, and to share what I have learned along the way.

One morning some months ago I left my hermitage before dawn, as I frequently do, to watch the world come to life outside. The monastery sits on a ridge overlooking a broad canyon; far below the main compound, at about a twenty minutes' walk, a lively creek winds its way along the valley floor through oak and maple and buckeye trees and beside sloping pastureland. Above all things I love to watch the day dawn beside the waters of that stream, or, when the days are too short to permit it, to sneak down in the darkness to study the moon and stars in its black pools. That morning, as usual, the deep tones of the monastery bell drifted all the way down to my ears, where I watched an ancient oak catch the first light of day.

As the day brightened a deep feeling of gratitude awoke within my heart for all that has been given me: for the energy that animates my body, heart, and mind; for the rich life I have; for the path of discovery I follow and the practice that gives me this life, which I would not otherwise possess. I suddenly perceived myself as if from a great distance, through the eyes of the unfathomable love that I feel holding me day by day, despite my stumbling efforts, and I was moved by the magnitude of my transformation these past years. Until I found this path and began to experience the possibility it awoke within me, nothing that was mine by right to enjoy—like the earliest light in the branches of that tree, or the sound of that bell—was mine. I had given them all away for my unhappiness. Now, oftentimes, I live the alternative. I understand the miracle of my existence and the profound spirit that animates me, and I know that I am a most fortunate human being.

My former sorrow still lives on, and yet, when I am able, I count even this among my blessings. I continue to suffer, but this suffering is the doorway to all the varieties of my human experience, to the loving kindness that I need, and to the clarity within me which can provide it. This is the work, it seems, that is mine to do: to become, as fully as I am able, the compassion I am searching for. I suspect that this is the work of my entire life; and so I go on, following the life that is mine to live with as much courage as I can muster and with a deep feeling of gratitude for this opportunity.

That morning beside the creek a wish arose that I might return something of what I have received to Life. Later that day, as I labored my way through the hours of the monastery afternoon, it occurred to me that I might write my story as a way of offering the gift of spiritual practice to others, as it was once offered to me. Just then a breeze sprang up from the depths of the canyon below; all around new spring leaves danced on the trees, the grasses bowed, and my heart sang a little joyful tune. The wind said to me that it is time to go adventuring once again, but this time not as in days gone by, with a hunger in my belly and a frown upon my face, but rather with a heart full of gladness and a happy gift to give. Today I set out in pursuit of that possibility.

In this I am most indebted to my teacher. Her own deep practice of the path of awakening has offered it to me, and this book is an expression of my gratitude. I have received so much;

even this opportunity to give is her gift to me, as my time as a monk is not my own. I would never have attempted it without her encouragement. I write with the very intention she taught me, and which she models so fearlessly for all who know her—the same intention that as monks we bring to all things, whether it be the nails we pound, the laundry we hang, or the dishes we wash—that in the doing of it I might discover how I cause myself to suffer, and let that go and end suffering. I hope my fellow monks will feel my appreciation, too, because their work supports me as I work. You are a most inspiring gang of folks, you monks, and I love you all.

Naturally, what follows will be full of my teacher and her teachings, simply because I am full of my teacher and her teachings, as I hope always to be. It should be made clear, however, that what I offer here is only my own experience. In many places in the following pages I will put words into the Roshi's mouth. I wish the reader to understand that, although they arise from memories of conversations that happened long ago, these are my words ultimately, not hers. This book is not intended as an authoritative presentation of the teachings, or even a part of them; it will merely be the story of their profound impact upon my life.

To the extent that it lies within the power of my words, I wish to give the same gift that was given me. The teachings I received reach through the Roshi to her teacher, and through him to his teacher, and so on through all of the thousands of beautiful human lives that have carried the enlightenment of the Buddha to this blessed day. My hope is that this work may reflect the power of the practice that has saved my life and the happiness available to those who follow it. I dedicate this effort to all those who have come before me and have carried the way of liberation through their lives to the present day. I wish for everyone to have the opportunity of that same choice.

Every evening when the day's work is done the monks gather once again in the hall to meditate. When the final bell rings we bow in unison, then file out into the open air. Another day of our communal effort ends, and I walk in blessed solitude back to my hermitage to sleep. In the summer as I go along I watch the daylight fade; in the winter the moon or the stars guide my way, but in every season I delight in the ancient oak trees, in the fields of green or brown grass, and in the shadows of the sun or moon. Some of these days I have resisted what Life offers to me. These are filled with hardship and pain. Other days I have let go, ceasing to clutch in fear at the movements of my heart and mind, and have fallen gracefully into my experience of myself, whatever that may have been. These are the days of ease, excitement, and awe. Either way, however, as I walk home to my hermitage, I feel the gratitude and contentment of my privileged life. This life is the one I am here to live; this practice that the Buddha taught has saved me, and I follow it with my whole heart. How could I not? It is the one open door to true happiness.

1

The Game Called "Life"

I remember one day when I was just a sprout, standing beneath the cherry tree behind my childhood home. I stared up through the leaves to the blue sky, wondering at how things are and if anything in the world moves without someone like me to cause it. I imagine I had experienced little beyond my own will before that day; likely, the thought of something larger than myself had never shown itself to me before. "Do we make it all happen?" I asked myself. Just then a breeze sprang up, the tree shook its branches cunningly at me, and I perceived the independence of the wind. In that moment my mind opened just a little to the infinity beyond human experience. It may have been my first glimpse of the mystery that inhabits this strange and wonderful world and my first step towards the life I am called to.

As I grew and as I traveled through my early years, I learned that whenever I chose I could simply look for this mystery within and beyond myself and find it. It was everywhere. I began to long for a way to understand the nature of the mystery and how it came to be. One day, much later, as I acted my part within the story of my life, I perceived that I do not even cause myself to happen—that I do not possess even my own life. There was no turning back after that. In order to negotiate the circumstances of my life at the time, however, I hid my love of the mystery from those around me, keeping it like a secret pleasure for the solitary hours that life offered. Over time as my body grew up and as the human world crushed my spirit into the little box it said was me, I gradually lost touch with the mystery in my daily experience. I never completely relinquished it inside, however. Nor did it relinquish me, and so, though distracted by a chaos of worldly things, and though I doubt I ever named it to myself, as I followed my unhappy way I ever watched and waited for the mystery.

During my late teens I became interested in chess. I was a book wormy sort of a kid, so this didn't surprise anyone. Gradually, however, as my interest became an obsession, and as I began to spend hours alone every day in my room poring over a chessboard, the people around me began to express concern. They asked me the same question (essentially) that they did later, when I became a monk: "What are you doing in there?" Part of my motivation was to escape from self-consciousness, and another was to deal these same people an underhanded sort of revenge for their role in my unhappiness, but by far the greatest draw for me was the beauty of the game. I perceived something divine in it, as if the pieces arranged on the chessboard offered a glimpse into the dynamics that construct the manifest world that we live in. Chess is all about energy and movement; it mirrors in miniature, you might say, the way our amazing world comes to be in each moment. Everywhere else in my life at that time I endured disharmony, but there in the silence of my room, in the practice of that subtle game, I found the mystery again. I could not have said at that time that this was so, but so it was.

I set the chessboard aside when I found another game to replace it. After surviving my formal education I discovered books, and for some time afterwards I dedicated myself to the study of philosophy. Here was a much deeper game, one that included my own inspiration and the beauty I perceived inside and all around me. I gave up everything to play it. I abandoned the life I had at that time—I was working as a baker in a small town in North Carolina—and drove up into the Appalachian Mountains. There, to my inexpressible delight, I found a little shack way back in the woods and rented it for thirty-five dollars a month. It had a tin roof, a glorious front porch, a creek just outside the east windows, and an outhouse. I loved that little house more than words can say. Many of my favorite memories come from the time that I lived there. For two years I worked odd jobs for my country neighbors when I had to, hoarding my time and money so that I might be free to peer through the lens of philosophy Life and my experience of it. All day long I read old books, and I walked in solitude through the forests and beside the creeks around my home, dreaming of the beautiful hearts and minds of those who wrote so majestically.

For a good while I believed that philosophy would be the game of my life, but ultimately it failed to satisfy me. Philosophy could not take me beyond my own thinking, which is what I longed for, though I did not understand this at the time. I wanted so much from the words that I read: I wanted peace and security, and I wanted to enjoy the life that moved my body and my mind, but words could not give me those things. As time went by the hope I placed in books gradually flagged. I began to look to nature alone for inspiration and wisdom, spending more and more time in the forests and beside pools of clear water, where the patterns of what we call "reality" lie so close to the surface. I knew that the mystery was near: it seemed to me at moments that I could almost grasp it. And yet I could not, because I still remained somehow outside of the deep workings of my life, able to see hints of the mystery here and there but not to experience it as myself. Always wondering, always wanting, I sought it, but more and more the mystery eluded me, and over time I came to doubt that it was real. As I did I gradually grew weary of my life.

When my solitude finally became unbearable to me I began to understand that I would never find the way beyond unhappiness alone. I did not know how or where to find the help I needed, only that I needed it, and so I decided to gamble my little shack for the chance that somewhere in the world of humans I would find the peace that I was looking for. This inspiration terrified as much as it exhilarated me—I had lost the ability to be happy in my mountain home, but I felt safe there, in a way—and I put off the change as long as I could, but my deepening angst and isolation proved that if I continued to search without guidance I would ultimately fail. And so I worked until I had saved enough money to buy six or eight months of independence, then one glorious winter evening, as the sun went down and a gigantic orange moon rose over the dashboard, I set out on my own into an unknown world. I had no idea where I was going, and did not care. "West," I told people. It wasn't running away, at first: it was running towards. It was the mystery that called me: this is what filled that glorious first night of my manhood and many that followed with the magic that they had. For the first time in my life I felt free!

It happened to be February and painfully cold, so I headed south. Over the next three weeks I traveled through Georgia and Alabama, then towards the Gulf through Louisiana, camping along the way. I moved slowly, staying often for several days in one place. One evening just before dark I pulled into a tiny free campground beside a wilderness area in Mississippi called "Black Creek", as I recall. It felt magical to be so deep in the south and so far from the places of my origin. I hiked most of the next day along the creek, enjoying the black water, the white sands, and the gorgeous magnolias that grew wild in this place. While I walked I began to feel lonely, as was frequently the case in those times. Suddenly the thought arose that what I needed was a dog to keep me company. This had never occurred to me before. A human companion would present complications that I had neither the patience nor the money for, but a dog, I told myself, would take the edge off my loneliness without cramping my style.

As I emerged from the woods at the end of the hike and started across the gravel parking lot towards my truck, I was startled to see a little black and tan hound in the ditch beside the road, foraging in the garbage there. "There's one!" I said to myself. She was a cute little thing, though terribly thin, with floppy ears and a tuft of white fur at her throat like a neck-tie. She appeared to be still a pup and I could see from her obvious neglect that she had been abandoned there. I walked over to the edge of the road, getting as close as I could without frightening her, and put out my hand. With that she began to howl most hideously, the way only a hound can do. I stood up instantly and put my hands on my hips. "Oh, no—I don't think so," I said to myself, "That's too much." And so I turned away, drove back to the campground, and forgot about her for the rest of the evening.

The next morning I packed my things early, having decided that this would be the day I would finish the journey south to see the Gulf of Mexico for the first time. On the way out, to my surprise, I saw the same little dog about a quarter mile from the place I had met her the day before. She was attempting to find the inside of a discarded potato chip bag, her head down and her rear end up in the air. I slowed the truck to a crawl while I studied her, wondering at myself while I did it, and finally pulled over. I dug a piece of bread out of the back of the truck and carried it over to her to see what she would do. When I held it out she hesitated for a long time, her tail wagging furiously but too scared to step within my reach. I talked to her soothingly, telling her that I was a very nice person who liked dogs and had no evil designs upon her. When hunger finally overcame fear she wiggled over, took the bread from my hand, and wolfed it down in one gulp. I got out another piece and repeated the offer. She accepted more quickly this time and allowed me to gently pet her while she ate. "Who are you, little one?" I asked her. "Do you want to be my friend?" She wagged her whole body with this, as if to say that, yes, she would like that very much. I sat there beside the road with her for another fifteen minutes, trying to decide what to do. Finally I said, out loud, "Oh, what the hell!" then scooped her up, put her in the truck, and drove off.

I stopped at the first store I found to buy her some food. She ate until she was fat as a tick, then looked up to me with such an expression of gratitude that it moved me to tears. I returned to the store to buy a collar and a leash, then we jumped back into the truck and drove until we found a place to camp within sight of the Gulf. It was such a novel experience that evening to walk with my new companion, suddenly not alone and with another being to care for! I felt pleased but uncertain. That evening I made a bed for her out of a blanket and put it at the head of my sleeping bag. I tried to sleep but was unable—I could feel her shivering with the cold. Finally I said, "C'mere, sweetheart," and lifted the mouth of the bag to invite her in. She dove in at once, wriggled until she was all inside, then squirmed until she had managed to turn herself around and lay on my chest with her nose pointed out of the bag for air. This was the first of several thousands of bed-times spent in just that way, heart to heart and nose to nose. "You're going to need a name," I told her. I thought of a book on Greek mythology that I was reading at the time. "I think I will call you 'Rhea'," I said. "She is the Goddess of the Earth. What do you think of that?" She wiggled in assent. We were fast friends and constant companions from then on.

For a long while I imagined that Rhea was the lucky one that day: that I had rescued her from the life she would have had without me, rather than the other way around. As time passed, however, and as I witnessed the changes wrought within me by her devotion and her love; as I felt the unfamiliar stirrings of unconditional love within my own heart in return, I began to see her as my first recompense for the surrender that had set me upon my current journey. I did not know it at the time, but Rhea's presence in my life would eventually teach me how to care for something beyond my own ego, preparing me for the much larger surrender that would begin when I entered the monastery.

From Mississippi we drove west, across Texas and into the southwestern states. Many beautiful, happy days followed. I spent the mornings reading in a folding lawn chair, protected from the cold by a huge coat, two hats, and three layers of socks, with Rhea under a blanket in my lap. All afternoon the two of us roamed the deserts and mountains that we found along the way, while I peered through their beauty into the mystery, savoring the silence and solitude that made it palpable to me. In the evening I cooked my food over a camp stove and gazed at the stars until time for bed. It was an exquisite, precious time. Often I wondered if I had found a way to lasting happiness.

I could not run fast enough, however, to leave my sorrow behind. Eventually it caught up with me, and as it did, my new freedom waned, and the fear returned. I fought to escape desperation, camping in a multitude of solitary places and praying to the spirits there to save me, but the gladness I had felt slowly passed. The running towards became a running away; discontent and longing hunted me wherever I went, and the more I ran the closer misery followed upon my heels. At last it overtook me and I began to feel that I could run no more.

Then one day someone taught me how to meditate. She was a stranger; I knew her only for a day, and she likely never knew the tremendous gift she gave to me. One spring afternoon I camped in a canyon in New Mexico and found her there, that generous woman, sitting contentedly in the grass beneath a rock wall two thousand feet high. She was just sitting there, doing nothing. I sensed at once that she had what I needed. "What are you doing?" I asked her.

"Sit down, and I'll tell you," she said. I sat, and she showed me how to practice being still. She taught me how to observe the workings of my mind and to listen for the faint guidance of Life within me. In return I showed her my confusion and my wounded heart, and I told her about the mystery. "You only need to look inside, and you will find it again," she told me. She was right.

I forgot her name, but I never forgot what she gave to me. She introduced to me that day the greatest of all games, ten thousand times more subtle and intricate than those I had played before. It is a masterful accomplishment of creation, this game, requiring every bit of all we have even to see that it is there. It is a game that must be played from within it—this is what so compelled me. It is not confined to a table in a room or within the confines of language. This game encompasses all of existence: every thought, every feeling, every action, every sensation, every outward circumstance is a part of it. Nothing, I saw, stood outside this game: it is the game of Life. It is the one open door to everything that is possible. And I knew at once that I wanted to play

My life began anew the day I met that angel in New Mexico. As we sat together in the shade of sycamores, beside the chattering brook that followed the base of the cliff towering over our heads, for the first time in my life I tried to willfully direct my attention. I doubt I succeeded much, but even so the attempt made a deep impression upon me. For the first time I sensed within myself the power to make a true difference in my life. I remember thinking, "You mean there is something you can do?" When she and I parted I promised her I would continue to practice what she had taught me, and I kept this promise eagerly. Imagine my delight when I discovered that at any point I could just sit down, be quiet, and have a pretty good chance of feeling better. Before long I became devoted to this exercise, sometimes spending hours in the lawn chair beside my pick-up truck, just being still. Rhea was my teacher in this: I learned from her how to just be and watch the world kaleidoscope over and around itself as time passed by.

From New Mexico I continued west. For several more months I traveled on through the western deserts, along the Pacific coast, then back east towards North Carolina through Idaho, Montana, and the Plains. All the while I practiced on my own, wishing to discover the secret of awareness. I had little skill, of course, but this did not matter: I was doing something, and that was everything.

Eventually I made my way back to the Appalachians. I found a spot in one of the forests there where I might safely live out of the back of my pick-up truck, and I secured a bit of work that would buy me food. Then I settled down to wait for whatever would happen next.

I continued to read and walk as I had before, but often during the day I stopped for brief periods, as had become my habit—by the creek near my camping spot, under a tree, in the meadow on the mountain top, under the stars at night—to practice formal meditation as I understood it. I did this in secret, imagining that

I alone loved stillness and silence. Everyone else, after all, appeared to thrive in activity; even those who obviously suffered from unhappiness seemed to adore busyness and hate quiet. Soon, however, I discovered that there were those who not only openly practiced awareness, but gathered to practice it together. I learned that there was a meditation group that met on Monday evenings in the small community just down the road. I could not believe my good fortune.

The woman who had founded and who organized the group would soon become a great friend to me and one of the true loves of my life. Her name is "Janey". Janey was and is a beautiful, silver-haired woman with a spiritual practice several decades deep, a heart full of kindness, and a smile that made my day every time she shared it with me. I met her the next Monday evening at her home, an ancient log cabin at the top of a hollow she called "The Valley of the Moon." The group met in her spare bedroom. She welcomed me at the door, ushered me in, and explained how things worked, then left me to enjoy my first experience with a spiritual community. At the appointed time six of us meditated together in silence. Janey rang bells to begin and end the session. Afterwards, each person spoke in turn about their experience while Janey reflected and made comments. I loved it, and vowed to return the next week without fail. I did, and did not miss a week for the next several months.

Then one day Janey invited me to accompany her to a week-long, silent meditation retreat. I had never heard of such a thing. To my surprise, I went—and my experience there changed the course of my life forever.

2

The Illusion of Suffering

As I look around at the natural world, as I turn my gaze upon the world within my heart, and even as I peep into the world of human things, I see everywhere the beauty that inhabits the forms of what we call "reality". We each exist as an aspect of the breathtaking harmony that organizes all that we perceive. This morning, as I fed the monastery cats beside their shelter in the woods, I felt how much my heart feeds upon the order within what is, and how so little else seems to matter. The rain had just ended. The branches of the scrubby oaks all around dripped from their creases and bends; the wet leaves on the forest floor gleamed in the sudden sunlight; the cats munched contentedly, and all was well. No pleasure that I know, not even those considered by many to be the greatest treasures of life—the intoxication of power or success or sexual love—compares with this. What more, I wondered, could I possibly desire?

And yet, there is much within my mind that would pull me away from the experience of life's beauty. My heart loves a wet fluttering bird or a puffy cloud more than all the riches of the world—but not my mind. My mind prefers worry and fear over sunlight and shadow, and any urgent cause over the sound of the wind in the trees. What I wish for myself the most—to be truly alive in whatever strange and wonderful way that appears in this moment—often is not available to me even in my own mind. Not long ago it never was. My mind works incessantly to deny me what I most want. How could it be that my experience is not what I choose? This seems absurd: it's my mind, after all. But so it is.

This habit of the mind to leave what is here, in this moment, right now, and to live in an illusion that is not here, is what the Buddha called "dukkha", or "suffering".

I have a friend who lives in the mountains alone with several dogs and cats. In the evening, when her day's work is done, she sits still with her animals all around and just feels what she is feeling. Isn't that wonderful? After a lifetime of busyness, she told me, she has discovered that this, the experience of her feelings in her body, is what she wants most for herself. I imagine her there, silently feeling the life within her while the earth turns on its axis and races through space, while human drama plays itself out all around and just beyond the reach of her senses, and while her animals doze—just experiencing herself.

This is what most people cannot do. Few are able to be here, in the present moment. Most blindly follow the mind as it wanders through the past and dreams about the future; it is this habit that we call "suffering." Suffering is that which deprives us of our capacity to experience life as it is in the present. We suffer when we leave the moment and lose the natural clarity and ease that is our essence.

Within a mind that suffers, instead of life we experience our thoughts: our thoughts about our feelings, our thoughts about our perceptions, our thoughts about our thoughts—our thoughts about darned near everything. Our thinking isolates us from our experience; when we believe what we think, when we believe that our thoughts are our experience, then we live in a bubble full of meaning but without reality. Our gravest confusion is that our thoughts are who we are. Nothing could be further from the truth. In fact, our habit of thinking tranquilizes the vitality of our present-moment experience and will eventually put our lives to sleep if we do not take great care to prevent it. The importance of this care cannot be exaggerated, nor the tragedy of a life wasted on the clutter of the mind. If we lose ourselves in thought then we cannot be: we can only do, and we risk squandering our lives upon nothing.

In the days before I began the work of ending suffering I rarely doubted the reality of the world I experienced. As I have learned to attend to the operation of my mind, however, and as I have caught on to the ways in which my thoughts steal my life away, I have seen how little of the world I believed in had anything to do with what actually existed inside and outside of me. I lived a dream, believing it was real. This is how it is for all of us who suffer: to live in the world of thoughts is to live an illusion. Anyone who doubts this needs only to place a flower or a piece of fruit or any other object before their eyes and attempt to keep their attention fixed upon it for five minutes. The person who is able to accomplish this without finding himself or herself suddenly and repeatedly in some place far away (in a plan, in a fantasy, in the memory of something come and gone. . .) has either done a great deal of inner work or is an unusual and blessed human being. This is inexpressibly significant. Any time we are not present to and aware of what is around and inside of us, then we are not here—where we actually are. And if we are not here, where we are, then where in heaven's name might we be?

When they look inside, most people discover to their horror that the world they inhabit is filled with dissatisfaction, isolation, discontentedness, frustration, envy, despair, and every other form of misery. Astonishingly, until we look deeply at our inner workings we may not recognize that this is so. When we are not conscious of our present-moment experience—when we are "asleep"—we cannot see our unhappiness, and so we live within an illusion that the life we want is just around the corner, and that all we need to do to have it is to be who we should be, or get it right, or some such thing. In the meantime we ignore the life we have in favor of the dream we imagine is about to happen—and it never does.

Tragically, it is possible to spend an entire life this way. Imagine the sickening feeling of arriving at old age and only then realizing that the life you dreamed about all your days will never be yours. It will never be yours not because you are old, but

31

because it is not real—it is a fantasy. Imagine understanding too late that it never would have happened, no matter what you did, and that the life you actually lived was wasted on want and deprivation.

What we wish for most intimately is only to be here, in the moment, where we experience the joy of simply being alive. This is all we truly need, also, beyond physical necessities: just to be where we are. This is something no one can do without training, but that anyone can train themselves to do. Just as the Buddha did over two thousand years ago, we can train ourselves to become aware of what is here, now, inside and around us. We can train ourselves to live in the present moment, where we are, and where the life is that animates us.

Before I began to practice awareness I could see that I was miserable, but I did not understand what misery is or how it comes to be. Gradually, however, as I practiced looking inward, I began to discern the violence perpetrated upon me within my own mind. I began to perceive myself as the subject of my suffering, not the author of it. The relief that came with this insight was incredible. In addition, I began to see that the habit of my unhappiness had *no external cause*. I was not, as I had always believed, merely the victim of an unjust world. This realization placed an enormous puzzle before me: if the cause of my suffering is neither myself nor the outer circumstances of my life, then what, I wondered, could it be? Suddenly this became the most important question in the world.

I had always assumed that my suffering was a feeling. It shook me profoundly when I understood that everything I had done—every choice I had made, big and little, through my entire life—was done in an effort to control my feelings, and through this, to save myself from unhappiness. Every decision had as its fundamental motivation the desire to make me feel the way I wanted to feel and to avoid feeling the way I did not, with the expectation that whenever I accomplished this my suffering would end. But it never worked. It appeared to work or that it soon would work because I felt myself in a way that I enjoyed whenever I got what I wanted. But it never ultimately ended my discontent, because suffering is not a feeling. It is something much larger, but without this understanding I remained a prisoner of my own emotions and a victim of my circumstances.

Gradually, with the help of the teachings that fill the following pages, I came to see that our suffering is caused by an independent entity within our minds. This entity dominates our awareness, focusing our attention on the illusion it creates that we are somehow isolated from what simply is inside and around us. It puts us in one place and everything else in another, so that we relate to life as if it is ours, as if we own it, and can therefore make it what we will. A person trapped in suffering is lost in an imaginary world of preferences, deaf to the soft voice of guidance that Life constantly offers.

This entity insists there is something wrong all the time and that a parallel reality exists in which everything is as it should be. It also tortures us with what we do not have, and then persuades us that the cause of our dissatisfaction and unhappiness is ourselves. It creates an empty and false world in which lack and deprivation appear as the obvious reality, destroying our natural joy and wonder. Who we actually are is peace, gratitude, love, and everything else our hearts desire, but we do not experience this when our attention is dominated by the entity. Suffering is an illusion—we do not in reality live in separation from life—but we believe it to be real, and as long as we do then unhappiness results inevitably. People infected by the illusion live as ghosts of their possible selves, empty of the spirit that would give them their lives without it.

The suffering that lives within me is the same suffering that infects all people. It is one thing. The same entity that drives groups of people to slaughter each other over an idea also teaches a young child to punish herself for not being good enough. The forms it may take are infinite, but the process by which it asserts itself within each person is the same. All of us who suffer are afflicted by the same invisible cause.

At the monastery we use many names to describe this entity. My favorite is "Conditioned Mind," pointing to the conditioning process we each endured when we were children (more about that later). The Roshi likes to call this same thing "Egocentric, Karmic Conditioning," a name that suggests its vast egoistic assumptions and the unconscious patterns it uses to cause us misery. Sometimes we will call it "Ego," or "Egocentricity," or "Conditioning," or even just "I" for short or for variety.

The world is filled with unhappy people pretending to themselves and others that they are well but who are not well at all. And it need not be this way. Another alternative exists—this is what the Buddha taught. There is a way to go beyond suffering. There is a way to end our separation from who we are, and to reunite ourselves with the joy that we have lost. There is a way to come to life again. This way is the work called "spiritual practice."

3

When the Student is Ready, the Teacher Appears

One cold afternoon in January I met Janey in the Valley of the Moon and climbed into her car for the two-hour journey south to the retreat center. I can still recall the excitement that accompanied us that day. As we drove off I remembered the evening I had departed from my cabin in the woods almost a year before and all that had occurred since to bring me both to the opportunity of that winter day. The events of that evening and much that followed seemed magical to me, as if I had fallen by accident into a story that someone else, some kind person, had authored and I just lived. I had no idea what to expect from the experience that was about to come, but I anticipated more magic and something good.

Along the way it began to snow. At first this gave us little trouble, but before long the snow began to pour heavily down and stick to the road. Janey was forced to slow the car down to a crawl. We made it finally to the retreat center, but not until after the retreat had begun. The first meal was finishing. One of the monks staffing the retreat sat us down and put some soup and bread before us. "Eat quickly," she whispered, quietly. "Group will begin shortly in the meditation hall."

While we ate I listened to the quiet. It was remarkable to me: I had never experienced such deep silence before. Around us people bustled to and fro, cleaning up from the meal and other things, but the whole while we did not hear the sound of a human voice, just the clicks of silverware and the clatter of dishes, the swish of a broom on the wood floors, and the rustle of clothes as people strode purposefully by. I had expected the silence to feel strange to me, but it did not at all. I felt held and supported by the environment of the retreat in a way that I had not known I longed for.

As soon as Janey and I finished eating we hurried to the hall. What I saw from the doorway amazed me. Nearly forty people had arrived before us, as near as I could guess. Instead of seating themselves in rows facing the front of the room, as I had anticipated, they had arranged themselves around the perimeter, each person sitting on a little round cushion, on top of a square black mat, facing the wall. While they waited for the evening discussion to commence, each one silently practiced meditation. I was struck by the solemnity of that arrangement and by the seriousness of intention that I sensed behind it. I noticed that as each new person entered the room they bowed, and that when they found their place they bowed to the cushion and then bowed to the room again before they sat down. As I hesitated at the door the same monk who had brought us our food recognized my confusion and whispered, "It's okay—you can sit anywhere. We'll explain how this works before long." I nodded, stepped into the room, then—for the first time in my life—put my hands together in prayer position, bowed to the room, found a place to sit, and faced the wall.

After I had squirmed on my cushion for a few minutes, faking meditation, all movement behind me ceased. Everyone, I supposed, had arrived. Then several minutes of profound silence passed, during which I could only hear the faint sound of the wind blowing outside and the gentle breathing of those around me. I heard footsteps slowly approaching from outside the meditation hall. The footsteps continued into the hall and around the room with startling regularity, then stopped opposite me. I heard someone sit down. Another minute of silence passed, then I heard a voice say, "Would you face this way, please?"

I spun around on my cushion like the others did, then looked across the room to the owner of that voice. It was the Roshi: the person who would become my teacher and the most significant and influential person in my life. She smiled to welcome everyone.

"What shall we talk about this evening?" she said.

The conversation that followed intrigued me. The first thing I noticed was that everyone spoke directly and only to the Roshi. I sensed that this was a part of the rarified retreat environment; that as retreatants we were not to engage in conversations with each other, even in group. The Roshi's authority impressed me profoundly. Whenever she spoke I listened, with all of my being. Here, I thought to myself, is someone who understands how things work. I was fascinated as well by the way people spoke of themselves. The topics discussed were varied, but the focus of the conversation always remained the same: what is the inward experience? How does suffering happen? How can we be free of suffering? I remember speculating as I listened that this was the most significant conversation I had ever heard. I had been waiting my whole life, it seemed, for the information that began to come my way that evening.

Finally I decided to speak myself, and so I raised my hands in prayer position, as I had seen the others do, and waited to be acknowledged. "I am brand new to this," I said, when the Roshi called on me. "I wonder if you could tell me—what are we doing here, exactly?"

The room filled with laughter, and the Roshi smiled. "We are here for just one purpose," she replied, "To pay attention."

"Oh." I said. Suddenly realizing I was speaking to a Zen teacher in front of a roomful of people, I was attacked by self-consciousness. That was all I could get out of my mouth.

"Let me explain," she said when she saw my hesitation. "Conditioned mind operates according to a fundamental law. This law says that our life experience is determined by the focus of our attention. This," she said significantly, "is worth a very long pause to consider. If your attention is on joy, you feel joyful; if your attention is on what you do not have, you feel deprived. It's as simple as that. This is why it is possible to say— as audacious as it may sound—that if you want to be happy, just

37

be happy. Happiness is available everywhere, all the time. All it requires is our attention, and then it is ours.

"Without the awareness required to keep our attention consciously ours," she continued, "it will continually go against our wishes and abandon the beauty of the sunshine or the tenderness of our feelings or whatever else is here, in this moment, and instead reside in discontent or envy or longing. It is as if our unhappiness decides for us who we are and what our experience of life will be. Suffering ends when we reclaim our attention from the illusion that habitually directs it. This is why we practice. Our attention wanders away from what is here, inside and all around us, and we practice bringing it back. It wanders away again, and we practice bringing it back. Moment by moment we practice in this way, and over time the tendency to wander erodes. We discover that our attention need not leave what is here at all."

"But why does our attention wander like that?" I interrupted.

The Roshi looked at me with mock severity. "In the old days," she said, "when a student asked a 'why' question, the teacher would knock the student on the head with a stick. What is your name?"

"Dave," I said, meekly.

"Dave," she repeated, and then paused, as if seeing me for the first time. In that moment, I think, the relationship began that would be central to my life the next many years. "You are new, however," she continued, "so we'll let you slide this time." Everyone laughed again.

"The secret of human happiness," the Roshi told us, "is this: the contentment and well-being we wish for reside in the very place we abandon to search for it. All we have ever wanted exists here, in the present moment, where our attention is ours. We only need to be here to have the life that our heart longs for. That's it—we just need to be here. It is true," she admitted, "that this is the most difficult of all human things to accomplish, but it is just as true that it can be done. We may have the life that we want simply by claiming our attention for ourselves, and we accomplish this through practice.

"Suffering cannot exist in the present moment—that's the bottom line. When we are present we are here, in the moment, with what just is. Nothing exists in the moment beyond what simply is, so there is nothing to suffer over. Once we understand how this is so, our confusion evaporates. What lies around and inside us in each moment is all that we can say is 'real.' We are never in fact engaged in some past embarrassment, or in some future hope, even if the imagination is: we are only ever here with what just is. We suffer when we abandon our authentic experience for a fantasy of the mind.

"We can learn to live in our present moment experience rather than in an illusion. All that is required is that we find the courage to turn our attention away from the one and give it to the other. That is all," the Roshi said, "and yet it is everything. Every moment of life we may practice this, turning away from thoughts about what is wrong or how things could be different and instead enjoying the gifts of our senses, our love for the people in our lives, and the depth of the mystery that surrounds and inhabits all things. Every moment we may practice and every moment we may discover again the joy of the life that is ours.

"What do you think?" she said to me when she was finished.

"I'll give it a shot," I said.

"I sense that you will," the Roshi replied. "Let me know how it goes."

I bowed in response. As the Roshi turned away and called on the next person, an unfamiliar feeling of well-being filled my heart and mind. Something had happened to me since I had ducked into the building from the snow only an hour and a half earlier. I had fallen in love with the environment of the retreat, with the silence and the bowing, and, especially, with the spiritual practice that lay beneath it. Somehow I knew that I had found what I had been looking for all the previous hard years: a way to live with myself, to learn how life works, and to be safely with other people. I sensed as well that I had found my teacher—though I had not even known that I was looking for one. As the old Zen saying goes, "When the student is ready, the teacher appears." For the remainder of the evening, until the Roshi concluded group and led a group bow, I sat in awe of that fact and of the serenity that filled my heart. For the first time in my life I felt at home.

I kept the promise I made that evening and began to pay attention in the way that the Roshi taught us. I had never felt so still inside myself, so aware, or so vulnerable. The next afternoon I had my first "guidance appointment" with the Roshi. It was explained to us that "guidance" was an opportunity for each of us to talk individually with the teacher about our lives and practice. I can remember perfectly how nervous I felt when the time of my appointment rolled around. I stood in a hallway on the second floor of the retreat center with a large bell in my hand. My instructions were to ring the bell exactly at the time of my appointment. I arrived early to be safe, which gave me plenty of time to agonize over whatever would follow. "How does one talk to a 'teacher'?" I wondered. "What in the world will I say?"

At precisely the correct moment I rang the bell. A minute or so later a door opened at the end of the hall, one of my fellow-retreatants emerged, and a bell rang from beyond the doorway. With all the courage I could muster, and with the best imitation of unconcern that I could paste on my countenance, I wobbled down the hall and stepped through the door out onto a porch that overlooked the main courtyard of the retreat center.

The Roshi was there, sitting in a wicker chair. She smiled pleasantly and motioned for me to sit down. She seemed not at all as fierce as she had the evening before—she seemed downright grandmotherly, in fact. "Greetings!" she said. Immediately I felt at ease.

I hesitated, unsure of the correct way to proceed. She leaned over and whispered, as if she were a fellow-student offering a tip the teacher was not supposed to hear: "This is where you talk about something you want to talk about, and then I say stuff about that."

"Ah!" I whispered back, then opened my mouth in a more formal way to see what would come out. "I don't know why I'm here," I said. "I guess I don't know what to do with my life."

"Tell me a bit about that, if you don't mind," the Roshi replied.

"Well, I live out of the back of a truck. I have almost no money. I have friends, but not many. I have no plans."

"I see…. And you don't want to live that way?" she guessed.

"No—I love it, actually. I just don't feel like I should."

"Oh!" said the Roshi, laughing, "I see! I think I can clear this up for you. 'Shoulds' all come from conditioning. Do what makes you happy."

I wish I could adequately convey the effect those words had on me. Countless times since then I have looked back on this meeting and that moment and recognized in it my first tottering step as a monk. I knew the instant the Roshi spoke that she was right. I could not have explained it in words, but it was perfectly clear both that what she told me was so—that I was victim to a thought that was not real—and that she understood how my mind worked in a way that I did not, despite all the many books I had read. Beside her I was a child. I needed desperately to grow up, but knew not how—and she did. I looked at her with renewed awe. "I didn't know that," I said.

"Of course not. How could you?" the Roshi responded, and laughed again. "None of us are taught how life works. We are only taught how to survive the fact that we do not know how life works. We are left to figure it all out on our own, and nobody can do that without help."

My relief at this reassurance overwhelmed the hesitation that had held me back so far during our interview. I opened my mouth and words poured out, I knew not from where. I told her about my struggles and the suffering I had endured; I told her about my love of the mystery and of the divine experiences I had when I was alone; I told her everything, in fact, that I had longed to say all those years of my young adulthood but had never had the courage to admit before. It was only later, when I had time to remember that she was a stranger to me, that I was amazed by the ease with which I opened my heart.

The Roshi listened in silence. "Yes," she said simply when I was finished. I felt completely held and embraced by her presence. It seemed as if she was absolutely there in present time with me and yet, at the same time, as if I talked with something universal rather than another individual human being. "I don't know if you know this," she added, "but what you describe goes on for everyone. Not everyone is living out of the back of a truck, but just about everyone is living in the prison of his or her own mind. The difference between you and some other people, it seems, is that you want a way out. Most people don't—not really."

"And so what do I do?"

"Well, this is a process, you know. It's a practice, in other words. If you will practice, then gradually you will see how you are imprisoned, and gradually you will find the way to free yourself."

"How do I do that?

"You pay attention, as we talked about last night. And more specifically, for now, I would suggest that you pay attention to your thoughts. It's your thoughts that trap you, and the assumptions that lie beneath them—like that 'should' we talked about a bit ago. See if you can watch yourself thinking."

Just then the bell rang from the hallway, signaling the end of our appointment.

"Okay," I said, somewhat sheepishly. The bell had brought me back to my previous self-consciousness.

The Roshi laughed heartily. I love it when she laughs like that—it's one of her ways of articulating the fact that everything in the world is okay exactly as it is, and of inviting everyone to share that understanding with her. "You can do it," she replied. "You are here in this life to do it, whether you are aware of that or no. Just pay attention, and the miracle will happen."

42

I stood up, bowed to her, and turned away. As I left the room I heard her ring her bell, calling the next person to enter.

The rest of that day I attempted to follow the Roshi's encouragement. I practiced seeing my thoughts apart from myself, as something occurring within me but not "mine". To my surprise, I could do it. Then a most amazing thing occurred.

On the third or fourth day of the retreat, during the break after lunch, I decided to take a walk down the road below the retreat center. The day before I had begun to notice the judgment within my thoughts—the Roshi had suggested this in another guidance appointment as a more concrete way to recognize my thinking in general—and as I walked along I toyed with my newly discovered ability to observe the operation of my mind. It was fun to me, like a game. I had no idea of the enormous implications of that shift in my point of view, from one who looks through thought to see the world it projects, to one who watches thought projecting. Technically, the shift in my identification with my thoughts had already occurred, or else I would not have been able to see them, but I did not understand that this had happened. As far as I knew, I was the same me I had always been, only with this neat trick of being able to watch myself think.

That afternoon as I sauntered down the empty road beneath the pines, suddenly I glimpsed the reality beyond the illusion I had lived within my whole life. I saw the person I had always believed I was, and I recognized that this was not me. At once I glimpsed who or what I actually am, beyond conditioned mind. In a moment this insight cut loose all of my thoughts, both the judgmental ones I observed and those that still operated beneath my awareness: suddenly I could see them all. I watched the thoughts bombard my mind, searching for some place to land with an impact that would rock me back into my habitual reality, but for several minutes I stood apart from them, completely unaffected. I just stood there, gaping at a world of beauty and promise I had never seen, and a simple state of being within my mind I had never known. For a few precious moments I was free.

There was only one thing I could do: I sat down right in the road and cried my heart out. I hadn't cried but once or twice in twenty years, but I just sat there and bawled. The relief I felt was unbelievable. I did not truly understand before that day how I suffered, but through those minutes of freedom I saw the desperation that my identification with conditioned mind had driven me to, the deep unhappiness of it, and the terror of life that it contained. I saw that I was none of that; that I am empty of all of the misery I had believed to be so real. After a while I got up, happier than I had ever felt before, walked another five minutes or so in perfect enjoyment of the beauty around me, then sat down again to cry some more. This went on for I don't know how long—maybe an hour—and never really left me after that for days. All it took was the tiniest thing to set me off again. I remember the next day at breakfast, as I ate my oatmeal in front of one of the windows that overlooked the front lawn, I saw a bird pluck a worm from the earth, and the world dissolved again before my eyes.

As soon as I had the opportunity I told the Roshi. "Don't let it ruin your life," she said. That sobered me up a little. But only a little, because the magic that came into my life with that experience intoxicated me. Everything at once was explained: why I felt the way I did, and why that feeling had always seemed to fall so short of what was possible. And yet, she was right. Without that reminder I may have made something out of those incredible days that belittled all the rest that followed. I willingly let them go, but I thank them still for the alternative they gave to me and the opportunity they left me with once the euphoria passed.

With this, an eagerness awoke within me to throw myself into spiritual practice as fully as I knew how, and so I did for the rest of that week. I had no idea what I was doing, really, but I did it with everything I had. It occurred to me that I might get help by going to the monastery that the Roshi had founded, where the monks lived who staffed the retreat, and I remember the thrill of joy that moved through me with that thought. It seemed so real and so perfect that I almost up and went.

The trouble was that I had not the willingness for it—not yet. The commitment to end suffering was not yet ripe within me. And so, as I left the retreat and the power of the experience wore off, and as ego drunkenly re-established itself within my mind, I set off to pursue the life I had known before instead.

4

The Path of Heroes

In awareness practice, "willingness" is everything. The willingness to renounce the fear of conditioned mind, to set aside our imagined limitations, and to choose the possibility that calls us towards our natural heroic lives, come what may, is the power that awakens freedom. As the Roshi often says, all we have to do is to show up and the transformation will happen. The showing up is the willingness; the power that we call "willingness" grows as practice grows; and practice grows as we experience for ourselves the life available beyond suffering.

Willingness is not developed in a day, however. It requires great effort and determination to achieve. At the same time, it could be said that willingness cannot be achieved at all, in the sense that it is not something that you can *make* happen. Willingness is something that happens to you.

That was my experience, at any rate. As I left the retreat center with Janey at the end of that eventful week and she dropped me off at my campsite beside the stream, the willingness that the experience had awakened within me began to carry me towards a new relationship with Life and my self within it. As I settled back into my strange but familiar way of living—cooking for myself within the grove of maple trees that surrounded my little camping spot, wandering through the long afternoons along the creeks and over the mountaintops nearby, sleeping on the ground in fair weather and in the back of my truck when it rained—and as I pondered the change that those few days of retreat had wrought within me, I began to understand that my life as it was then was not the life that I am here to live. It was a beautiful life in a lot of ways, and I can truthfully say that I loved it, but I began to sense that there was something more than solitude and old books that I was called to. I longed for Life to

46

challenge me, and for the possibilities I felt within me to be forged upon the anvil of experiences that were beyond my control and apart from my own choosing. I loved the freedom I had at that time to explore this amazing world that we live in, but I did not love the discontent and unease that followed me wherever I roamed, nor the fear of other people that I suffered from. I longed for a different sort of freedom: one that permitted me happiness wherever or however I might be. In addition, I understood with even more certainty than before how helpless I was to discover that freedom on my own. I saw that my isolated efforts to save myself from unhappiness could only further deepen my misery.

Slowly, as I practiced awareness and began to explore the authentic "me" I had discovered on retreat, something interesting began to happen. I fell in love. To my astonishment, I did not hate the person that I found beneath the illusions of conditioned mind, as I had thought I would. I found myself to be beautiful, loveable, and good. A love sprang up that was sweet and quiet like the first day of spring, when the earth is pregnant with the life that will soon erupt from the ground. It was as if I had spent my life as far back as I could recall in winter; now there were clusters of daffodils along the road, flocks of geese flying high above my head, and peeping frogs in the trees. Held within the loving arms of my new awareness, I felt a part of Life as if for the first time.

This was my "honeymoon period". I felt wonderful for several weeks. "I am a new man!" I told myself. My happiness felt so solid and true that I imagined it would never abandon me, but of course it did. As the euphoria wore off my old habit of suffering gradually returned, and I slid back into my ancient miserable ways—only it was worse than before because I now had new awareness to bring to my unhappiness. I learned much later that this stage of practice is called "going farther and faring worse." What in the world, I wondered, had happened to the bliss? Where was the joy and excitement I thought would surely last forever?

47

I had awakened the sleeping giant called "conditioned mind"—that's what had happened. Until this point in my life all was well for the entity within me that orchestrated my unhappiness. As long as I was willing to suffer according to its dictates, as I most enthusiastically was without realizing it, there was little conditioned mind needed to do: only to alter the deception occasionally so that I would not catch on to it. It guided me to suffer over this difficulty, then that one; this problem, this situation, this bit of trouble, and on and on. Meanwhile, it fed upon my obedience, gradually becoming fat, lazy, and weak. Then, suddenly, with the assistance of the guidance I received during the retreat, I began to see the entity operating behind the scenes and to question its authority. Conditioned mind responded to this change with remarkable violence. I had caught it off guard and out of shape, and it lost control of me for a bit—that was the honeymoon period. But not for long: conditioned mind lives upon suffering and cannot tolerate love or joy. Unhappiness is its life; freedom is its death. When it finally caught up with me the ferocity of its reaction was such as I had not seen since childhood.

I was an easy match, alas. How it punished me for my disobedience! It pulled out every mistake I had ever made, every hard or harmful thing I had ever done, every humiliation I had ever experienced, everything I might feel bad about from my entire life, and rubbed my nose in it all. It crushed me with supposed proofs that there was something wrong with me, pointing out in painful detail every way I had failed in my life so far, all the ways I had disappointed myself and others, and on and on. I began to live again as I used to do, in fear of the next beating—only now it was overt. In the past the punishment had always been in the background, where I could not see it. Conditioning was no longer able to hide behind my awareness because I had learned to see it, but that did not stop the abuse. I still believed conditioned mind was real, and so the violence was real to me as well, and the fear of it followed me everywhere.

As might be expected, when conditioned mind reasserted its authority I reacted as I always had before. I ran.

I sold my truck, bought a backpack, and put the remaining money from the sale aside to support me as long as it would. I also put away the obvious fact that once this money was gone I would have nothing, and without a vehicle I would have little chance of finding work to bring me more. I also bought a tiny pack for Rhea and a week's worth of food for us both. A friend dropped us off at the nearest access to the Appalachian Trail. For the next six months we hiked north, from that spot in North Carolina all the way to Maine. As in past adventures, much of what occurred during that time was wonderful—glorious, even— but I could not escape the sense of doom that followed me. It weighed me down more than the load on my back: I dragged it up and down mountains, I dissipated it in every form of distraction that was available to me, as broke as I was, but I could not shake it. On some level I must have known that my life as I had created it before was over, and that I had no choice but to face conditioned mind in order to go beyond suffering and access the freedom I had recently tasted. All the while conditioned mind did everything in its power to compel me to stop looking, to stop watching it perpetrate its violence upon me, but I would not stop. Something within me had changed; I refused to go back to my former unconsciousness, and so I endured the beatings and the awful, aching fear day after day.

It was horrible. Most people quit at this juncture. "If it's going to be like this," they say to themselves, "what's the point? I was better off before, when at least I didn't know how unhappy I was." But to stop here is a terrible mistake. It is a tragedy to give in to the abuse once we have seen it, and to consent to suffer once again, when the courage to go beyond suffering stands so near. If we can only see that the horror and the pain of confronting conditioned mind may lead us *towards* freedom— that it implies that we travel in exactly the right, not in the wrong, direction—then we will not falter. Few, however, understand this. Most will ultimately choose to suffer rather than experience the pain of their awakening. And then they truly suffer, because the possibility of an end to unhappiness, which they have just glimpsed, will never completely disappear from memory. It will haunt them for the rest of their lives. Some will be driven back to spiritual practice eventually; others will attempt to return to their former ignorance, enduring the misery of this choice as best they can until death.

In my own case it was more dumb luck and stubbornness than insight that kept me going. I was fortunate in that I had nowhere to go and nothing to turn to for relief.

So what happens if you don't quit? Here is what happened to me. First, things got worse. Like everyone else, I had to spend a period of time making absolutely sure that conditioned mind would not, after all, provide the life I wanted. This is the most frustrating and painful pursuit there is, but nevertheless it is very popular.

I finished the hike and then reluctantly made my way south with Rhea, flagging rides with my thumb beside the road. Finally we landed in a town back in the North Carolina hills with but a few dollars in my pockets and not much anywhere else, inside or out. I felt profoundly helpless and alone. For the first time in my life I feared for my physical survival in this world. Something, obviously, had to be done. I set about determinedly to avoid the one thing that would save me from my unhappiness, which was to allow my heart to choose my way, to surrender to the life that was before me to live, to throw myself upon the mercy of the monastery, and ask for help. As long as it seemed I could escape the inevitable, I did, or at least attempted to. I tried to find a job—no luck. I tried to find a place to live—no luck. I tried to make friends—no luck. I tried harder—no luck. An acquaintance took me in temporarily out of pity or I don't know what I would have done. Words cannot communicate the desperation of my predicament: no matter where I turned I found a closed door. I began to grow seriously low (even for me) on funds, but I still had no luck finding work. It was as if there was no such thing—and it wasn't from pickiness, either: janitor, bicycle pizza delivery guy, cook, street sweeper, construction grunt—I was willing to do anything that paid, but I wasn't wanted anywhere I went. The whole experience mystified me. Could it be, I wondered, that Life desired my death? In hindsight it seems obvious that people merely responded to my hysteria, but even today I am in awe of how completely circumstances denied what the fear of my true life convinced me I must do.

Next, things got worse still. The closer I was to making the inevitable choice, the more vehemently conditioned mind resisted. Because I remained fundamentally confused about who I am—because I believed I *was* conditioned mind—then I experienced that resistance as "me", and so I suffered. I went on trying to make unhappiness happy, and I failed over and over again, as of course I must. Over and over it got as bad as it seemed it could get, and then it got still worse. At last it became more than I could bear. I hit bottom. "That's it!" I told myself, "I can't take it anymore!"

Right about then I found a copy of <u>The Odyssey</u> by the ancient Greek poet Homer at a used bookstore. I had read the story before, but even so it called to me that day from a dusty shelf above my head. The Odyssey, I knew, is one of the greatest adventure stories every told. I also knew that its hero Odysseus endured trials that were far worse than mine. It would be pleasant, I thought, to compare my predicament to his and come out the more fortunate, and so I decided to buy it if I could. I peeped fearfully inside the front jacket—it was eighty-nine cents. I could afford it, I thought, just barely, and so I bought it and took it home.

One part of the tale affected me profoundly. The story goes something like this.

Once upon a time, way back in the days of myths and heroes, there lived a fellow named Odysseus. Odysseus was born into an age of great conflict. Even as he became a man and acquired the fearlessness and depth of spirit that people have since loved in him, war erupted with a kingdom across the sea. Like many others, Odysseus responded to the call to arms and set sail with a band of sturdy companions to join the contest.

As often occurs in the lives of heroes, however, all did not proceed as he desired. Just as Odysseus set sail, the worst of all possible disasters happened: he offended the gods. I do not recall exactly what he did or didn't do, but the gods were touchy in those days, you know, and they were mighty ticked. In retaliation they sent Odysseus off with a curse that condemned him to eighteen years of separation from his wife and family and nearly unending trials and trouble. The war itself required nine years to win. Afterwards, Odysseus and his remaining followers struggled for nine more years against the curse to make their way back to their homeland. Along the way they underwent various strange adventures, of which this story is one.

In the midst of the return, Odysseus decided to steer their ship through a famous strait between the Greek mainland and a rocky island. This particular sliver of water had won the fearful admiration of all of the sailors in those parts because of the extreme danger in its navigation. It was not currents or reefs that terrified people about this place, but rather the Sirens who resided there—supernatural beings, part woman and part bird, who sang so seductively that sailors on passing ships would become maddened by desire and leap to their deaths into the waves.

Other people avoided this place, but not Odysseus. Instead, here is what he did. He told his sailors to fill their ears with wax to save them from the Sirens' song, but he did not fill his own. He commanded his men to tie his body to the mast of the ship, exhorting them to check the knots well and to leave him fastened there no matter how he might beg or order them to set him free. Once this was accomplished, onward they went, and as they passed through the strait the Sirens sang and Odysseus's heart surged within him. He cried out to be released, and insanely struggled against the bonds that saved him from his own destruction. The cords held, his sailors remained true, the ship passed safely through the strait, and Odysseus emerged, unharmed.

Reading that story, I saw myself in it and realized that I must do as he had done. I must choose the narrow and dangerous way, and I must follow it with all of my senses open, knowing that the force of suffering that possessed me would torture me with every sort of fantasy, from the loveliest to the most horrible, in an effort to seduce me from the way. It would not serve me to avoid the call of Life as I had been doing if what I wanted was freedom. I sensed that everything I had ever feared or longed for would arise to be healed if I chose to end suffering; that many times this would seem too much to bear, and that I would wish to abandon myself again, closing my heart to the pain of it, as I had been taught to do. A time comes, however, when the hero in us rises up. A time comes when the heart takes the helm, and we realize that what we truly want is not safety: what we want is our experience of Life, however it may be. This is what is required, and the reason why this way is called "The Path of Heroes."

At last! Without knowing it, this is what I had been waiting for. Willingness finally arrived and brought the necessary courage along with it. At last, after all of my resistance, the day came when the misery of my banishment from my own true life exceeded my horror of the unknown, and I became ready to risk letting go of my unhappiness. I had arrived at the point that is called "having suffered enough."

That happened at the end of January. Magically, just then I learned that the Roshi was returning to the area in February to offer another retreat, just like the year before. I can still recall the sick thrill of horror that accompanied that piece of information. Imagine the way a running felon would feel at the idea that he might confess and end his flight. I knew that I would go—that I must go. What choice did I have? Every other door was closed.

It became clear to me instantly upon arrival at the retreat center how my heart had been left out of my recent struggles. I had forgotten how much I adored the silence of retreat, the meditation, and, most of all, the compassionate teaching that I found there. Slowly, over the hours and days of the following week, a wish grew within me to give myself over to what my heart wanted, come what may. I began secretly to consider actually going to the monastery to get help with my life. The thought terrified me, but the hope and joy of that possibility often overcame the fear, and the idea grew and grew. I hardly slept, I think, all week. Early in the morning until late at night I sat in the meditation hall, with all of my life, it seemed, in pieces around me. Finally the terror abandoned me completely, and the wish became a determination. I cannot even say it was a choice: it was a necessity. Finally, on the last full day of the retreat, I asked the Roshi if she would accept me as her student and train me as a monk. Tears come to my eyes even now as I remember it.

I'll never forget what she said: "What about the dog?" Rhea's future, of course, hung in the balance at that moment. I was flabbergasted. I had expected that the Roshi would require me to defend my worthiness, but she took my request as a matter of course, as if she had been waiting for me to make it. The short conversation that ensued cemented an agreement between us which included an invitation to Rhea to accompany me to the monastery. Not without a warning, however: three times during those few minutes the Roshi leaned over and said to me in the most significant manner imaginable: "You must be aware that it will be very, very strict."

As I departed, in a moment of panic, I asked what I might expect for myself at the monastery. "You will get to see how you cause yourself to suffer," she replied. Boy, was she right!

The retreat ended the next morning. I was the last to leave. I took the little pick-up truck I had borrowed and drove it back to the room where I had been staying. I piled my remaining belongings in the truck and spent the rest of the day going about to various people I knew, giving away everything but what I would take with me to the monastery. These were the most ecstatic hours of my life so far. In my mania I gave away things that I would later need, but it was worth it. Finally, with all but the most necessary possessions remaining, I retreated up into the mountains and far away from the city that had failed, mercifully, to support my suffering. There I resolved to wait patiently for the day six weeks out when I would make my journey to my new life.

5

In the Valley of the Moon

The pick-up truck I had borrowed belonged to Janey. I returned it to her the next day. When she saw my pile of things in the back, and when she noticed my wild eyes and sensed my immense vulnerability, she perceived the tremendous change that had happened inside of me. All my defenses were destroyed—I must have been absolutely transparent to her. "Oh, Dave..." she whispered, with a gentleness that could only come from a heart as full of awe as mine was. I responded only with tears, but they said everything.

I mentioned earlier that Janey lives in a beautiful log cabin beside a tumbling stream, at the top of a wide hollow. Above her house, just before the forest begins its ascent to the mountain top above, is a flat piece of ground that overlooks the entire valley. Janey invited me to make a home of that place while I waited for the time to head off to my new life. One of my few remaining possessions was an old canvas tent, the sort that a miner might have used in days gone by, with a hole in the roof for a stove-pipe. I set it up beside the creek and settled down to wait. The next day it snowed, and as I sat there in that little tent, with a fire burning in the stove and a new faith blazing in my heart, I felt stronger than I ever had before.

The six weeks that followed until my journey west were the longest and fullest I had known. The anticipation, at times, was awful. I remember lying awake at night suffering over what would happen when Rhea met the monastery cats, of which there were said to be at least two dozen. But that was nothing: more than anything else I feared I would not be adequate to the demands of my new life. Solitude was a habit with me—that was not a problem—but silence was not. Before entering the monastery I never allowed myself a blank hour out of fear, I think, of what I imagined would appear in the quiet. Just in case, I had always kept plenty of distractions within easy reach. On a day when nothing worldly required my participation, I might read for eight to ten hours to avoid myself—this is how I had learned to survive. This would not be possible at the monastery, I knew. The silence of retreat had been challenging, but softened by the newness of the environment and the thought that it would soon be done. At the monastery there would be no escape for months. Daunted by these thoughts, I wondered often through those long, deep days how I would endure what would soon follow.

At other times joy touched me. At last I had something I wanted in my heart to do! To pass the time, I did good works for free for anyone who would enjoy the fruits of my labor. I don't know what inspiration gave me that idea, but it saved me. For the first time in my life I had no need for money—moved, I think, by the audacious decision I had made, people fed me wherever I went—so I worked simply for the pleasure of it. I had never worked so willingly or happily before.

Looking back I can see how well life cared for me through all of this. All the while that I suffered, all the while I approached my own transformation without knowing it, all the while that Life like a patient father guided me towards the way that I now live, I never was abandoned by the mystery. It is true that it was my helplessness that brought me to the threshold of spiritual practice, but this was as far as it could take me. If my own suffering were the only issue I doubt I would have found the courage to become a monk. What called me to step through that door and embrace the dazzling but appalling possibility I perceived beyond it was the joy that practice gave to me even through my stumbling efforts at it. To sit still with a stalk of grass, or with the bubbling sounds of falling water, or with my best friend in the world, Rhea the dog, and to see through them as through a window the mysterious law that animates all things—this is what drew me forward through my life, and finally led me beyond my addiction to unhappiness.

Day after day in the Valley of the Moon, as I gathered wood for the stove from the forest floor, as I worked, and as I took sweet refuge in the love of my friend down the way, I felt the mystery living within me and through me. What a happy, innocent time that was, despite the fear! The trees around my campsite still waited for spring to begin; their branches were bare, and I peered curiously through them into the valley below, wondering at the human world of busyness that I saw there. It was a world, I realized, which I had relinquished. So many of my expectations perished during that time, leaving me alone with the naked trunks of the trees, the crispy leaves beneath them, and the sky! Those sweet days taught me to loosen my grip upon my life, to give myself over to the larger intelligence within all things, and to allow it to do the work of my transformation. Gradually, and with perfect tenderness, the practice I did each day, even as clumsily as I did it, soothed the fears that troubled me and prepared me to give myself over to the unknown life that lay ahead.

My instructions from the monastery were to write an official letter—called the "letter of intention"—that included a "statement of commitment" laying out the exact ending and beginning dates of my stay, as I proposed it. I was told that I could commit to whatever period of time I chose (so long as the Roshi agreed), but once the commitment was made I would be expected to honor it, come what may.

I understand now what I did not then, that it is essential that we monks train within a non-negotiable commitment. This is because the choice to train monastically—or in any context, actually—arises from the heart, as it must, but at times the heart is nowhere to be found. One's commitment at such times serves as an anchor in a sea of fear and resistance. You might commit to a month or to a year, it doesn't matter—even those of our neighbors who come down to the monastery to work with us for the day know exactly when they will arrive and depart. In every case, for all of us who have accepted the guidance of the monastery, the necessity is the same. Having committed from the heart to end suffering and having no honorable way to escape from that commitment, when we lose touch with our willingness to face what we must face, our commitment will continue to guide us until we find our willingness once again.

In addition, the letter of intention ratifies the essential agreement that a monk makes to give over his or her will to the guidance of the monastery. This is what grants the training its power: in order to give over the will, one must let go of ego—there is no other way to do it—and this is what monastic training is all about. If we cannot give up our lives to something larger than ourselves—to something larger than the conditioned mind that we imagine is who we are—then we cannot be free.

Once in the middle of the various adventures I described earlier (somewhat condensed in order to fit within these pages) I took a job as a whitewater river guide. Over the course of my short but glamorous career I trained a number of other people to guide, and I noticed that their learning always took the same course. Everyone's first instinct was to attempt to control the river. To get my boat from here to there, they reasoned with themselves, I must exercise my will upon the water until it yields to me. Now, if you have ever stood near a river during a spring flood (when the paddling is the best) and seen the awesome power of rushing water, you will recognize the futility of this approach. The results were dramatic: urgency, anger, desperation, and a fierce resentment of all that ignores human will—not to mention capsized rafts, people swimming rather than paddling through dangerous rapids, boats crushed against boulders, and so on. It was entertaining, it is true, but it wasn't pretty.

New guides who were unable to discover an alternative would soon quit in frustration. For those who stayed, however, a tiny but powerful shift occurred. They learned to work with the river rather than against it. The ways of the waters are subtle and deceptive, and to master them each new guide is required to set aside every notion of how the river should be so that she might see how it actually is. Sometimes the laws of the waters work in exactly the opposite way than people expect; the water in a large eddy, for example, will often flow upstream. Once she gives herself over to be taught by the river, the guide learns with awe and excitement—and she learns not with her mind, but with her body, feeling the teaching in the boat as it moves.

Just so, we may give ourselves over to Life so that it can teach us freedom. Our commitment is the same as the river guide's: to set aside what we want to happen so that what can happen may. The current of our lives moves with many times the force and subtlety of the river, so we must pay exceedingly close attention if we are to master it. A river guide remains ever watchful of the water, no matter how long he has practiced his craft. A moment of inattention and the river will pound you mercilessly. In the world of whitewater adventure this is considered a good time ("getting thrashed" they call it), and the equivalent in spiritual practice can be thrilling, too, if you're up for it. But the ultimate point of training is mastery. This sort of mastery is not a holding on, but a letting go; complete mastery is complete willingness to turn in each moment where Life asks us to turn.

When we are fully committed to that willingness, all of Life gets behind us. The river will take a wise guide wherever she wants to go; in the same way, Life will carry us inevitably towards real happiness, once we understand its laws. We just have to want the same thing for ourselves Life wants for us.

The letter of intention, I was told, must also include a statement of special needs. A "special need" is any need that will interfere with the normal course of training. If I were unable to eat a certain food, for example, this would constitute a special need. Every time a monk ends one commitment period and begins another, he expresses any special needs he has once again.

On one level there is a practical reason for this, as there is for all the monastery requires. For the monastery to agree to train a monk, it must be certain that it will be able to provide for that person's needs. On a deeper level than this, however, the

60

question of needs points to the heart of practice. Practice teaches us how to meet our own needs. Any unmet need that we have stands in the way of freedom. And so we must learn to grow into people who can take care of ourselves.

In the beginning I understood nothing about my needs. I did not even know I had any, really. As I have gone along through practice, however, I have discovered bit by bit what I need as a living creature upon this earth and what I do not. I have seen what I must relinquish for my life to be purified. It is true that I have surrendered more than I ever imagined I could, but never once have I been required to give up what is necessary and good.

There is a delicious paradox in this. People generally imagine that spiritual practice involves deprivation. This is exactly opposite from the truth. Spiritual practice unites us with what we truly long for. Our transformation requires us to abandon everything that ego holds dear, it's true, but it never asks us to renounce what we love, because love—in the deepest sense of a heart open to all that is—is a function of the Life that animates. Now, practice has demanded countless times that I sacrifice what I *believed* I needed, but this is a different matter entirely.

There is nothing wrong with needs and wants. It is a part of being human to have them. Before we can choose freedom, however, we must see through the falsehood that says a life spent attempting to satisfy the cravings of ego will result in real happiness. When we no longer want to suffer, suffering is easily set aside. The trick is to learn the difference between what we need to grow and live fully and what we need in order to suffer. Practice will ask for us to let go of the one, but not the other.

None of this, of course, was clear to me as I sat down in my tent on an early March afternoon to write my letter to the monastery. I only knew I had to write something, and that it was important. With a trembling pen, I committed to an initial period of six months. Now, in the world of monastic practice six months is like a single grain of sand in an hourglass. Still, I had to commit to something, and I figured that if I hated monastic training I could survive it, just barely, for that amount of time. I said I did not need anything—that seemed safest.

Carefully I folded the letter, sealed and addressed it, then held it in my lap while I listened to the fire snap and pop in the stove. After a few minutes I stood, put on my coat, and walked outside. It was a quarter-mile walk to my friend's mailbox. I remember how brilliantly the bare trees shone in the light reflected on the snow. I remember the singing creek I walked along, and the icicles that clung to the fingers of the trees that reached towards the water's surface. I remember most of all how my heart beat as I marched through the forest towards the road—these were the most courageous moments of my life so far.

A crow called out as I emerged from the trees and strode towards the mailbox. The universe churned around me, but I did not hesitate—I could not hesitate. I opened the mailbox, placed the letter inside, closed the box again, and then turned back the way I had come.

I must have sensed the significance of that moment, but I had no idea really what I was committing to. In that act was the end of my life as I knew it. From that point on there has been no turning back. How many times since have I wished I could return and undo that simple act of faith! How many times have I tearfully thanked the innocent wisdom I somehow possessed, to have made that heroic choice! I must have understood even then that the choice was more than for a half-year's adventure, but I could not have known it was a choice for a lifetime.

Over the next few days I wrote to everyone I knew explaining my decision, and I held many earnest conversations with those who loved me and feared for me most. After that there was nothing left to do. I sat and sat, and I breathed and breathed, and I waited and waited until at last the day came to go.

Janey dropped me at the airport early on a spring morning. It was March 25th. I played the hero bravely while we remained together, but as soon as she left me my spirits plummeted. By the time I landed in California I was in a state. I saw a movie once where a man stood in a skyscraper window, threatening to leap to his death, with a crowd tensed behind him, pleading with him to save himself. There I was, it seemed to me, just like that unfortunate fellow, ready to leap into the unknown and leave behind forever everything I knew. The fact that my life would follow me to the monastery in all its weary ways might have offered me some unhappy comfort at that moment, but I had no idea this would be the case. My habit of suffering protested the awesome choice I had made and the supposed freedom that moment by moment slipped away.

From the San Francisco airport I was to take a puddle-jumper to another town, where someone from the monastery would pick me up. I walked to the designated gate and then collapsed onto the floor, all but undone by the unknown fate awaiting me. I had never been so scared, I think, in all of my life.

Then the most wonderful thing happened: a Buddhist monk walked by. He wore orange robes and thin sandals. A tiny satchel hung over one shoulder and across his body. He was in his late middle-age, it seemed to me, and looked exceedingly strong. I knew at once that he was the real thing, and I admired him instantly. As he strode by me our eyes met. He nodded, as if to say, "Yes, I understand," and as he passed my anxieties were carried away. It was a gift, I knew at once, of the life I had chosen.

In that monk I saw the dedication of all the many people who have carried the teachings of the Buddha moment by moment through more than two thousand years all the way to me. In him I caught a glimpse of the great nobility of the ancient path I had embarked upon, and this granted me the courage to set self-doubt aside. If he can do it, I told myself, then so can I.

A monk from the monastery picked me up outside baggage claim. She wore jeans and a t-shirt; I recognized her only by her beads. We arrived at the monastery after a three-hour drive. By then night had descended.

The first thing I noticed when I stepped out of the car was the silence. My logical mind tells me that silence is an absence of something, but no monk would ever agree. Silence is a something, not a nothing. The quiet I observed in that moment was palpable, as if all the years of voiceless work in that place and all of the deep attention originating within that environment had created a physical feature just but not quite beyond the reach of human senses. It moved me deeply. I gathered my things together and, with Rhea following on a leash behind, was led by the monk to the main monastery buildings.

The place seemed uninhabited at first; everywhere darkness and stillness filled my eyes and ears. Then I noticed that a large room in one of the buildings was lit; as we passed I peeked through the glass doors and saw inside a group of men and women seated on the floor in a very formal manner around the outside of the room. They were receiving the teachings, I realized. The thought thrilled me that these people in this place, so remote from the urgency of the world, had dedicated themselves to discover the freedom that resides within each human heart. I felt in awe of their sincerity. Even more, I was amazed that I was to add myself to their number; it seemed too wonderful and too terrifying to be true.

The monk handed me a flashlight and led me down a wide trail through the night shadows of overhanging trees, then past a broad, grassy field, lit by a crescent moon. Abruptly she turned into a path that ducked behind some large bushes and steeply down and away from the main trail. At the end of the path stood a small square structure, almost completely hidden by the darkness. We stepped inside. She lit an oil lamp and explained to me that this place was mine for the time that I remained and that no one would ever trouble me there without my permission.

I adored it. It was and is, to be completely honest, a plywood shack, but nothing could have seemed more wonderful to me. To have my very own hermitage! I hadn't expected such good fortune. A small bell rests by the main path, she told me, in case I should be needed urgently, but she also let me know that in the several years she had lived on the property her own bell had never sounded once. She further explained that the next morning at six I was to be at the main buildings. She encouraged me to rest, and then she left me on my own.

For the next several minutes I explored my tiny home. Never was a king in ancient times more enchanted with his palace than I was with my little shanty. It had everything—even its own outhouse! My heart, which until then had guarded itself in fear of this strange destiny of mine, opened like a flower to the warmth of my gratitude.

Despite my excitement, before long I began to feel my need for rest. Still reluctant to spoil my delight by trading it for sleep, I sat up for a while before crawling inside the bed with Rhea. Slumber came quickly, but not before the thought arose that, of all the people in the world, I was the luckiest of all.

6

The Last Resort

The monastery lies in the foothills of the Sierra Nevada Mountains, in gold country. At one time, it is said, the area was packed with miners and unruly towns tucked here and there to serve their needs. Now it is a country of vineyards, olive groves, and cattle ranches. Along the way here from the west the highway rises out of the dry and bare Central Valley into the hills, where scrubby clumps of trees and hardy bushes dot wide, grassy slopes. Clear creeks run in the creases, their banks overhung with maples and oaks. It is beautiful country.

The monastery property begins at the end of a long gravel road that winds its way through a country neighborhood of small ranches. The road gets smaller and smaller until finally it becomes our driveway. A gate guards the entrance to the property. Bolted onto the gate is this large sign:

STOP!
This is a silent religious community.
If you are expected, welcome.
Please enter and leave the gate as you found it.
If you are not expected, please do not enter. No
exceptions.

Beyond the gate the driveway winds through a dense forest, then out into an open field offering a view of the main monastery compound. On the left are the gardens, surrounded by a tall fence that maintains our friendly relationship with the army of deer that shares the property with us. Just beyond the gardens, banks of solar panels reflect the sun and moon. As a part of our commitment to sustainable living we generate all of our own power. To the right, beneath a towering ponderosa pine, stand two gorgeous buildings, joined by an open archway that shares the same red tile roof. They are constructed with rammed earth. The monks who built them, after carving out a flat spot for the building's foundations, mixed the resulting dirt with a bit of cement and packed it into walls eighteen inches thick. They are of a light brown color, dotted here and there with quartz pebbles. Those same monks made all the windows and doors from old redwood wine casks. Perched at the apex of a high ridge, the buildings command views in one direction of hills that rise towards the high Sierra and in the other a rolling valley stretching off into the distance towards the sea.

One of the buildings houses the dining hall, with its broad tile floor and its lofty ceiling. The center of the room stands empty except for the antique table where the food is served. The monks eat at benches along the outside, facing the walls or windows: in this way we may practice meditation while we eat, without distraction or the interference of others. The other building accommodates the meditation hall, with its fat black cushions lining the perimeter and the Guide's place at the end. From the main buildings the monastery property spreads out in all directions. Three-quarters of it is wooded. The remainder is covered by expansive fields of grass. Here and there, tucked away in the trees, are the tiny hermitages that shelter the monks. Each is spare and simple, but comfortable. At the bottom of the road the property borders a lovely creek, with a nearly unused public road on the other side.

When people come to the monastery they generally notice the silence first, as I did. Of all our possessions this is the one the monks value most, and we take great pains to maintain it. Those of us who live here keep the silence all the time, through all the hours of the day, and through all the days of the year. Our visitors follow the same practice so long as they stand on monastery grounds, no matter who they are. In the dining hall hangs a large note board, which serves as the main vehicle for conveying information between members of the community. In this way we can communicate without breaking the silence. Should I need to request or give information, I would write my message on a slip of paper, address it to the correct person, fold the paper in half so that the message will not distract those for whom it is not intended, and then pin it on the board. There are times, of course, when verbal intercourse is required—someone might need to explain to me how to accomplish a work assignment, for example—but this is kept to a minimum, and, when necessary, is accomplished through whispers.

As a further way to deepen the stillness, we practice "custody of the eyes" as well. We avoid making eye contact with each other, keeping our gaze towards the ground whenever others are around. This practice, in conjunction with the silence, creates what we call the "privileged environment." Those of us who live and practice at the monastery enjoy the privilege of an environment that does not include personality. There is nothing in the monastic world that requires us to indulge our own conditioned perceptions or to suffer the delusions of others. We are safe to just be who we are.

Posted on the note board is the schedule that we follow. We all do the same thing at the same time all day and night: we eat together, work together, and meditate together. We do not sleep together, however, as we practice celibacy as a part of our monastic commitment, but we do sleep at the same time in different places. We begin and end our days with sitting meditation, and most days we sit a couple more times in between. Two nights a week and on Sunday mornings we gather to share our practice verbally in group discussion. Otherwise, we work. We build, we clean, we cook, we type on computers, we garden, and many other things. We work hard, in fact: for many, this is the most intimidating part of the training here, even beyond the emotional and spiritual challenges involved.

The days go by, one pretty much like the other—or at least so it appears. Beneath the regular cycles of monastic life a mysterious transformation occurs. You can see it in the eagerness of the monks as they go about their daily tasks, and you can hear it in their laughter at night in the discussions. We are practicing happiness, and for this reason life here is very, very good.

At the same time, it is far from easy. On one side the monastery provides protection from the unconscious cruelty that dominates life outside the gates; on the other it offers without choice a gentle hand of encouragement to face whatever it may be that we have run from. Together these two structures put us in the very place that most people have avoided all their lives: right here. We all get here kicking and screaming, but we all do it sooner or later. We have to. To survive even a few days in the silence you have to find your way to the present moment—where the pain is, yes, but also the refuge from pain. To be anywhere other than the moment, in this environment where there is no distraction, is to be stuck in the hell of conditioned mind. It's just too awful to choose.

Life here is as beautiful and exciting as it is horrible and terrifying. We have a nickname for the monastery that expresses this paradox perfectly, I think: we call it "The Last Resort".

I will admit that it took me some time to see the compassion in the approach after I arrived. At the beginning the training seemed brutal to me, uncaring, and despotic. I wanted the monastery to assist me to escape from myself; I wished for sympathy and excuses; I longed for someone to save me from my unhappiness—this is what I understood "compassion" to be. Alas, it was only more suffering. True compassion requires us to learn to provide for ourselves the understanding and the mentoring that we were taught to look for in other people. We will never receive what we truly need from others, or from any material thing, no matter how fondly we might wish it—but we may absolutely receive it from ourselves. To do this we must stop running and face the fear-driven habits of the mind that separate us from the goodness and compassion that we are, no matter how painful this process may be. The monastery exists to provide support for this journey.

Few choose it. Even those who do generally exhaust every other option first. There have been those who have stepped onto the property for the first time and begun weeping with gratitude and relief at having submitted at last to the guidance of something larger than conditioned mind. Most folks, once they have recovered from the shock of the transition, flower most beautifully in the privileged environment. There have been those, however, who have slipped secretly away in the night. The difference is a matter of willingness. A monk has only two choices: to suffer, or to end suffering. Sneaking around or over or under suffering is not an option. You wake up every morning with a long day ahead of you in the silence with yourself, knowing that you may either resist what occurs and suffer, or give yourself over to the compassion of the moment and be free. That is the practice.

How, then, does the change happen? How do we escape from the illusion of our suffering, realize who we truly are, see the miracle Life actually is, and then remember to live from that place?

The answer is easy to say. It happens through the practice of now. All of spiritual practice, we might say, and all of the transformation that occurs as a result, comes down to the fundamental skill of turning our attention away from conditioned mind and putting it on our experience in this moment instead. It happens as we attend to the breath. It happens as we hold the body in our awareness as it inhales the air of life and as it lets it out again. It happens as conditioned mind releases its desperate grasp upon our consciousness, as we set our thoughts free, as our feelings arise and pass away, and as the moment cradles us in its nurturing arms.

The answer is simple, but to live that answer—to be here, in this moment, where life resides—is, as far as I can tell, the most difficult of all things for a human being. It is so difficult because we cannot see the difference between conditioned mind and Life. In the beginning, most of us are so lost in unconsciousness that we think conditioned mind *is* Life. Practice offers a way to

70

see the difference. As we practice keeping our attention on the breath, the body, and the senses; on the emotions that pass through; on the thoughts that come and go—as we practice experiencing what is here, we begin to notice when we lose sight of the moment and become lost in the past or future. We begin to see what, in terms of our attention, leads towards suffering and all the many forms of unhappiness, and what leads towards peace, joy, connection, clarity, compassion, and everything else the heart longs for. We begin to see patterns in the way conditioned mind manifests within us. We begin to see how it works; through this growing understanding we begin to acquire tools, ways of looking, which assist us in more and more deeply seeing how we suffer and the choice that is available to end suffering.

7

The One Rule

My first morning at the monastery I awoke to the horror of what I had done. "I'm a what?" was my first thought. The gladness that had gone to bed with me the evening before had vanished in the night. There I was, I imagined, suddenly three thousand miles away from all I knew myself to be, with a future full of unknown disasters before me, and without a single steady thing to hold on to—only Rhea. There I was, by some twist of fate cast adrift upon a life that was not mine. All that remained of my former life, which I longed for suddenly as if I had been happy there, was a single duffle full of clothes.

Incredibly, it had never occurred to me to wonder what it might mean to be a monk. What does a monk do all day long? I didn't even know that. My imagination, which was not a friend to me in the best of times, churned out a wide range of hideous scenarios, all of which ended with my dying from humiliation. "Oh my god! What have I done?" I wondered aloud. I understood suddenly with panic what I had experienced with relief the night before, that I no longer needed to be the person I had always been. Nothing around me said "Dave," even as much as I wanted it to; instead, everything questioned me. Everything wondered spookily who I was.

Of course, whenever anyone ventures beyond what is known, he leaves his familiar self behind, but everywhere else—everywhere other than a Zen monastery— an individual may easily survive the resulting uneasiness through the expectation that he soon will create himself anew out of his new circumstances. Usually this happens so immediately that people don't even notice it; it is just what we do. What alarmed me that first morning was the realization that some madness had carried me to a place where nothing and no one would agree to support my conception of myself. This was all I understood about monastic training, that nothing in it would accept "me".

In addition, I recognized that nothing I believed I needed to be happy was available to me now—nothing. One day I was a vagrant, the next I was a monk, and though it is true that, as a vagrant, I had little that anyone else would desire, I had the one thing that mattered, which was the freedom to choose suffering through whatever vehicle happened to be available at the time. The moment I arrived at the monastery, everything I habitually used to compensate myself for my unhappiness was torn away. All that remained was silence and my experience of myself within it. There was, I saw, no way to escape from myself, no away to avoid what the silence required me to face. On top of that, I had little skill or experience in sorting out the mental chaos that erupted in the quiet. I had no tools, and without tools I had no choice but to submit to the misery of my domination by an egocentric mind suddenly jerked from its position at the center of the universe.

Luckily, before I arrived I had no idea what I was in for. If I had I doubt I would have made the journey. Like many, I believed that a life of silence protects a person somehow from pain. If anything, what monks do all day long is float around in bliss, six inches off the ground, or something similar. Nothing could be farther from the truth. The entire point of monastic training, as I quickly discovered, is to force into your awareness whatever you have avoided all your life, again and again and again, no matter how you may resist, until at last you let it go.

"We've made a terrible mistake," I told Rhea. "But don't worry, sweetheart—we're outa here tomorrow."

Having no choice, I got up, dressed myself, and made my way to the main monastery buildings. I wish I could return for a moment to that first morning of my training, as I trudged towards the meditation hall and saw the lower path, the outhouses, the outshowers, and, finally, the red-tiled buildings by the light of day for the first time. Even in my tumultuous state of mind, the sight of the archway took my breath away. My heart beat fiercely as I approached. A number of monks passed me as I hung my bag on the coat rack and took off my jacket, but none made any sign of welcome or, in fact, gave any indication that they had noticed me. With a gulp I reached out my hand, turned the handle on the meditation hall door, and stepped in for the first time—for the first of many thousands of times. I sat down on a cushion, faced the wall, and did my best imitation of a monk deep in contemplation. The sitting period lasted just thirty minutes, but it seemed forever. I was in hell. When it was over I couldn't stand up: my legs had fallen asleep. The other monks left me there on my own. When my limbs finally came to life again I hobbled to the door and back out into the archway, where I found a monk waiting for me. "I have been asked to orient you to breakfast," she said.

After breakfast the same monk showed me how to help clean up from the meal, then we sat together in the dining hall while she gave me the first pieces of information I needed in order to understand the expectations and opportunities of my new life. At the end of the lecture, which I heard as if from a great distance, as we passed the message board together the monk stopped and pointed at something hanging there. "Read this when you have a moment," she said. "You may find it helpful."

Later that day I returned to the message board to see what she had indicated. On a small piece of laminated paper pinned in one corner I read the following:

The One Rule:
We have many guidelines, but only one rule.
Our one rule is that we will use everything in our experience
to see how we cause ourselves to suffer,
so that we may drop that and end suffering.

I did indeed find it helpful. As I only vaguely understood before I arrived, the primary agreement that a monk makes with the monastery is to follow this one rule. I quickly discovered that this is far from easy to do, as our training as children has made it deeply habitual for us to use everything in our experience to prove how we are right, or inadequate, or deprived, or a host of other unhappy things. I shudder to remember my ignorance at that time, how blind I was to myself, but I admire the innate intelligence and willingness that taught me, even so, how to follow the One Rule in those first days and weeks and, through that rule, to begin to see the cause of my unhappiness.

I understood that I suffered—just this, in itself, was a blessing. I even understood, though not in a way I could have articulated, that I suffered because I lived within a fiction that said that I am this one, small, separate thing named "Dave," with needs and wants, and with likes and dislikes, that are not mine. What I did not understand was how this illusion was constructed. I had no idea how it was created and maintained. But I sensed that somehow my own thoughts created my misery, and that there must be a way to see into the chaotic workings of my mind to the ongoing processes underlying the mirage.

Conditioned mind resembles a machine. It operates with mathematical precision according to fixed and inflexible laws. Like a machine it is utterly predictable: this stimulus produces this response without fail, over and over and over. This is a fortunate thing, because if conditioned mind possessed its own reasoning, which it does not, in addition to the infinitely complex and subtle arrangement of gears and pulleys that it uses to cause us to suffer, we would never be able to see through it. Conditioned mind's automated nature is, in fact, our greatest asset—because we, as the spiritual mechanics that we can train ourselves to be, can learn to dismantle it.

Slowly, as I learned to follow the One Rule, I began to see glimpse how conditioning works. Like a shaft of light that beams through the foliage to the forest floor, here and there a moment of clarity pierced the dark confusion of my mind, illuminating bits and pieces of the processes that caused my suffering. Gradually I began to trust this clarity, and to yield to it despite my fear and doubt. Over time I recognized that to live the One

Rule was to accept the only opportunity I would ever have to escape from the grief and isolation that had poisoned my unhappy life. And so I set about the enormous work of discovering how I cause myself to suffer. This was the gigantic life choice that I made, without even understanding it, when I became a monk. I chose to submit to the process of my transformation. Since that first day the One Rule has guided me through all of the changes I have witnessed in myself these silent years, through untold upheaval and emotion, and through every sort of trouble and scrape you can imagine.

The first assignment I was given for working meditation that same morning after my orientation was to wash the meditation hall windows. Now, you wouldn't think a job like that would be terribly intimidating. You might even admire the kindness in giving such a simple assignment to someone so fresh from the world beyond the gates and so unsteady in his new role as a monk—but you probably do not know, as I did not, our windows. The monks made them from some antique glass that they scrounged up somewhere, and though they are beautiful because of this, they are also impossible to clean. No matter what you do, you leave streaks behind: that's all there is to it. So there I was on my first day as a monk, completely terrified, with squirt-bottle and rag in hand, clinging desperately to the hope that it all would go okay and that I wouldn't have to suffer this one time. Those darned windows, however, just wouldn't cooperate. I scrubbed and scrubbed and scrubbed, and the more I scrubbed the more they streaked and the more my anxiety grew. I nearly cried in frustration. As with most everything at the monastery, the metaphor in this was perfect, but the profundity of it was lost on me. I only wanted the windows to not have streaks so that I might feel myself to be okay, and when they refused, I despaired.

It only got worse from there. In my imagination, everything I was asked to do in some public way proved that there was something wrong with me. Everything seemed to display my incompetence. It did not matter what the job was or how it actually went; inevitably I finished each task (in my mind) as a failure. The irony is that I did not actually fail at all; in fact, I succeeded so well that I was continually given more and more challenging jobs to fail at. A few days after the windows I found myself to my dismay with a level and a shovel in my hands, and with the assignment to pour a concrete stoop beneath the back door. "I can't do that!" I said, but nobody listened. What could I do? I poured it, and it stands to this day as a monument to the lie of my inadequacy. But for the person I was at the time it was not good enough, because in my mind I was not good enough, so that for me was how it for a long time remained.

On and on it went like this. Every day the monastery gave me yet another list of ways to prove my incompetence to myself, and every day I succeeded in failing to be the person that I thought I should be. I can see now that if I had really wanted all this to stop, I could have just sabotaged everything, leaving a trail of disasters behind me—that would have taken care of it—but I did not think of that. The trouble was, in my heart I did not want to fail. And so I went along, helplessly succeeding but failing in my imagination, and continually setting myself up for greater and greater reasons to fear.

One day, perhaps two weeks into my training, I was asked to paint a sign. The sign was to say "private," I was told—it was for somebody's hermitage. The head monk (the general manager, you could say, of the monastery) laid out the job for me: "Here is a board, here is the paint and brush, and here is a sign to copy. Make it like this one," she said, pointing, then left me to my task.

I blinked in the dim light of the woodshop for several moments. "Hmmm...." I said to myself.

The task seemed simple enough. There was just this one problem. I couldn't do it, not in the way she had asked. My fear of my incompetence had exhausted me by this time, and so I had changed tactics. In order to compensate, I decided that I would have to be different and better than all the other monks. It made no sense, as conditioned mind generally does not, but I was unaware that I had made this decision, so that didn't bother me

77

any. This was the path I had followed my whole life and I was not about to abandon it here, at the time of my greatest need. "These people are peons," I said to myself. "They don't even know how to paint a sign."

There was no way in hell I was going to paint my sign just like the old one—too small and wimpy, too humble—so here is what I did instead. First, I scrounged around and found a board three times as big. Next, I reasoned that simple black on brown paint would never do. "Everything around here is brown," I said to myself. "Nobody will ever see it." I hunted for a while until I found some leftover fire engine red. With innocent delight I painted the background black, then painted "PRIVATE" in the most fearsome lettering I could come up with. Finished, I stepped back to admire my work. "Now that's a sign!" I said to myself.

Along came the head monk and asked to see the sign. I handed it to her, and to her credit she didn't even flinch. She just said, "I'm afraid I'm going to have to ask you to do this over, Dave."

"Huh?" I said.

"We need the sign to look like this one," she added, pointing to the old sign that I was asked to copy.

What? I was stunned. "But mine is better!" I insisted. She just bowed and walked away, leaving me to my humiliation.

I did not know that I was having the quintessential monk experience, one that would be repeated in ten thousand different ways over the next years of my training.

There was nothing I could do. As a monk I had no option but to bow and accept the guidance. I could not protest, or complain, or apologize, or anything. Just start over and paint.

As I painted the most hateful and bitter (but humble) "private" sign you can imagine, I began to feel rage rising within me. Finally, after those two weeks of intense psychological stress, I had had enough. In my heart, I cursed the head monk, and the monastery, too, and everything else in it down to the flies that feasted on my sweat while I worked. My anger grew; it went on for days, and I suffered and suffered and suffered.

Meanwhile, Rhea was having some challenges of her own.

Rhea brought her issues with her to the monastery, just as I did. She had big critter-chasing karma, that dog. At the time she and I entered the monastery, she chased everything, not just cats—she would have chased the cows down in the valley if they'd have run—but it was the thought of the cats, in particular, that had intimidated me. Before we arrived I could not imagine a future in which she would not destroy the opportunity that I so much wanted. Afterwards, I depended upon her to save me from the new life I was embarked upon, but in both cases I miscalculated. From the Roshi's point of view, I learned, Rhea had come to the monastery for the same reason I had: to train. You see, the Roshi is not troubled by such distinctions as "human" and "non-human." In her mind, Rhea was to be officially and just as much as me a "monk." The others referred to her from the beginning, in fact, as "the four-legged monk." She was to participate in the same spiritual work that we are all here to do, with the same ambition to end suffering that motivated me. I had never heard anything so absurd. "How can a dog be a monk?" I complained to myself. And yet, being but a monk myself, I conceded to the wisdom of the Roshi, and so together Rhea and I began our training.

It wasn't quite true, I found out, what had been rumored about the cats: the monastery had six, not twenty. Six, however, was plenty to destroy my peace of mind. I discovered also that they are a wild bunch of boys and girls, those cats, remaining invisible most of the time to all but the initiated—and, unfortunately, to Rhea. Almost immediately she got us into trouble. The cats all lived down by the old "kitchen tent", which had served as the kitchen during the years that the monastery was being built. No sooner had she discovered this than Rhea ransacked the place, scattering the terrified kitties into the woods. It was days before some were seen after that. When Rhea returned from her conquest, panting and furiously wagging her tail, just as happy and satisfied with her new life as she could be, I could only shake my head. "What are we going to do?" I wondered.

As bad luck would have it, one of the other monks was down there feeding the little buggers when it happened. "There is going to be trouble," I said to myself. I was right.

8

What is "Hard"?

My days continued to pass in fear and anger. Each one seemed interminable. I counted the hours that I had endured as a monk, then the days, then I began to count the weeks. I longed fanatically for escape, but there was no way to accomplish it. I had no choice but to continue and practice as best I could. People often talk of the spiritual advantages of willingness and courage and such, but when it comes right down to it, no better incentive to practice exists than having three thousand miles between you and your freedom to suffer, with no car and no money to get you there.

The time came at last when I had my first interview with the Roshi on the property. When I saw her sitting under the spreading oak that stands just outside the monastery gardens, speaking with the monk whose appointment preceded mine, it was the first time I had laid eyes on her since the day I had asked to be her student several months previously, in North Carolina. Finally she rang the bell by her chair, indicating that I was to approach. I bowed respectfully and sat in another chair before her. "Howdy!" she exclaimed cheerfully. "You made it here, I see."

I nodded. We talked for the next fifteen minutes, and though I cannot say I understood what occurred between us, something happened that changed my life forever. I sat down a man of the suffering world, and I arose instead a monk.

"How is it going so far?" she asked.

I tried to lie at first. I wished her to see in me strength and wisdom that I did not possess. I affected them mightily, but did not even fool myself: my heart was just not in it. I wished also to show her my secret experience, that sitting before her was not a man, but a child—a boy overwhelmed by life and in terror he would not survive—but that I could not easily do. I feared to see, myself, what I longed to show her. At last my pretense failed; my distress sat nakedly before her, and I had no choice but to admit it to both of us. So I screwed up my courage, and I said: "It's really hard."

"Hmmm..." she replied, and studied me closely. "What is hard?"

I could not answer. The compassion I saw in her appalled me. I could not even meet her eyes. "What is hard?" she asked again after a few moments, though more gently this time. I tried to speak once more, but what could I possibly say? *Everything* in life was hard as far as I could tell.

In my heart, as I sat there with the Roshi that afternoon under the oak tree, I wanted to tell her that. Hard, I wanted to say, is what life in its cruelty has forced upon me. I am here against my will, the prisoner of merciless circumstances. I am desperately unhappy and confused and I want to go home.

"Everything," I said.

"No, no," she replied, then leaned forward significantly and whispered, as if passing to me a great secret: "What *is* hard, with the emphasis on 'is'."

"I see," I said, but I actually didn't. Her cheerfulness distracted me. She seemed quite pleased with everything, in fact. After a few moments of silence she commented on the beautiful spring weather and the loveliness of the day, even as I labored on and on within myself about my misery.

Suddenly I saw the obvious: she was just plain happy. This captivated me, despite my determination to suffer. What, I wondered, is the difference between her and me?

"I thought I would be happy here," I said.

"And so you will," she replied, "But first you must discover who you are."

That startled me. I thought I knew who I was. "How do I do that?" I asked her.

"Good question! You used the magic word: 'how'. That must become the most important word in your vocabulary. Whenever anything happens, you must ask, 'ow'? How am I causing myself to suffer? How can I let go and end suffering? 'How' is the key that unlocks the mystery."

The *how* of life is everything. This is the fundamental understanding behind the One Rule and the basis, as I later became aware, of spiritual training: freedom from conditioned mind begins when we learn to see life in terms of *how* rather than *what*.

The *what*s are the content of experience: this situation or that situation, this relationship, this job, this feeling, this thought, this behavior, this anything that is a particular something. The *how* is the subjective process behind or underneath the *what*s: how feelings happen; how I create this world or that world to live in; how I come to believe in a "me" that is separate from all else that is, and so on. "How" is a name for the mysterious way life manifests in form.

Conditioned mind uses the content of life, the whats, to cause us to suffer. As long as we remain caught in believing that the outside circumstances of our life cause us to feel the way we feel, or to think what we think, or to be who we believe we are, then we have no choice but to live in obedience to an illusion. The whats of life, in fact, do not cause us to feel or think or be anything; it is the how of life that does. The secret to happiness is the discovery of this truth.

I can remember as a boy being shown how to put a quarter beneath a piece of blank paper, and how to rub a pencil back and forth across the top until, to my immense wonder and delight, an image of the coin appeared as if by magic. In the same way, as our minds race here and there through the content of life— through the *whats*—an awareness of *how* can trace the processes through which suffering creates itself and give us the power to choose what we could not without it.

There is nothing real going on outside of the mind—neither here at the monastery nor in the world beyond the gates. That is, there is nothing in what we believe to be going on that actually is. Without make-believe life is perfectly simple: there is only sensation, the amazing phenomena that seem to cause sensation, and our awareness of it. It is the nature of conditioned mind to create meaning out of our sensations: to make up "perceptions", to think about what we supposedly perceive, then assume these thoughts contain independent truth and reality. We fill our lives with whats, in other words—with thoughts we believe to be real—and allow them to sweep us away in a story about our unhappiness.

At the monastery there is little to create whats out of. You are eating lunch, you are washing the dishes, you are sitting on the porch—that's it. You might go the whole day without anyone saying anything to you; there is little to have or acquire or in other ways use to suffer over. Even so, people manage to re-create their whole accustomed reality from the way the person sitting next to them is chewing his or her food, from some innocent note on the board, from the assignment they are given for working meditation, and so on. The purpose of the silence is to put a mirror up in front of this process so that we may see through the illusion. The fantasy becomes impossible to believe eventually: there just isn't enough to hang the fiction on. Everybody here hates me, says the fiction. How do I know? I can tell by the way they crunch their toast.

I had little understanding of this that day I sat with the Roshi under the ancient oak, while the breeze ruffled her grey hair, while the sunshine played with shadows over her shoulders and arms, and while daffodils along the garden perimeter shyly displayed their yellow and white petals behind her. I only knew that I was miserable. "Ah!" I said, feigning comprehension. "How!"

"Very good," agreed the Roshi, though I doubt she was deceived. Then she leaned forward in a friendly sort of way and added, "Now—what about little Rhea? How is she faring as a monk?"

"I don't think she's realized yet that she is, in fact, a monk."

"Apparently not. There was some business about the cats, I understand."

I gulped as the dread descended. "Cats?" I said innocently. She frowned, and her eyes pierced me to the heart.

"Yes, cats," she said. "She must be tied."

The horror of that thought flushed me from my defensive posture. "You can't tie her up!" I cried. Seeing how little my urgency impressed the Roshi, I tried again. "She didn't choose to be here!" I moaned. "It will kill her! To be tied up the rest of her life...."

"The rest of her life?" the Roshi interrupted. "No, only until she stops chasing the cats."

That stumped me for a moment. The thought had never occurred to me before. But only for a moment: "She will never stop chasing the cats," I pleaded, "That's the problem. She can't. She chases cats—it's who she is!" I did not know at that point that you do not say to a Zen Master who somebody is. Alas, there was a great deal more than just that which I didn't understand. Most importantly, I did not doubt the person I believed my own self to be. That was the trouble.

"It is not who she is," said the Roshi sternly. "You must train her."

I was flabbergasted. How could it be that what was so clear to me was not clear to her? I knew she was asking the impossible, but what could I do? She is the Roshi. And so began Rhea's default commitment to end her suffering.

Here is what the Roshi told me to do. Everywhere I went, she said, Rhea was to go, tied to my waist with a piece of rope. That way "support" would be always available to her. Whenever we saw a cat I was to teach Rhea how to not chase it. In fact, I was to take Rhea down to the old kitchen tent twice a day to practice not chasing them. I was never to punish her, the Roshi said. Instead, when Rhea saw a cat and tried to chase it, I was to grasp her head in both hands, put my nose to hers so that I looked her directly in the eyes, and say "No!" several times very earnestly.

Over time, the Roshi promised, she would get it. Her love for me would teach her what she needed to let go of.

Just then the bell rang, signaling the end of our interview. It was another monk's turn to speak with her. Conditioned mind attempted to distract me with thoughts of injustice and revenge, but it could not keep me from the admission that what the Roshi suggested might work. Her clarity had touched me. I also could not avoid the bit of understanding about my own training reflected in her outline of Rhea's: the issues I faced were different, of course, but the letting go required was the same. I bowed, and as I walked away I recalled the question from the beginning of our interview—"What *is* 'hard'?"—and suddenly grasped the radical change in perspective that it entailed. She did not ask me, I realized, what is hard about life—what in the content of my life story felt hard for me—but what this thing is that I believed in called "hard" that made my life so difficult. This is the question that made a monk of me—this, and the obvious difference between my life experience and hers. I wanted what she had, whatever that was, that turned the same world that sickened me into a place of joy for her.

Now I can see what she did, that almost nobody knows who they are. The Roshi, of course, was right: this is the difficulty. I would guess from my short study of humanity that few are completely lost to the beauty and magic that surrounds them, to the reflection of who they actually are that nature provides. But few seem to experience this beauty *as themselves*. We are too deeply trained to separate ourselves from anything that suggests our inherent goodness to admit the wonder that each of us is. We, like everything else that we perceive, are natural beings; how could it be that we do not participate in the harmony that we see? Who we are is everything that life is; but, just as I had done for so long, we deny this reality to live in isolation and deprivation instead.

That afternoon the Roshi modeled for me an alternative: that we may live in awareness. After much effort and time I learned that it was not something she *did* but something she did *not* do that made her perception of the day so different from mine. She did not carry before her in her mind the need to be other than who she is. She just was.

That evening, as I walked along the porch outside the hall on my way to the last meditation of the day, I spied one of my fellow-monks inside through the window where he sat. The lamp at the far end of the room silhouetted the figure that he made, so that his face lay half in darkness, half in light. His hands, I saw, were held before him, palm to palm, and his eyes were closed, gazing inward—completely unselfconscious in his sincerity. I saw in that image of a man's perfect devotion to himself and his own transformation a glimpse of my own. True, it lay deeply shadowed by the many fears that towered over it, but there it was, available to me should I find the willingness to embrace it. Gratefully, I did have that willingness. Over time this devotion became less of a stranger to me, I became more its confidant, the fear lessened, and the resistance began to pass. I found at last that what I wanted most was not to run, but to stay and be still, and to work to end my suffering. I found, in fact, that this was all that I actually wanted, and so I stayed and set out to learn what it is to be a monk.

9

The Sickening Dread

A number of days passed. The determination I had felt after the talk with the Roshi eroded quickly, as I might have anticipated with more experience. Even after all these years I am still amazed at the ceaseless tenacity of conditioned mind, at its perfect consistency, its unremitting daily brutality, and at the invisible power it manages to employ even within the monastic environment. Once again I was plunged into misery. I wished ardently to free myself, but no matter how hard I tried I could not do it. I could only suffer, and I could only imagine suffering for the interminable months that remained of my commitment. "Heaven help me," I said to myself as each day passed in hopelessness and desperation. "What am I going to do?"

One day I was assigned to dig an irrigation trench between the greenhouse and the garden. The head monk described the task to me as if it were the simplest thing a person could do. "No problem," I said to myself. I went to work with great hopes, thinking that surely I'd be done in no time at all. I quickly found that she had failed to mention the stones buried in the earth, the sun that blazed on my back and neck, the clouds of dust that filled the air with every blow I struck, and the flies. In no time at all I stood knee-deep in a muddy hole, covered in dust and sweat and tears, reduced to a state of desperation—as green a monk as could be.

I did not understand at the time the kindness behind that wretched work assignment. I entered the monastery the way a meteor enters earth's atmosphere: with tremendous heat and momentum and a need for some solid place to crash. I could only see the great misfortune, as I imagined it, of being me. Nobody on earth, I decided, was more miserable. Nobody had more reason to hate the life he had, to resent the unkind destiny that had brought him to it, or to wish it all would somehow, miraculously, be over. My mind rumbled on like this for I don't know how long, despising my existence, envying the hordes of people beyond the monastery gates and their unconscious lives, condemning myself and the other monks, and other unpleasant things.

I might have agonized away the whole afternoon and completely missed the experience of those precious few hours, but suddenly the sunlight fell upon my filthy arm where it flexed against the handle of the mattock, and in that moment I realized that I lived. In that moment a whole world opened up that had been unavailable before: for an instant I just *was*. I noticed the feel of the sweat that trailed down my legs and smelled the raw earth. I noticed the breeze that teased the leaves on the trees nearby. I noticed the feelings that moved like clouds through my body as I worked. Suddenly I was here.

I stopped digging and stood still. "Oh my God!" I whispered as I perceived the implications of this little awakening. What if it had not happened? What if I had not woken up from my unhappiness? Worse, what if I had *never* awakened but had gone on perpetuating misery in this way for the rest of my days? To do that would be to miss my whole life! The horror of that possibility and the excitement that came with the insight kindled a determination within me to find a way through my unhappiness, come what may.

As usual, the clarity quickly passed and I tumbled back into my old unhappy ways. The trouble was that I did not know how to end suffering. My recent experience and others had shown me it was possible, but not how to do it. I wanted to escape from the sorrows that overwhelmed me; I even understood that an entity called "ego" resisted that escape from within my own mind, but I did not know how to get past resistance into the place of freedom that I knew existed just beyond the reach of my awareness. All I knew how to do was wait and hope.

Luckily, this was all that was required—that, and a bit of willingness.

On Sunday afternoons the monks are given a few hours to rest and take care of personal needs. Ordinarily, the meals here are a communal affair, but on Sunday evenings we are on our own to forage what we can from the leftovers. One Sunday evening not long after the insight just described, as I went to make a meal for myself from the available odds and ends, I found something in the refrigerator that I never would have expected. Right there on the top shelf, as plain as day, was a great big jar of peanut butter. I was amazed: monks do not eat peanut butter (or at least, not these monks). The Roshi does not consider peanut butter to be healthy food, so we do not buy it.

Now, I have always hated peanut butter. As a boy I was the only kid on the block who preferred egg salad sandwiches to peanut butter and jelly. I doubt I had peanut butter in my mouth even once between the ages of five and twenty-five: I just couldn't stand it. Then I moved to the monastery and discovered that peanut butter is something I could not have. You would think that someone with my abnormality would experience relief at finding himself at last in a world without peanuts: that just seems intelligent. But no, instead I developed an overwhelming craving for peanut butter.

Then suddenly there it was, that Sunday afternoon. Heaven only knows where it came from. I understood immediately both that I should not take any, and that I would. Very cautiously I looked around to see if was alone. I was. In an incredible hurry I made myself the biggest peanut butter sandwich anyone has ever seen, then I slithered off to my hermitage to consume it in private.

One bite and I saw how I had been swindled—it was awful.

For a long while I stared at that cursed sandwich, wondering what in the world had come over me. The conclusion suddenly became obvious: it was conditioned mind. More than I hated peanut butter, I (it) loved dissatisfaction. How else could it be explained? A little thrill of excitement moved through me with this insight. It was the first time, I think, that I could see for myself what the other monks seemed to understand so clearly—that which they called "process". They were always talking about having "done a process" with this or that, and it thrilled me to realize that I had done a process with the sandwich and had recognized that. "I think I'm catching on to this!" I told myself.

The suffering in it, I realized, had nothing to do with the peanut butter. When I remembered all the pleasures I had longed for all my life—all the glorious places I could not travel to, all the possessions that lay beyond my grasp, all the people I had loved who seemed to turn away—I understood the cruel deception I had been a victim to. Here it was again, only in miniature. I only wanted what I could not have. Whatever I did have was never enough, no matter what it was. What a perfect way to suffer! No wonder I had felt so dissatisfied! Through my whole life conditioned mind had robbed me in this way of everything I was given, and of the deep satisfaction that comes with what just is.

Seeing this, I instantly experienced choice. I saw how it would be possible to live without the life-long assumption of deprivation. I experienced myself as I rarely had before: without wanting and utterly content. As I felt the sudden freedom move within me, I understood the nature of the lie I had believed. "This is what they mean when they say 'how'," I thought. "Maybe I can do this after all."

Soon afterwards it came time for my next opportunity to meet with the Roshi under the oak tree. "How's it going?" she asked after she had greeted me.

"Well….," I answered. Her eyes questioned me. "I'm having a heck of a difficult time. I have suffered almost every moment since we last talked."

To my great annoyance, the Roshi smiled at this. "Of course!" she said. "We could hardly have expected ego to rejoice at this new life choice you've made."

"For six months," I reminded her.

She continued to chuckle. "We'll see…."

91

I told her about those moments of freedom I had experienced while digging the trench. I did not tell her, I confess, about stealing the peanut butter.

"Yes! Yes!" she said. "That was a glimpse beyond the illusion. There will be more of those coming your way shortly. I guarantee it. Just hold on."

"The thing I don't get is that my practice went so much better before I came to the monastery. It was easy out there. Since I arrived here I've felt as if I'm going backwards."

"Don't believe it. It only appeared that you were better off out in the world because conditioned mind had control of you there. It could not prevent you from having awarenesses from time to time, but there was never any danger that it would lose its fundamental mastery of your attention. That changed radically when you set foot on the monastery property. Nothing here reflects ego, as you know—it all reflects and supports the heart. Conditioned mind is in real danger here, and so it has had to do here what it did not have to do out there—it's turning the big guns on you."

"It's working," I said. "I'm getting blasted all day long."

"Do you know about the Sickening Dread?"

I nodded. "I've heard the other monks talk about it."

One of the things that I recall most clearly from my first months at the monastery was the awful sensation that often filled my chest and throat, like physical nausea, only a hundred times worse. Imagine being in a car accident while you have food poisoning—it was something like that. It afflicted me especially first thing in the day. Getting out of bed was a work of pure determination. I longed each morning to sleep the rest of my life away rather than face the fear that I knew would dog my unsteady footsteps if I got up. Usually once I did get going the sensation eased a bit, but not much, and it always waited like a jealous lover for me to return to my hermitage at night. The experience, I learned, is a common one. The monks even have a name for it. That's what they call "the sickening dread."

Once as a teen-ager I rode a train from my grandmother's house in the Illinois countryside into Chicago to explore the city. There was a place I saw through the window along the way that I will never forget. Imagine a canal full of thick-looking water that doesn't seem to move, a muddy dirt track full of pot-holes on the far bank, two leafless and probably dead trees with a listless bird perched on one of them—and, beyond the wasted road, the hugest pile of trash you could ever imagine: gigantic heaps of twisted and rusting metal, thousands of them, one after the other leading off to the horizon. I had never seen anything like it: it was an entire countryside full of waste.

Now, imagine this: that gigantic pile of garbage is yours, and it is your job to clean it up. Imagine as well that it has always been with you, right there overflowing from your back yard, and that you have lived most all of your life in denial of its existence. One day you look outside your kitchen window and you see it for the first time. Imagine that every single piece of garbage in all those piles is something that you left there long ago because it terrified you. Finally, imagine that you know in your heart of hearts that you are going to clean it all up because you simply cannot stand to live with it any more. The feeling you would have if all of this were so is what is called "the sickening dread."

The dread comes when no way out exists but into and through what we have avoided all our lives. It comes when we have suffered enough, when it is at last too horrible and too late to return to ignorance and delusion. Few can bear it. This is why people enter the monastery, to get the support they need to face all of the hurt in that enormous work.

"What do you think?" the Roshi asked.

"Yes, I'm sure that's it," I replied. "It just seems so real."

"Of course. It is designed to seem real—but it isn't. Here's the thing I hope you will consider: the decision is already made. You have committed to ending suffering. It's done, over, too late to go back—even if you have not accepted that yet. The dread is ego's reaction to that fact. You might as well let go of the resistance and get on with it, because you are going down the path of awakening whether you like it or not. You can either go willingly and easily, or you can fight it the whole way through. Now, it's true," she continued, laughing suddenly, "that everyone fights it, but it's good to know that you don't have to."

"So what do I do now?"

"You must learn to see how conditioned mind does what it does. That is the way you free yourself from it. Gradually, as you do that, you will align yourself with the transformation that is happening rather than with the old programming that controls you now."

"I'm not sure I know how to do that," I admitted. "Any tips?"

"Yes. The easiest and most direct way to see what ego is up to is to practice recognizing what I call 'the voices'. Do you know what I mean by that?"

"I think so," I replied. "What I'm saying to myself."

"Yes and no. It would be more accurate to describe it as 'what ego is saying to you.' We have a couple more minutes, I think— I'll explain."

10

The Voices

"Within our minds is an unseen force that talks to us in our own voice," the Roshi continued. "During every waking moment it speaks to us, telling us who we are, who other people are, what we like and don't like, how we feel, and what we are experiencing. It uses the first person, "I", to talk to us, with the implication that the thoughts it creates are our thoughts, and the experiences it tells us we are having are our experiences. It says that it is who we are, and we believe it, and so we live its life, not ours. This is how it causes us to suffer. To live as a conditioned human being is to live as one possessed."

Isn't it amazing how life works? We are all born with the same ability as any sentient creature to feel our portion of the life energy that flows through all things, and to respond according to our nature with this energy. As human beings, we are also born with the capacity to be aware of ourselves as we participate in the mystery of our existence on this earth. As we awaken to this world we live in, however, ego awakens also. Almost from the moment we open our mouths to take our first breath a seed is planted deep within our minds that sprouts with the awakening of our consciousness, that grows within us as we grow into the opportunity of our self-awareness, and that takes this opportunity for itself. It assumes our identity; we presume its reality, and so it becomes something, even as unholy as it is, that abides in this world of miracles.

"In order to be free," the Roshi continued, "not only from the suffering that troubles you now, but in the largest sense, you must learn to recognize the voices—to see what in your mind is you and what is not you—so that you may live this life that you have rather than the life the voices would prescribe for you."

"What really *is* me?"

"Well, technically there is no 'you' beyond compassionate awareness, but that's a matter for another time. It would be best at this point to just hold that question in front of you and allow your experience to answer it. The key practice in this is to keep your attention on the conversation in your mind. That's how you will see the difference between what we might say is authentically you—what is here, awake, alive—and the voices. Almost everything going on that involves language is egocentricity. You will notice that it always demands unhappiness of some kind."

"To keep my attention on the conversation in my mind...." I repeated.

"Just do the fundamental practice, in other words, with the awareness that it is the voices that cause you to suffer. Keep bringing your attention here, to this moment. Remember that your breath is here, and your body. Anchor your attention in the present with the help of the breath. The voices are not here— though your perception of them is—so if you are here you will see them through the contrast. That's a good principle to remember: the only place from which we can see conditioned mind—where we can see how we suffer—is here.

"Expect to suffer," she continued. "There is no way around it. You will suffer until you are not willing to suffer any more. It won't go on forever, though. If you will ground yourself as courageously as you can in awareness, and if you will watch conditioning do what it does, it will gradually lose its power over you. It's in a really bad spot right now. It has been required to get out the big stuff, which it never likes to do unless it has to, because the danger is so great that it will be seen."

A bell rang, ending the interview, and I headed off into the silence to practice. I immediately began to see the voices more clearly. In fact, they attacked the Roshi's credibility as soon after the appointment was over. "She's a crackpot," they said.

"Ah-ha!" I said to myself. "That's the voices!"

Against the background of the silence and armed with my assignment, I could not fail to notice how I talked to myself through every moment of the day—or rather how I was talked to by that unreal entity that we call "conditioned mind." A running commentary followed me from my first to my last moment of wakefulness. Every instant was filled with voices that told me what I thought about myself or the other monks, that planned for the future and rehashed the past, that argued with themselves about what they wanted, or about what was real, or about what was right or good to do. They talked and talked and talked and talked, on and on and on and on, as if this conversation were necessary for my functioning in the world.

The next Sunday afternoon I went for a walk down to the creek with Rhea. As a special treat I packed a picnic from the leftovers that were available. When we arrived I sat down on a stone beside the water to eat, and, as always, Rhea began to negotiate for her fair share. Now, Rhea just happened to be the most adorable dog in the entire world, and the world's foremost master in the art of begging. She sighed and groaned and wagged her tail and did every other thing she knew to win my heart. She gazed longingly at my cheese sandwich as I ate it, she performed her little act of angelic starvation, she made herself more pitiful and deserving than a human can stand, until at last I broke down and gave her some.

As I did, and as I delighted in her delight, I suddenly saw how perfectly she understands herself without language. I saw the fundamental difference between her and me—that she does not suffer. There is no confusion within her mind about who she is. Clearly she knew just what she wanted, and just as clearly she understood how to get it from me, but without, as far as I could tell, the need to explain it to herself. She employed her deprivation act and all of her beguiling ways without, it seemed to me, any voices. Surely, I thought to myself, I must be blessed with this same capacity, even if I do not often experience it. How is it that I cannot live as she does, doing whatever is before me to do, being whatever I am in a given moment, without a cascade of

97

words to disturb the gentle pool of my experience? How have I lost this capacity?

The voices pull us out of our present moment experience: that's the entire point. Without an interior conversation there is just what is happening: I am whatever my life presents to me in a particular moment—the breeze that ruffles my hair, the sensation of hunger in my tummy, a feeling of loneliness or of joy, and so on—plus the awareness of these things. With a conversation a separation arises between me and my experience. I become something outside of my life, looking in; I am the subject, and my life is the object. The advantage of this arrangement (from the point of view of ego) is that it places me in a position from which I believe I am able to control my experience; the disadvantage (from the point of view of the authentic human) is that I am, in this place, no longer alive. To be alive is to participate in the creation of the moment, as Rhea does. To position myself outside of the moment of life—to objectify my experience—is, in a manner of speaking, to die.

Time passed and I practiced as hard as I could. Here and there I began to have small moments of awakening that heartened me and gave me the strength to carry on. They were always unexpected, I noticed, and without a cause. I would just be walking from here to there, or performing some simple task, or listening to my fellow-monks in group, and suddenly my mind would open to the startling fact that I am alive. The voices would cease and I would see the objects around me for a moment with new clarity, as if they were infused with light. Joy would arise in my heart, and I would feel glad and at peace. Then I would grasp at the happiness I experienced—I would think about it—and it would pass. Usually it would not return for many days, but over time I began to trust that if I would continue to pay attention eventually the opening would happen again. I started to feel that the hope that had brought me to the monastery was being fulfilled, and that I would succeed. I finally celebrated my half-way point—three months—then the worst of all possible things happened.

One afternoon I found the following note addressed to me on the message board. (FYI: the word "gasshō" is Japanese. Our translation is "my heart and your heart are one". To put one's hands in prayer position and bow is to "make gasshō". The word is used to communicate respect and gratitude, among other things).

Dave,
      Please take over as the cook beginning tomorrow morning. The current cook will meet you after breakfast for an orientation.
Gasshō

I stared at the note for a long time. "What?" said the voices.

11

The Hot Sauce Episode

What a blow that was! I most desperately did not want to be the cook. I would rather have been anything—*anything*—than the cook. Why? Because the cook is the worst of all possible jobs at the monastery. Even someone with perfect confidence has good reason to hate the cook's job, but for someone like me, whose whole ambition in life was to avoid the failure I believed myself to be, being the cook is a nightmare. There are just so many ways to mess up. The details are endless, and if you overlook just one you've had it. In addition, the preparation of the food is the most visible work in the entire place, so if you mess up everybody knows it. To make things even worse, everyone considers herself or himself to be an expert on food, even if they've never boiled water, so no matter what you do it is going to be the wrong thing. Success under these circumstances is not possible.

I went to the Roshi to complain. "But I don't *want* to be the cook," I said.

"Of course you don't want to," she replied. "Nobody does. If you wanted to, you would be disqualified. The question is: are you willing?"

"Well..." I replied.

"In case it's any consolation to you," the Roshi said, "I can sympathize. I would even let you off the hook if I could—but I can't. I don't make these decisions, you know." She rolled her eyes upwards significantly.

I nodded knowingly, but I didn't get it. "What?" said the voices. "If you aren't making these decisions, then who is?"

The next day I found myself in the kitchen with a knife in my hands, wondering if I should use it to chop the carrots or to end my miserable existence. I chose the former, and so began my career as the monastery cook.

The next three months were pure torture. Every meal was a dizzying opportunity to prove myself to be the person I believed I should be or wretchedly to fail. I threw myself frantically into my work—it was life and death—and the other monks quickly learned to avoid the kitchen lest I run them over in my hysteria. Every morning after breakfast I decided that this would be the day that I would produce the food that would proclaim once and for all to everyone that I was not the flawed person I believed myself to be. Nothing I did was ever enough, but even so the near possibility of success intoxicated me. I never left the kitchen, even at the end of day: instead, I took it home with me at night and turned it over and over in my mind, imagining all of the various schemes and inventions—the salads, the soups, the sauces, the soufflés! —that for sure, if they would only work, would set my mind to rest at last. It was horrible.

One of the jobs of the cook is to go to town for groceries. Considering my distracted state it is hard to believe I was allowed to leave the property, but I was. Once a week I made the long journey to the local grocery store. Now, a grocery store, as everyone knows, is filled with of all sorts of seductions. For this reason it was made clear from the beginning that I was to buy only what I set out to buy, and nothing more. Poor me, I obeyed this guideline scrupulously at first, but as time went by I sort of forgot the importance of it, and sort of decided that I was in charge instead of the monastery, and in this way gradually became vulnerable to the tricks of conditioned mind.

And so it was one day that I found myself there in the grocery store, standing in front of a bottle of Vietnamese hot sauce. It was the most glorious jar of hot sauce I had ever seen. It even had garlic in it. In the hidden places of my mind the voices of conditioning began to make a case for buying it. What they actually said to convince me I don't know, but the implication of their words, even as crazy as this will sound, was that this little jar of hot sauce would get me the approval I had always been looking for. Somehow this would be the thing that at last would cement my right to exist as a human being and would capture the love and acceptance for me that I had always been denied. At last, this was it! If you ever feel tempted to doubt the insanity of conditioned mind, remember the tortured young man I was that day, putting his whole life in a jar of cayenne peppers.

Everything hung in the balance in that moment. All of my past misery had led me to that fateful choice. All of the known universe held its breath as I debated what to do: would I choose at last to let go of the lie that I was not good enough, and walk away without the sauce? Or would I succumb to the illusion of my incompetence yet again, and buy it?

I bought it.

Before long the Roshi found out—she has spies everywhere, you know—and invited me to visit with her under the oak tree for a little chat. When I arrived I saw to my astonishment that she held the hot sauce in her hands. "This is not okay," she said, pointing to the jar. "Take it back."

I was stunned. "Take it back?" I said.

"Yes, take it back," she replied, then she leaned forward significantly as she repeated, in the most serious voice imaginable, "This is not okay."

I will not even try to describe the violence that followed those words in my mind. The Roshi represented to me then, as she still often does now, the possibility of the unconditional acceptance that I had always wanted. I had learned to love and to trust her; to have her speak in this way devastated me. I heard her words through the woeful filter of conditioned mind. What I heard her say was this: '*You* are not okay....'"

There it was at last, the very thing that all of my life I had avoided.

Oh, the rage and defiance that followed! Day and night for weeks anger and rebellion dominated my mind. I hated the Roshi passionately, and I despised the other monks as well. I still cooked for them as I had to do, but I seasoned their food with bitterness and fury. I longed to leave and find some safe if unhappy way to survive my life until finally it was over. All day I fantasized about all the places in the world where I could be instead of the monastery kitchen. Every evening I hiked as far as I could beyond the front gate, and when I could go no farther, I stared down the road towards my imagined freedom. Every morning when I awoke I subtracted one from the days until the end of my commitment, when I could turn my back without defeat upon this place and finally go.

I still followed the schedule, as I had no choice. I still dragged myself out of bed in the morning, trudged to the meditation hall to sit with the other monks, and spent the whole long day by myself in the kitchen. There I was accompanied by the sound of the knife on the cutting board, the warm water flowing over my hands, the sunlight reflecting on the tile floor— and the voices, who screamed furiously all day long that I must quit and run. It was hell.

Perhaps a week into this I was asked to take one of the monastery's computers in to be repaired while I was out shopping. I was surprised—I had not been asked to run that sort of errand before. The place that does this sort of work for us doubles as a satellite television outlet: half the store displays computers, the other half TVs. Only someone who has lived for four months in silence and solitude can understand what a shock it was to be suddenly surrounded by televisions. Right by the door was a screen the size of a billboard. It played a movie of some kind that was full of sharks and women in slinky bathing suits. Luckily, the store is arranged in such a way that while I worked with the technician behind the counter my back was to the television; he faced it, but I faced him, so I did not have to wrestle with the distraction.

At first our conversation was energetic and focused on the difficulty at hand. After a while, however, there came a moment when the technician was required to perform some sort of test on the computer, and we were left for a few minutes with nothing to do while the machine groaned and crunched and did its thing. While I waited I turned my attention, as best I could under the circumstances, to my breath and to my body and to my sensations, as I was training to do. There was no way I was going to look at that television. Instead I observed the beams of sunlight that streamed in through the windows and the tiny particles of dust that swam in them; I felt the clothes on my body and my feet in my shoes; I touched the anger that burned in my heart over my life circumstances, but with a gentleness and understanding that surprised me. Against the backdrop of that worldly scene I sensed the changes practice had wrought in me those four months, and I was moved.

After a bit I looked over to the technician to ask him something, but I stopped short in amazement. His attention had been captured by the television. His eyes were open, but his face was so fixed that he seemed without life or intelligence. He had lost consciousness of himself, of me, and of everything else but what occurred on the screen. He was gone, checked out, absent—however you want to say it—and I was alone.

Now, I do not know this, but it is possible that even when the technician and I resumed our interactions he remained unconscious. He had the appearance of life again at that point, but the chances are good that, unless he had done an enormous amount of awareness practice prior to our encounter that day, his attention simply moved from the images on the television to a conversation in his mind. Instead of a world of skin and sharks he likely lived in a fantasy about some conflict in his life, or something as trivial as what he would have for dinner. This would be a more subtle level of unconsciousness, it is true, than his stark disappearance into the television screen, and it would permit at least some awareness of his surroundings. The effect, however, would be the same.

I saw myself reflected in that man in a way that was most helpful. I lose consciousness, I realized, in exactly the same way as he.

What interested me most about the experience was the realization that the images in the television possessed no reality until the technician gave his attention to them. Without anyone's attention—his, or mine—there were no sharks: only light, shade, color, and movement. Nothing exists within the TV to make these into "shark"; the sharks became "real" only when organized by the intelligence of an observer. In the same way, the conversations in our minds have no life until we give it to them through our attention. Without our attention they are but sounds moving through on their way to who knows where; with the infusion of our attention they take on the appearance of reality. This appearance is so convincing that it eclipses our actual perceptions. We do not see that we are being talked to by voices; we believe they represent reality, and so we listen, and in our listening, we lose touch with our lives.

One who is possessed by egocentric, karmic conditioning assumes that she or he has self-determination, but in fact does not. The choices we think of as "my" choices are not actually ours: they are the dictates of the system that causes us to suffer, and we act them out unconsciously. No matter what we choose, if we listen to the voices our choices will result in separation from our authentic lives and union with egocentricity. Sometimes a radical life event, like a death or falling in love, will wake us up for a time to the real choice that our imprisonment denies us, but sooner or later, unless we are practicing awareness with all of our hearts, we begin to listen to the voices once again, and our capacity to choose life over suffering disappears.

This is exactly what had happened, I realized, around the hot sauce: I was merely possessed by the voices. Seeing this, it became obvious that all I had to do was to turn my attention away and put it on something that is here, in this moment—like my breath or some other physical thing—and my misery would end. A great rush of energy and hope arose with that insight. "Ha!" I said to conditioned mind. "I've got you now!"

Nothing could be simpler—I just could not do it. Try as I might over the next days, the story of injustice that had attached itself to recent events commanded me through my attention, demanding that I suffer over it, and I could not keep my attention away. Most of the time I did not even remember it was a story—I just lived it as if it were real. Occasionally, however, I did remember, and though I could not break the spell it held over me, gradually the questioning I applied began to undermine its seemingly seamless aspect. Eventually its believability began to erode.

The violence stormed within my mind for what seemed like an eternity. Then at last the illusion broke down. One evening, as I once again walked off my outrage on the road beyond the gate, a little something suddenly caught my eye. It was a leaf, turning slowly over and over in the wind. In that moment, through no willful effort of my own, I let go of the story and suddenly I was there. This was not the "I" that steals our lives away, pretending to be who we are, but the clarity that sees beyond conditioned mind to what is. I saw in that moment that I was not the flawed person who I believed I was: I was merely a man trapped in the agonizing world of his own misperceptions, each of them telling him that he was bad, and wrong. I saw that I was something else, something infinitely larger and full of space, something full of clarity and compassion, and just like that the entire edifice of my suffering collapsed, and I was free.

12

Everyone You Meet is Your Mirror

Next chance I got I told the Roshi what had happened. She listened with the utmost gravity. "Well done," she said at the end of my narrative.

At that moment, all of the resentment and anger dissolved that still hovered around the edges of my awareness, and I basked in a feeling of pure love for her and acceptance for myself. "I think I'm back," I said. "Thank God!"

She laughed. "Luckily for us," she said, "this is a practice of exploration, not a practice of perfection. It's these sorts of experiences we are here to have. You are fortunate in having aroused conditioned mind to such an extent and to have come out the other side."

"I suppose I might expect to have to do that again?"

"Of course! But that's a good thing. Every time we get lost and then find our way back, we learn more deeply how to do that. In this case, every time you believe a story like the one you've described and then wake up from it, you get to see again how we create the world we live in—not just when conditioning is aroused, but all the time. Every moment of every day we make up a world to live in so that we can suffer."

"We project it, you mean," I said.

Everything we believe we experience outside of ourselves is actually a reflection of our own internal processes. This is the teaching I had learned to call "projection". There is no self that perceives an other, says this teaching. All there is, in any way we can know it, is ourselves.

I had run across this idea initially during my first retreat with the Roshi. Every evening, as I described earlier, she led a conversation in which people shared what they had seen about life and practice during the day. I loved these talks and listened to them attentively. As I did I began to notice that people generally spoke in a peculiar way that avoided any assertion that what they observed outside of themselves was so. Everything was presented hypothetically. This puzzled me, as of course it would, having never witnessed anything of the sort before. I think I had never questioned the integrity of my own perspective; it had never occurred to me that something I perceived could be illusory. And I just couldn't figure out why these people, who seemed so pleasant and fairly normal in other ways, were talking in that bizarre manner.

One night in group I asked about it, and everything tilted inside of me as the Roshi explained. "There is no outside," she said. "All that you can ever experience is you." I went around for the next couple of days saying to myself, "What? There is no outside. What?" I still didn't get it, then one evening—this is one of those classic moments in spiritual practice that you never forget—I caught myself "projecting". It happened right there in the kitchen of the retreat center. I observed myself as I condemned a fellow-retreatant for being a slacker because he wasn't washing the dishes fast enough. It was sort of like catching it out of the corner of my eye: suddenly I spied myself doing judgment. Then an interesting thing happened: I looked to myself, and noticed with a start that I happened to be in that moment leaning against a broom, watching this fellow not work fast enough while I wasn't sweeping the floor. I nearly laughed out loud. Who, I was forced to wonder, is the "slacker" here, and who is actually being judged?

Armed with this experience, and fortified with my brand new practice of awareness, I began to watch for my projections. Sure enough, they were everywhere. In the retreat environment, I found, it was easy to see how I made up everything I perceived. The silence just refused to ratify the inventions of my mind;

instead, it reflected them for my observation. I saw how I projected onto the Roshi (she's bossy, I decided), onto the cook (she's sweet and loving), onto my roommate (he's insincere). Likewise, I projected onto inanimate things, like the retreat center itself (warm and compassionate), and the mountains (wise and serene) that surrounded it. I even projected, I discovered, what other people thought of me. Nobody liked me—that seemed clear: I could tell by the way they walked, or bowed, or swept the floor.

"Yes, we project it," replied the Roshi as we sat together under the garden oak, two years and many trials later.

"I get that I'm projecting," I replied, "and I can see to some extent how I do it, but I don't see how to use it in a way that would make a difference in my actual experience. It's not much more than an idea for me, and as an idea it doesn't have any power over all the suffering in my mind."

"I see. Good! We need a project. Do you have anything unpleasant going about any of the other monks, by chance?"

I did, indeed! I have detailed already the various forms of unhappiness that attended me when I began my life as a monk. I omitted, however, the primary way by which I relieved myself of the resulting desperation. I did what any normal monastic would do under the circumstances: I blamed it on the head monk.

Oh, how I hated her, that woman! How I despised her evil ways! Her entire mission in life was just to afflict me: to punish me for no reason, to humiliate me before the others, to grind my poor, innocent heart under her heel, just for the sick pleasure of it—of this I felt sure. I loathed her blind arrogance, her haughty superiority. I detested her simple-mindedness and her ignorance. I abhorred her duplicity: she pretended to be so pure, so spiritual, yet she was rotten to the core. Anyone could see it; I only wondered why the monastery did not throw her out on her ear, to suffer the disgrace that she deserved.

"I am having certain…. feelings…about the head monk," I admitted.

"Of course," laughed the Roshi. "The trick, then, is to observe yourself projecting onto her, remembering that there is only one monk involved here: you. Instead of believing the projections, let go of their seeming relationship to her and follow them back to the place where they originate within your own mind. See how you are or do what you project, in other words."

"You mean I have to stop hating the head monk?" I asked, only partly in jest.

"Alas, yes," she replied, her eyes gleaming, "The sacrifices we must make in spiritual practice are almost too much to bear, aren't they? And here's a little something more to play with. Most of the time, you are telling me, you are going around in various states of unhappiness, even though—hard as this may be to believe...," with this she smiled again, more devilishly this time, "there is truly nothing here to be unhappy about. See if you can find the life, the experience, you want here. See if you can project it, in other words."

"That seems like cheating."

"Conditioned mind would love for you to believe that, certainly, but it's not cheating at all. You can live from whichever place you choose, heaven or hell. It's up to you. Here's another way to approach it if you get stuck: just let yourself be still, without the voices, and see what you project."

"Okay. I'll give it a try...." I said and prepared to go.

"By the way," the Roshi said, "how is little Rhea coming along in her training?"

Rhea, who always lay beside my chair during these interviews, looked up at the sound of her name and wagged her tail. "Surprisingly well," I answered. "We are practicing diligently, at any rate, and it seems to be doing some good."

Every day, in fact, Rhea and I practiced not chasing the cats. I had resisted the idea mightily at first, but to my surprise I learned to love this little exercise. It gave me a way to be with Rhea without frustration, disappointment, and anger; it gave me a way to step beyond my own doubt and pessimism, and to create a possibility in which both she and I could win. I did not know at that time how to truly care for her, but in my heart I wanted to learn more than anything, and so once my reluctance passed we had gone to work. Everywhere we went we kept an eye out for the cats. Pretty quickly they learned to avoid our habitual haunts, but that did not stop us. Whenever we had a spare moment we snuck down to the old kitchen tent, to see if anybody was home. "We're going cat-hunting," I would tell Rhea.

I never punished her, not once. That was my guidance. In fact, her training was identical to mine: when she acted from habit I just made it clear to her that this was not what we were going for. If she sensed a cat nearby she would tense up, her hair would stand on end, and she would plead for me to let her go—and I, in a soft but clear and authoritative voice would growl in her ear: "No, Rhea. No!" We practiced and we practiced and we practiced, and gradually Rhea started to get it.

"Of course!" replied the Roshi, patting Rhea on the head. "Anyone can see she's smart as a whip and as willing as they come. Not to mention cute," she continued, bending towards Rhea and talking directly to her. "How can you stand to be so cute?" she asked her. Rhea wagged her tail furiously, as if to say it was no trouble at all. "Talk about a projection exercise!"

I thanked the Roshi, then Rhea and I headed off into the silence. As we did I looked over to my little companion. I will be forever grateful for that furry being and the support she provided during those difficult times. Every night before we went to sleep I cuddled with her in her bed on the floor; every morning, as soon as she sensed I was awake, Rhea would jump into my bed with me, squirm under the covers, and lay on my chest, just breathing, until it was time to rise. It was her loyalty, her sweetness, and her deep and constant love that moved me and indebted me to her. How wonderful, I thought, to get to own these projections, and to see that I also bring loyalty, sweetness, and love to my life and to those around me. Before I went back to work I stopped and held her head in my hands, looking into her eyes as I often did, and thanked her for the gift she was to me in so many ways.

One day a couple of weeks later the head monk sent me to her office to fetch some papers she had left there. I had not been inside her office before, so I took the opportunity to spy a little. Above her desk, taped to the window, I found a tiny piece of paper with these words:

A hostile person lives in a hostile world;
A loving person lives in a loving world—
Everyone you meet is your mirror.

I stood there for a long time, pondering those words. "Everyone I meet is my mirror," I mused, "including the head monk! Everyone the head monk meets is her mirror, including me." Remarkably, it had not occurred to me that the head monk was human as much as I, with the same struggles and the same desire for liberation. She was attempting to free herself from illusion just as I was. Something shifted within me as I considered this fact. I realized that I could not see her. I could only see what I projected; what reality lay behind those projections—what real woman, full of hopes, fears, and feelings of every kind— was a complete mystery to me. I am, I realized, essentially alone.

Over time, slowly but driven steadily by the pain of my narrow world, I began to understand how I created my experience of her and everything else I perceived. It took a great, long while, but gradually I let go of the assumptions that colored my experience of the head monk and admitted that none of it was true, no matter how real it seemed to me. As I did I was forced to admit that all that I experienced in that innocent woman was only myself: that all the meanness and judgment I perceived in her, and all of the hostility, came only from the projection of my own disharmony.

In the beginning, I must admit, I regretted this little awakening. I most definitely did not want to know that such hatefulness and other unpleasantness came from me. How could I admit to my own arrogance and duplicity? Deeper than this, I did not want to know that I alone created my suffering. I was appalled by the responsibility that this implied I must accept for my own life and intimidated by the massive piece of work my new awareness required. If I alone create the world of my isolation and helplessness, it seemed to me, then I alone must end it, and at first this necessity seemed more than I could bear. As I practiced, however, and as I came to realize how much I wished to end the judgment and other conditioning that lived inside of me, I began to feel gratitude for the gift of this insight as a doorway into a world that does not reflect conditioned mind. I found in it an amazing tool that I might use to acquire understanding of the illusion that caused my unhappiness.

Here is how I practiced with it: whenever I caught myself judging the head monk, I dropped the projection and turned my attention to my breath. It was simple, really. The judgment, I saw, always happened in the form of language. Since this was so, I had only to observe the voices spilling out of my mind to see it happening—and once I did it lost its power over me. Residing through my attention in the breath, I found I could look out over the landscape of my conditioned "reality" with no involvement in it, and just observe what happened there.

As I practiced in this way I began to realize the power I have to create the world of my own happiness. My own internal landscape, I saw, is the one place where I have influence; if all of my suffering originates there, as it does, then it all is subject to the compassionate work of healing I can provide. How to actually provide it was, at that point, still a mystery to me, but that did not slow me down. If everything is me, I figured, and if who I am, as the teachings say, is compassionate self-acceptance, then all of the suffering of the world can be embraced within my own being, and I can live in real happiness.

13

Home

One day in my late teens I took a ride in the back of a pick-up with some school companions along a tiny dirt road way back in the mountains. This is one of the most vivid memories of my youth. I remember how I sheltered myself from the cold behind the cab, hunkered down amongst backpacks and piles of camping gear. I recall the way we bumped and jerked along the road, the way the tires crunched the gravel, and the thrill of excitement and wonder I felt as my eyes roamed through the misty hills all around, the thick green forests everywhere, and the patches of blue sky here and there between the leaves. The beauty of those mountains, which I had not seen before, and the adventure I was engaged in, absolved me from the lonesomeness and desperation that so often troubled me during those days.

It was a journey of two hours to our destination. Along the way, as we drove around a bend, hugging the steep bank beside the road, then rattled across a wooden bridge over a creek, and as the view beyond opened up before us, I spied the most wonderful home place in all the world. I saw a small cabin with a tin roof tucked way back in a hollow and in an elbow of the stream. It had gardens bursting with plants, an old log barn with a tractor in it, a clothesline neatly hung with overalls and plaid shirts, and three dogs on the porch. My heart leaped up with joy at the humble beauty of the place. I was enchanted: the sight of that tiny paradise said "home" to me as nothing ever had before.

Looking back, I can see that this was one of several visions that gave birth to the yearning that carried me through all of the sweet but hopeless adventures in the years that followed. I had never seen anything so wonderful as that place. I tasted in those few moments the heart's food that I starved for, and the memory of it never left me afterwards.

The truck growled on down the road, carrying me onwards into the life that was prescribed for me. As that little cabin disappeared behind us into the distance I despaired: the beauty that I saw was not mine to have, it seemed, and I did not know how it might ever be. And yet I knew it must, because without that feeling I called "home", or at least the hope of it, I felt I could not live.

In the years following that adventure, as I completed my formal schooling, I began to make a habit of journeying up into the mountains whenever I could to recapture the feeling of that day. Sometimes, I found, I did. Other folks noticed, and before long I had a band of cronies to accompany me. It was a wonderful time, but not a happy one. Our common sadness bonded us as outcasts from a world we did not belong to, and though our friendship was precious it was not enough to cure us of our angst and melancholy. It was the best we had for that time, however. Every weekend at the first possible minute (after classes were finished), we took off for the hills to sooth our weary spirits in the deep woods and on the craggy points above them. One day we found a spot of leafy ground overlooking a creek and a waterfall; it was so beautiful that we all just stopped and stared, and to my immense joy it said "home" to me as the other place had done. Over time this became our favorite refuge. We called it "The Magic Place." Over and over again we journeyed there, and every time, as I recall it, the joy awoke within me once again. I spent many hours during those years lying in the leaves above that cascade, feeling the wet breeze of it against my face, listening to the talk of the rushing water and the voice of peace within my heart. Over and over again, as we left for our necessary lives in the world, I left that peace behind me in that place. It never accompanied me into the life that society demanded, as much as I wished it would. It appeared that it existed only there.

Years later, after my school days were done, I found my way back to The Magic Place. By that time I had years of traveling, years of searching behind me, and enough experience with disappointment to know that my true home would never be found the way I looked for it. I remember walking through the crunchy leaves towards the magic place of my school days, the flutter of fear that it would be gone or that I would not recall the way, and the fond hope that the feeling I yearned for would be waiting for me as it used to do. It wasn't. My familiar companion, loneliness, greeted me instead, and we sat down together by the waters of the stream to wonder why it was that what I wanted most in life most eluded me.

I did not understand that I projected my inner onto my outer world. My ignorance of this fact is what kept the home that my heart longed for always beyond my grasp. I only knew to run from the circumstances of my life that I believed caused my loneliness, and this is what I had done those many years. It always seemed about to work: I would land in some new place of beauty, and for a time—sometimes just hours, sometimes days— I would feel myself to be home again, and at peace. But soon the same self-doubt that troubled me since the earliest days of my maturity would creep like a fog into my happiness and cover it over. What I did not understand is that I carried my unhappiness within me. It did not work to run away because it ran with me as an aspect of my suffering mind.

My isolation followed me wherever I went, but so did the experience I called "home." Except in rare instances, I projected my unhappiness rather than my joy, but both were inside of me. After I entered the monastery and settled into the silence of my new life, gradually I sloughed off the habit of sadness and despair, as I have described. As I did, and especially after I began to practice seeing the world I wished to live in, as the Roshi had suggested, I began to have glimpses of home again. It seemed quite miraculous to me: somehow that which I had searched for my whole adult life would suddenly appear, with no visible cause other than the fact that I looked for it. Over time I

116

realized that it lived continually inside of me, and if I could only claim it as my own it would be mine. I saw that everything in my world was a looking-glass, reflecting back to me, if only I were willing to see it, all that I longed for, even the origins of my salvation within myself. Every perception of beauty or harmony or peace might teach me the way I had lost to the home that lives inside.

In the mornings and evenings on my way to and from the main monastery compound I walk past a broad field. Right now this field contains millions of straw-colored stalks of grass shooting in every direction, massive reaching oak trees, lord knows how many insects buzzing and leaping here and there, an indescribable complexity of light and shadow, and much, much more. As I pass it by, when I can remember, I look to it as into a mirror for the reflection of my own harmony. Knowing that it speaks to me about myself, how can I pass it by without wonder? Sometimes in the mornings, or especially when a big moon guides my steps at night, I will stop for a while beside that field to just look and hear and smell. In that field exists all of the splendor and inspiration of my internal universe, and it is all mine to have if I am present to it without thought and meaning. With the assistance of that place, or of the people in my life, or of anything else I perceive, I discover all that I am inside. I become in a way as gigantic as the universe, able to contain all of the marvelous multiplicity that I am.

The days passed one after the other, and gradually the term of my commitment began to expire. As it did I faced a terrible decision: would I stay or go? Things would have been much simpler, of course, if I had not witnessed the transformation occurring inside of me. I could have then left the monastery without regret, and never thought of spiritual practice again. As it was, because I could see the change, because I had felt the joy of the steps I had taken towards freedom, and because of the tremendous resistance that ego threw up against it, the choice I must soon make haunted me terribly. It was one thing to blindly accept a distant life, as I had done before, then survive the reality once it was known; but to actually choose it, knowing the struggle and pain this life involves, that was a different thing altogether. The day approached when I must decide, but I knew not what to do.

Then, one September evening, after the day's work was done, I walked out to the end of the property with Rhea to watch the sun set. I remember how the yellow light filled the green leaves of the trees and how my heart sang at the sight of it. I remember how I felt: so strong, determined, and brave. As I watched the sun go down behind the grassy hills towards the west, I felt something shift within me. Suddenly, I knew I would return. I would go and visit my family, assure them that I was safe and well, and then I would return to the life of a monk. It was amazing to watch this clarity just appear out of nowhere. Much as it had been when I first entered the monastery, something too big and deep for me to understand moved inside of me, and I moved with it. I did not decide it: I just knew.

I turned to little Rhea, who rested there at my side. "Honey, what do you think?" I asked her. "I need to come back. Will you come with me?" She wagged her tail, then jumped up to lick my face, the sweetest and best friend a monk could have. "Thank you, sweetheart," I said. "Let's return, then, and be monks for a while more." The thought arose that we might be monks for good, but I banished it. That was just too much to consider at that time.

Two days later I had my last guidance appointment with the Roshi. She smiled when she saw me, and even giggled a little. We both knew it was the Big Moment.

"Ummm...." I said. The intensity of her eyes bewildered me. I felt as if I looked up at her from the bottom of a swimming pool. She waited expectantly. "So.... can I come back?" I asked her.

"Ha!" she replied, and laughed out loud. "You've become an awareness junky like the rest of us—I thought as much." Never was her love so apparent to me. "Of course you can come back!" she continued. "Just pick the day."

Then I laughed also, more with relief than anything. It was a good time to laugh. Neither of us said it, but both of us understood the intensity of the contest that would follow.

Two days later I left for North Carolina.

I flew from San Francisco International Airport, a three-hour drive from the monastery. Now, a trip like that would probably not be a big deal for most people, but for somebody who has lived for six months in silence and who has not traveled further than the local grocery store in that time, that's about as wild a ride as you can take. There we went, my monk chauffer and I, down our long gravel driveway and past the gate. I said a prayer as I went past it that I would have the strength and willingness to see it again before too long. We drove the two miles down our small gravel road to the main road, then down that small paved road to the town, then through miles and miles of pasture land to the nearest middle-sized town, way in the middle of no place. Then, suddenly, we found ourselves speeding along a four-lane highway with big trucks everywhere. Soon the road widened to six lanes, then eight. By the time we got to the airport there were six lanes of traffic on each side of the road, bumper to bumper, and we were going eighty. Wow. I arrived at the airport in a state of mild shock. When I found myself standing at last on my own two feet again, I just stopped and stared with wide eyes and open mouth, as if I had never seen concrete before. My confusion must have been obvious, because just then a fellow came up to me and asked, "Did you have a tough time in San Francisco?"

He was one of those guys who check people in at the curb. He grabbed my bags and went to work, but then some complication required me to wait with him for a few minutes while he helped some other folks. This provided me with the opportunity to study him, which I was eager to do. He was terribly funny, for one thing, but there was something odd about him—I couldn't say what—that attracted my curiosity. Immediately I noticed that he said the same thing over and over to everyone he came across, in between jokes. "It's all good! It's all good!" he shouted in the most cheerful way you can imagine. No matter what he was doing, that is what he said, and he attempted to get people to agree. Some scowled at this, but most seemed to love it. This man appeared so much to enjoy everyone, and so to love his work, that I couldn't help wondering how he pulled this off, here in one of the deepest strongholds of conditioned society. "What's he got that I don't?" I asked myself. My envy and resentment of this man can easily be imagined: after all, I had relinquished a life of dissipation to achieve only occasionally what he seemed to enjoy without effort. I began to watch him more closely. Then I became suspicious.

The man noticed how I observed him, evidently, because, after bawling out, "It's all good!" again for the umpteenth time, he turned to me—suddenly a completely different person, and with a tortured expression in his eyes and said, "You know, it really isn't."

As he spoke I glimpsed the being within him that lived behind its self-conscious shell; I perceived for a moment the authentic life that survived the tyranny of conditioned mind. I was filled with dread and amazement: so little of the man remained. And there was nothing I could do. I could only nod to him my sympathy and agreement and go my own way. As I gathered my bags together and left him there to continue on in the way that he knew, it was with a new understanding of my own dedication to self-awareness and a renewed commitment to my own liberation. I felt a deep compassion for that man. I train as a monk, I realized, that I may never be again as destitute as he.

It had been arranged that I was to call my mother from the airport to make plans for my pick up at her end. My fingers trembled as I dialed. "Hello?" she answered. Instantly my heart was flooded with emotion—it was the first time I had heard her voice in half a year. "David!" she exclaimed when she learned it was me. I explained I had little time to talk, as I had to board the plane. Quickly we arranged when and where she would pick me up. As the conversation concluded she said, "You must feel so proud of yourself! You've done a really hard thing. Now you're off to your next adventure!"

I knew that I should tell her of my decision. I knew it, but I could not: at the critical moment my courage abandoned me. I could only say, "Good-bye."

A number of hours later she picked me up at the airport in North Carolina. She was in fine spirits, full of excitement at seeing me and glad I was there. I was glad to see her also, but troubled by what she did not know. I did not see a way to break the news to her without spoiling her pleasure. Poor thing, only she understands the cross she bears in being mother to a monk.

That evening some friends of hers came to visit. I was something of a curiosity to them, I think: they came to marvel over me, like a creature in a zoo. Finally, the inevitable occurred. "So what do you plan to do next, Dave?" one of them asked.

All but honesty failed me. "I'm going back," I said.

It was a bad moment. The conversation halted with these words, and all eyes went to my mother. For an instant her gaze met mine. I could not read the emotion in her eyes; I could only plead with my own for understanding and forgiveness. Abruptly she left the room.

I wished so much to explain to her the turmoil that seethed within my own heart and mind over this decision. I wanted her to know how much I struggled with this strange advent in my life, myself. I had other plans for me, too! I did not want to go back—I had to. As long as I believed that outward circumstances caused my inner experience I could still choose the path I was brought up to follow, but I did not believe that anymore. I had seen another way. I had come to understand that I alone caused my unhappiness in my addiction to conditioned mind. Knowing this, I could only choose to end suffering. This is the only real human choice, and the only option that I had.

Over time she came to understand, also. She could see how I was moved by the challenge that lay ahead of me, and her love

121

taught her to see it through my eyes. The days passed until it was time for me to go. She bade me farewell with tears, knowing it would be a year before she would speak to me again. "Stay true to your heart," she said.

As I boarded the plane for California the storm began to gather in my mind that I anticipated would pummel me as soon as I passed through the monastery gates. My commitment to freedom had deepened exponentially since the day I had made this same journey more than six months before. Before, there was every reason to expect that my determination would one day flag, and I would choose to suffer once again; now my commitment said otherwise. It remained to be seen if I had the courage to fight to the death with Egocentric Karmic Conditioning—this remains to be seen even now—but I knew I would attempt it, come what may. I expected the response from ego to be just as earnest.

The same monk picked me up at the airport as had greeted me the first time. She smiled at the irony of that fact, and as if to acknowledge the change that had occurred within me since the former day, so seemingly long ago. As we travelled down the broad highways, then passed into the narrow, twisting roads on the way to the monastery, I noticed how differently I felt than I had formerly. This time I knew what I was getting into. I understood the daily horror and wonder of a life of silence, of a life devoted to a ceaseless struggle with the relentless oppression of conditioned mind; and yet, even as hard as I knew it would be, I craved that challenge.

Bumping down the driveway, coming to the place where the view opens out upon the gardens and the red tile roof of the meditation hall, my heart was filled with happiness. Conditioned mind hates everything about this place—every physical object, every person who passes through, every experience of freedom it has offered me—but the heart thrives here and cherishes it all. Stepping out of the car with Rhea, as we had done once before, watching her bounce and run with delight as she discovered where we were, I realized that the joy I felt came from the fact that, despite my constant struggles, I have often been at peace here, that I have experienced my true self in this place. Everything mirrored that for me. I saw my authentic nature in the rammed earth walls and in the tiles of the dining hall; I felt it in the cool air and the breeze that drifted through the archway; I even smelled it in the food cooking in the kitchen. "Ah!" I whispered to Rhea. "Isn't it good to be home!"

14

Gratitude

A little while ago, as I enjoyed my evening meal in a chair on the west monastery porch, I realized once again, as I have ten thousand times since I became a monk, how fortunate we are in this path of awakening, and how profoundly we are called to follow it in whatever form Life presents. That particular spot is my favorite in the evenings, especially in the summertime when the light pours down into the valley below, when the cooling breezes rise through the trees, and when the birds sing here and there in the branches above my head. This evening, as I peered down over the grassy-topped hills into the canyon, I saw a shadow of my former suffering self down there, wandering alone and without much hope, as I always used to do. Then the leaves above me glittered in the receding light, and as I looked up to wonder at their brilliance that old life fell away and I remembered: I am here, in this moment, in my life. Here is where my love is, and the peace I longed for. Here is the place where nothing is left out, and where all that I am is welcome, even my sometimes unhappiness. Here is the place where doubt is gone, and where I experience the joy that is my reality and my substance. It is all right here for the having.

As I continued to eat, and as the day slowly reclined across the valley, my heart filled with gratitude for all I have received. How is it that I have been so fortunate? By what strange wrinkle in the fabric of human fortune do I come to be here in this place, in this time, on this day, with this opportunity? By nothing that I may understand, that is sure, and so I let it go, and I drank in the blessings all around, and then I went to wash my dishes.

So much has happened since that day I first set foot on the monastery property! I think of all the thousands of hours spent sitting in formal meditation in the hall; of the many thousands of meals eaten in silence, facing the dining room wall or the greenery of the courtyard, just me, my food, and my breath. I think of the hundreds of group discussions with the other monks, all of the guidance appointments with the Roshi, all of the countless silent hours of work, all of the tasks begun, completed, and forgotten. I think of all the long, solitary Sunday walks, and the hours I have spent by the creek at the bottom of the property, just sitting there, watching the water flow by. I think also of all the nights I have lain in bed alone, gazing out of the window, finally falling to sleep with stars in my eyes; and all the early mornings I have woken up with only myself for company, with a day of joy or sorrow ahead of me. This has been the stuff of my life these past many years. As I have sat in meditation, and worked, and received the teachings in various ways, gradually I have begun to realize who I am.

There is much that stands between a socialized human and the possibility that exists for each one of us to live in freedom. There is much we need to see through and let go, much we need to accept and embrace in unconditional love. There is a process of awakening that we must go through in order to access the life that each of us is here to live—a process that is unique to each person and yet the same for all. I remain in the midst of that process, of course, having come a long way and with a long way to go. I am blessed and fortunate, however, in the years of training that are behind me and the experience I have gained. I am blessed in the guidance and support I have received as I have learned to study my own mind, to break free of social conditioning, and gradually unravel the mystery of the life that animates us all.

15

The Heart Knows

My first morning back, as I returned to the kitchen from the nearest outhouse, suffering as anticipated over the inescapable fact that I was once again a monk; I rounded the corner of the building onto the back porch and suddenly there was the Roshi. I stopped abruptly, overtaken by surprise and awe. In the time since I had last seen her the Roshi had grown to mythical proportions in my imagination. I felt like a worm in comparison.

"Ha! There is our cook!" she exclaimed, with her usual energy. "Boy, are we glad to see you! We've had nothing but bread and water since you left, you know. The other monks are growing thin. How are you?"

"Uh…" I said, completely confounded.

"Hmmm…." The Roshi studied me with mock concern. "Were they hard on you out there?"

I pulled myself together to respond. "No, I'm okay. Good, really. Just a bit…scared." There—it was out. I felt better immediately.

She smiled. "Of course you are! You would be a fool if you weren't."

I thought she did not understand, so I attempted to explain. "I just don't know if I can do it," I said.

"'I' can't do it and never will. But *you* can, or else you wouldn't be here."

"I can't do it?"

"You have to put little quote marks around the 'I'. 'Dave' can't do it, in other words. You think you are 'Dave'. That's the trouble."

"I think I'm 'Dave'," I repeated, considering the notion. Intellectually I knew at that point that I am not this entity I called

"Dave", but I had little experience of it. Grateful for this unexpected guidance opportunity, but self-conscious in my use of it, I added, "And…I'm not?"

"A self that is separate from life, a 'Dave', will always be unhappy because it *is* unhappiness. As is the case with all of us, you must learn to live from a place that is not separate."

"Is there a 'me' that is not separate?"

"Absolutely. The 'you' that is not separate is the same as the life that animates this…." She gestured to indicate my body and hers, then opened her arms to include the buildings, gardens, and everything else that surrounded us both. "That's the tricky and fun part. That you is you and yet not you at the same time."

"Hmmm…." I said. "I understand the words you are using, but not what you are pointing to. How do I get at that which is truly me?"

"By seeing and letting go of everything that you believe yourself to be that is not that. But we wax philosophical!" she cried, and prepared to leave me in my perplexity. "We have work to do! Shall we have something tasty for lunch?"

I nodded and she left. "I am not 'Dave'," I said to myself, trying it on. "Then I wonder who I am?"

With that I rolled up my sleeves and started back in both as a monk and the monastery cook. I did not fall headlong into my former misery, however, as I had expected to do—or at least, not for a while. That is to say, I was often confused and terrified, and often resistant; lots of painful things happened every day, and I got into all sorts of tangles with the Roshi and the head monk as I had from the beginning, but I did not suffer so hideously over all of this as I had before. Beneath my surface experience I felt cradled by a new sense of confidence in Life and the great compassion that it offered to me every day, even as small as I am, while I did the work of ending suffering. I was surprised: it was as if conditioned mind had played its best cards before I had gone away, had lost, and so forfeited its power over me for a time. As the days passed I felt myself expand, blessedly, into an understanding of my own adequacy that was larger than I had known before. I felt comparatively awake and aware, grounded in myself and settled in the life I had chosen, however long it may last. I even accessed joy here and there. As always, it was the small things that made the largest impression on my opening heart, when I was present to them: the flash of the knife I held above the vegetables, the exquisite beauty of a pot of soup coming to a boil, the sweet flow of emotion in my body all the day through, and so on. For the first time since I had entered the monastery I experienced ease, relaxation, and confidence for more than just fleeting moments.

I saw that, as the Roshi had intimated, when I was happy it was because I was not "Dave". I could not have explained this to anyone, but I sensed it in a deeper place than words can go. When I was happy it was because I was not involved with the conditioned illusion. There was no "Dave" in that place of clarity: there was just the breath, sensation, and awareness. When I was unhappy it was because "I" was there to be unhappy. It was as simple as that.

Within the illusion of conditioned mind, everything that happens, happens to "me." "I" is the most important thing in the universe, and the fulfillment of the needs and wants of this "I" is all that matters. The point of all that we invent and project onto ourselves and our circumstances is that it supports this identity, this "I". It is only because we so cling to identity that we do not see how ridiculous the fictions are. Nothing in conditioned thinking is real in and of itself; all of the values through which we relate to the world that we perceive are built upon unexamined assumptions, and as flat mental constructs are meaningless when applied to the dynamic movement of life. We create the illusion we live within so that we can be "I"; we assume a fantasy of power and invulnerability, believing ourselves to be here, in the moment, when in fact we are only surviving the fact that we are not here and cannot see anything of what actually is.

Ego assumes itself to be real, even though it does not exist in the moment. Further, it supposes that "reality" and the illusion it projects are the same. Ego puts itself in the place of God, you might say, assuming an omniscience it does not have. This is the way we find ourselves seemingly at the center of the universe: we believe we know what everything is. There, I saw, I had been all of my life: emperor of the world of my creation, passing judgment over all I surveyed, dispensing opinions in all directions, assuming this and assuming that, never questioning and never questioned (if I could help it), and suffering from my separation from life in this imagined autonomy.

I found this "I" incredibly difficult to let go of, but I also found it wonderfully intriguing to try. Every act of every day presented the same challenge: could I just be, could I just act, without assuming a subject or object—without making myself into a separate entity that dominates the world through "my" perceptions.

Soon after I returned from North Carolina we hosted our annual Precepts Retreat at the monastery. The Buddhist Precepts are a set of guidelines that assist in applying practice to daily life. They are not so much moral commandments as areas to pay attention to; they point out places where conditioned mind tends to seem real and draw people away from their authentic path. For example, the first precept is "Not to lead a harmful life". The second is "Not to take that which is not given". The Precepts provide a mirror to look into as we go along, where we may see the difference between what the heart and conditioned mind want for us in this life.

We had a full house. People came from all over the country to attend. I did not grasp the significance of the occasion as it approached—for me it was all about what they were going to eat and how I was going to survive feeding them—but the first evening of the retreat, in group, I suddenly realized what I had gotten myself into. As people expressed in turn their willingness to accept the Precepts as their guiding influence, and as the Roshi reflected the commitment and deep responsibility involved, I

129

sensed that the week would be about the decision we may each make to put the work of our transformation at the center of our lives. As the Roshi said to us all that evening, "This is not about bringing spiritual practice into your life. This is about bringing your life into spiritual practice."

As the week progressed I began to see the choice I had made to live as a monk from a much larger perspective. At that point I still clung to the idea that this was a temporary phase I was going through—like going to school—that would end one day and release me to return to the life I had followed before. Now I began to understand that my life was asking me, in the form of my teacher, the monastery, and this retreat, to make a deeper commitment to this life that my heart had chosen. I had always wanted to be free, even when I was unable to articulate this to myself. Looking back through my experiences as a child, as a young man attempting to find his way, and at the calling that had carried me to the monastery, this was clear: I had always wanted to truly live. Now I was asked to let go of all that remained inside me, to the extent that I could at the time, that was not this true life.

Towards the end of the retreat it became evident that I, along with all the others, would be asked if we wished to make a formal commitment to a life of practice. This stirred up conditioned mind to no end, as might be expected. The voices had everything to say about why that was a bad idea, why I had to think it over until another time, and so on. I believed them enough to throw me into confusion, but not so much that I could not ask for help. "How do I know that this is the best thing for me?" I asked one night in group.

"You can't," said the Roshi.

That surprised me. "I can't? Then how can I decide?"

"You *cannot* decide," she replied. "This is critical to understand. If you decide—that is, if "I" decides—then you will only choose to suffer. If you allow Life to decide through you, then you will choose what you actually need."

As she spoke it became obvious to me both that she articulated my recent experiences and, paradoxically, that I did not understand what she was saying. "How do I know if it's me or 'I'?" I asked her.

She smiled mischievously. "You can't know that, either." With this I covered my face with my hands while the others in the room laughed good-naturedly at my stupefaction. "This is both the hardest and the best thing about the way life is arranged, in my opinion," she continued. You cannot do it, you cannot know it, you cannot decide it—you can only allow that which animates to do what needs to be done through you, as the vehicle.

"Here's the thing," she continued. "Knowing is not helpful—not when it's coming from here...." the Roshi tapped her head at the temple. "We must give up knowing so that we can see, and so we can be available to the larger intelligence that will show us the way if we will allow it."

"So we can see?" I reflected.

"Yes. We need to drop 'knowing' so we can see what Life wants for us, what Life is calling us to. This is infinitely better than 'knowing' what we want to do and then doing that. It's the difference between happiness and misery."

"Oh...." I said. Something had moved within me as she spoke. It came out of nowhere and surprised me. I felt suddenly that I wanted to cry.

"Good," said the Roshi. "Now, look into your heart. What do you see? Or, more directly, what do you want?"

What happened next has always intrigued me. Arising along with the emotion was a wordless certainty. In the same way I had known that I must enter the monastery, and had known that I must return after my first commitment was ended, I suddenly knew what the answer was: it was simply "Yes." Yes, I wanted to give my life to service and to spiritual practice. Yes, I wanted to be a monk. Resistance arose immediately to meet this insight. For a few moments the two forces opposed each other equally, then the resistance gave, the uncertainty slid past, and suddenly I was there, in my body, in the moment, with the truth. Tears bubbled out of my eyes for a few moments, and I could not speak. The group waited for me in silence.

"I understand," I said finally.

Unlike any of the other retreats I had participated in, Precepts culminates with a solemn ceremony. I'm not going to tell you what the ceremony entails because I do not want to spoil the surprise. I can tell you, however, that it is a perfectly formal affair and conducted with the deepest possible seriousness. It is the ceremony in which the student "takes the Precepts" and accepts the beads that represent our commitment to put ending suffering above every other priority. And so I found myself on the final day of the retreat in a beautiful grove of ancient oak trees on the far end of the property, standing in the shade and in silence with the monks and others who, like me, had chosen to take the Precepts on this occasion. We had come to the climax of the ceremony. The Roshi stood in front of us in her formal robes. Each of us waited in awe and suspense for what would occur next, all of us practicing with all of our hearts to be present to that moment, with our teacher and all those beautiful people on that wonderful day. We stood in silence for a long time, then at last the Roshi opened her mouth to speak.

Suddenly a tremendous howling broke the silence. It was Rhea. Out of fear that she might disturb the proceedings, I had closed her up inside my hermitage, which happened to be hard by. She must have heard us as we had filed past.

I was horrified. In deep mortification and fearing punishment, I looked to the Roshi to see what to do. She laughed heartily. "I think Rhea wants to take the Precepts, too!" she said, feigning a whisper, but loud enough for all to hear. She then nodded in the direction of my hermitage and I hustled off to set Rhea at liberty. When we returned, Rhea bounded into the group, as happy as she could be. And so it was that Rhea and I took the Precepts together, both of us committing to a life of spiritual practice, each in our own way.

I spent two years as the cook. It was during that time that I learned how to be a monk: I learned the required toughness and determination, the unyielding self-love, and the courage to bend my will to the guidance of the monastery. I learned how to be silent, and still. After a while I got used to being the cook. I began to experience peace and ease in the kitchen rather than hysteria. I even started to enjoy myself. That was when the Roshi made me the work director: the person—get this—in charge of the whole physical operation of the monastery.

This is how monastic training works. Over time the monastery repeatedly forces the monks to step out of the areas where their conditioning can remain safe, and into the unknown, where we may discover for ourselves our adequacy to the new challenge, whatever it may be. Then, as soon as we get cozy in that new expanded place, the monastery flushes us out into the open again, over and over, until we learn to leap willingly into the unknown ourselves.

I went to the Roshi to complain. "But I don't *want* to be the work director," I said.

"Of course you don't," she said. "Who would?"

"But why *me*?"

"There is no 'me'," she replied sternly, "or, in our usual language, there is no 'I'. That's the trouble. Wanting and not wanting comes from 'I'. Suffering comes from 'I'. The end of suffering comes when we let go of 'I' and align ourselves with the life force that lives us. Life wants you to be the work director. 'I' doesn't want that, and so you suffer."

"I don't want to be impertinent," I said, "But how do I know that it's Life that wants me to be the work director and not just you?"

She frowned deeply. "That question is not worthy to be answered," she replied, "But I will answer it anyway. Next time I'm going to have to clobber you with my chair." She grinned for a moment so I would know she was jesting, then resumed her serious manner. "I have nothing to do with this. I am not responsible for the fact that you are here, or even that I am. As I said once before: I don't make these decisions. I only respond to the information that is in this moment. Look at the trees. What is in charge of them is the same as what is in charge of both you and me. All of the guidance that Life offers is available to everyone, here in this moment. The difference between me and most people—and you can join me in this if you are willing—is that I can see what is here, I am in touch with the information, and that I do what I'm told."

"I see...." I said, aware of the great significance of her words. They were not enough to extinguish my resistance, but as I considered that the Roshi was obviously not going to give ground, and since I had no choice anyway, I figured I might as well go along with the program. "Okay," I said finally. "So, what do I need to know?" And so began my career as the monastery work director.

So also began an earnest exploration into the fact that I did not access Life in the way that she did. It was clear that Life had guided me to the monastery, but it was equally clear that on a day-to-day basis I remained a separate self, full of resistance and complaints, and did not experience the joy that comes with surrender to that which animates. I remained "I", in other words. This was not a problem in itself, as there was no expectation from the monastery that I should be some place in practice that I was not, but the suffering in it was awfully painful. How in the world, I wondered, can I get past "I"? More specifically, how is it created and maintained outside of my awareness?

16

Why Nice Guys Finish Last

It must have been in the fourth or fifth grade when it happened. I recall a covered walkway at the edge of the schoolyard, a grimy wall without windows, and the feel of my bones beneath my sweater as I walked towards home at the end of the day. I remember tracing the grooves between the bricks with my fingers, and trailing the soft wonder of my boyish mind over the sadness in my heart. All was not right with me that day. I was not experienced enough with life, however, to know the cause of my unhappiness; I only felt my loneliness, and to soothe myself I dreamed of the most beautiful angel of a girl that I had ever seen. I cannot recall her name, but I can see her as if she stood before me even now, her hair flowing like a waterfall over her shoulders, her enormous eyes, and the sweet but sassy delight in her smile. There was an enchantment about her that I searched for in every woman I ever met afterwards—such is the magic of a boy's first love.

Suddenly, as I rounded the corner of the building, I stopped short and gawked in astonishment: there she was, the very enchantress that I dreamed of. She did not see me at first. She faced the other way, talking with another girl. The few words I heard were about a boy—some other boy than me. "He's just so *nice*," said my angel. My heart pounded so fiercely I feared she would hear it, and my thoughts spun like a wobbling top. I could not just stand there, feigning deafness, so I pulled myself together and went on—but as I did I resolved in my heart of hearts that from that moment on I would be, like that lucky fellow, whatever it was that little girl desired.

And so I began from that day forward to be "nice." Little did I know the sorrow this would bring! Being nice, as I perceived it, required me to set myself aside: it meant giving to others whatever they wanted, regardless of my own wants or needs. It meant sacrificing the little boy who overheard those words for someone else I never was and never my whole life could be. I am not "nice"—I am just who or what I am—and so I set about to put "nice" where my innocence had been. This is what it seemed I must do to win the notice of those whose tenderness I craved—first that little girl, then many others afterwards. This strategy never worked once, not in the manner that I hoped it would. It never won for me the affections, or even the notice, of that angel-eyed girl. I discovered in my teens that girls do not like nice boys—they like boys who are not afraid of being themselves—but by then it was too late. I had become a nice guy, and there was no going back.

This strategy did work, however, in a way that I could not have predicted. Being nice never got me what it promised, but it did provide me with a certain unhappy safety as it hid my heart from the world, and this, in the absence of the joy I wanted, seemed enough. Bit by bit I abandoned my desire for love and settled for that safety. It was all that I knew to do.

Being nice finally failed so miserably to produce happiness that it drove me to monastic life, but even there I could not give it up. Even here I attempted to win the love I hungered for by denying my own needs in favor of the imagined needs of others. Nothing is more impossible than to be a nice monk, but I did not know this at first. All day long people ignored me—we don't talk to each other, you know—no matter what I did or how charming I managed to be without speaking. I smiled at them incessantly, and in surreptitious ways attempted to give them little pleasures, but all I ever received in return was silence and a bow.

When I was made the work director—the guy in charge—and finally had the power to give people what they wanted and receive their black-market appreciation in return, being a nice guy started getting me in trouble. Two days into my terrifying new job a monk approached and told me she needed to see a doctor. Those monks know a sucker when they see one, I'll tell you.

"Sure," I said, so she jumped in a car and went.

When the Roshi found out, she hit the roof. That decision I had made, as I did not understand at all and as she heatedly explained to me, was too important to be left to me and my conditioning alone. The whole point of monastic training is to submit one's needs to the guidance of the teacher, so that they may be examined from a perspective outside of conditioned mind. Was it true that the monk needed to go to the doctor? Possibly. But if not—if what she actually needed was her own love and attention—then I had just robbed her of the opportunity to provide this for herself.

That got me thinking. Until then I doubt I had ever considered the possibility that "nice" is not who I actually am. Dave is nice, I had always thought—that's just who he is. Suddenly I saw the truth. As this understanding grew within me, and as I turned the eyes of my awareness upon the nice guy I had been, I began to see the deprivation and the suffering that hid beneath it. I began to see how I was swindled. No wonder I had been so unhappy! I had never lived my life—because the nice guy had, instead.

This thing that I called "nice", I saw, was merely a story I had manufactured. In addition, I saw that because I am not actually "nice" I was forced to tell myself that story over and over through time so that it would remain real to me. Otherwise I would just be who I am. I talked to myself all day long, weaving a pretty tapestry full of drama and emotion so that I might hide within its fibers. My stories—this one and many others—told me who I am, who or what everything else might be, how I felt and what I should do about those feelings, and so on. They scripted every thought and action from the first moment of every day to the last.

Like any good story, mine needed a plot to build itself around. There had to be some unifying theme convincing enough to fool my natural intelligence. Being the child that I was when it was

137

invented, I was not clever enough to create a believable drama on my own, but this was not required. The story was handed to me as a finished work of deception by the world I was born in to: I had only to trade my own good sense for it, and it was mine. The theme was made out of the various half-truths that I inherited about myself from parents, teachers, and others in a position to give them to me. Those who had traveled farther than I through the suffering world understood what I needed to do to survive, and they trained me well. The day I decided to be "nice" I only confirmed the path I was started on nearly the instant I was born. The theme was made from what I was taught to believe; the plot of my story was the series of life circumstances that seemed to prove this theme's reality.

As children we all go through this process. It is sort of like being potty-trained: when we attain the ability to fool ourselves with our stories all the time without any "accidents"—without accidentally dropping into the clarity of the moment—then we can be said to be, by the common definition, adults. An adult, from the point of view of conditioned mind, is one who needs not fear acting spontaneously. I can imagine the precious boy that I was in the beginning, as he struggles to teach himself this skill. There he is with his pile of curly hair, his bony limbs, and his freckles. There he goes, just being himself, just doing whatever it is that lay in front of him to do, pretty much as happy as anyone can be—then suddenly he remembers the artificial story that tells him who he is supposed to be instead. I see his body tense and the loss of his smile as his attention is seized by self-consciousness. His eyes betray the fear and self-doubt of the conditioning he is learning; they lose focus as he searches within his mind for the boy he is supposed to be. A moment later he pastes a look on his face that is his best imitation of this boy, and he carries it before him like a stack of china plates until some distraction invites him to enjoy his own self again—say, a butterfly flutters by—and the story drops and shatters to pieces.

Whenever this happened, whenever I accidentally became myself instead of the person I was trained to be, I was punished.

This is what happened to all of us: our socialization as children required that we be disciplined for being ourselves. The terror of this punishment taught me to practice being who I was in my story as often as I could remember to do that. The "boy I should be" kept me safe from the punishment. The older I became, the more consistently I was able to keep my attention fixed upon the fiction I was required to believe. As my body grew the flat pretense I wore became what I thought of as "myself," and I forgot the freedom I had previously enjoyed. In other words, I finally learned to believe my story. At last, at the point when the world had completely socialized me, the story was not even conscious anymore—it was assumed.

It remained a fiction, however, and so needed something to support its believability against my natural intelligence. To underpin my story, my parents and other representatives of society handed me a collection of beliefs about the way things are inside and outside of me. These were all false, but I was trained to believe them before I had attained the ability to see things for myself, so they were never questioned. I was taught to believe that people wished in their hearts to take advantage of me; that I was inadequate to an authentic experience of life; that I had better be safe rather than happy; that I needed to get what I wanted from the outside, and in particular from other people; that having what I wanted was bad, and not having it was good—and a host of other things. The most pernicious belief was the most fundamental: that who I am at the core is a bad person. This was the message delivered by the punishment I received.

I grew up, and the story thrived. How could it not? It was assumed, and so everything in my experience appeared to confirm it. I became unable to see beyond what I already believed. Every time somebody frowned in my direction, or preferred a rival, or criticized an accomplishment; every time life did not go the way I imagined it should, evidence collected that supported the story that I lived in a hostile world and that there was something wrong with the person who I was. Life simply became a series of experiments in which this was proven over and over.

In this way our socialization trains us to believe we are victims to our lives. We assume the way things are, and each assumption closes a door. This door closes, then that one, then this one, and on and on until we find ourselves trapped entirely within the tiny box of our ideas, being the false person we have learned to believe that we are, completely out of touch with our physical, emotional, and spiritual life.

I learned to be a "nice guy", but nice was not all I was. Beneath my smiles and cheerfulness and eagerness to please, there seethed secret resentment for all I relinquished to function in that unnatural way. I gave up everything to have that misery: most of all, the natural man I might otherwise have become, with a sense of who he was and what he might accomplish, and with an understanding of his deepest heart's desires. I gave up the possibility of uncontaminated maturity to protect myself behind the fears of a child. And though I made this deal in every moment of my life, I did so with terrible bitterness, and behind the wall of a nice guy I lived in rage.

As soon as I could I ran away from the world that required this sacrifice of me, as I have described. It was too late by then—my inner world too had come to demand it—but at least it felt powerful to run. At last I landed in the two-room shack way back in the mountains that I mentioned earlier. I rented the place from an elderly couple, Bruce and Mildred, who lived just down the road. They were mountain folk, those two, and I quickly grew to love them. They welcomed me as their neighbor, and with great excitement I settled into my new life, for the first time completely on my own.

Two months later Mildred died. I was there when the medics carried her away for the last time from the only home she had known as a woman. Poor Bruce, alone suddenly for the first time in fifty years, went absolutely to pieces. He had family all around, but they ignored his desperation after the first few days, so I offered to comfort him in his grief. Every day I sat with him on his porch while he mourned, and over time his pain mellowed. We talked of next to nothing, but we shared an unsaid loneliness, I think, that brought us together. I visited him every day for months out of pity and compassion, and I enjoyed this service that I offered him, but as time went by the pure motivation that I started with began to sour. I began to do it out of duty instead of love, and because he demanded it: if I did not go to see him, then he would come to see me, and if he did there was no getting rid of him. I started to be "nice" to him. I did not have the ability at that time to express to him what I felt or what I needed so that he could return my gift, and so I gradually fell into my lifelong habit of resentment as I gave him what he wanted and ignored myself.

This went on for about a year and a half. Then one day a friend of many years, my dear comrade Lisa, came to visit from the city. We enjoyed ourselves so much that we forgot the time, and so Lisa asked if she could spend the night, and I agreed. The next morning, she departed and I went over to see Bruce. It happened to be the first of the month, so I took a check with me for my rent. To my surprise he refused it. "It's just not right," he said over and over as I begged him for an explanation. Finally he motioned with his eyes the way Lisa had gone and I understood: he assumed that I had slept with her. I still do not know if he objected just to that, or because he figured I had cheated on my girlfriend at that time, who had been a friend of Mildred's. It did not matter: in a flash my entire world changed. At last the indignation I had suppressed those many months found the righteous outlet that it sought, and it erupted there before his eyes. Thank heavens I cannot remember what I said. I crumpled the check, threw it to the floor, and walked out, never to see poor Bruce again.

An hour later I was gone. I tossed my few possessions into the back of my pick-up and took off for I didn't know where. For good measure, on the way out of town I quit my job and broke up with my girlfriend. It was as glorious and as hideous as I

141

could bear: for hours I was intoxicated by the explosion of my repressed energy. At the end of the day, emotionally and physically exhausted, I landed at Lisa's place in the city. I saw her concern as she greeted me. I did not explain, but as I reached into the back of the truck to get something, a lamp fell out onto the ground, and she knew. "I see," said Lisa, smiling sympathetically. It was not the first time I had shown up on her doorstep with my life in pieces around me.

Looking back, I wince at the destruction and the dishonor of that day, but I sympathize with the confused young man that I was then. I had no understanding of how the chaotic world that trapped me had fixed itself within my mind, and no experience of an alternative. Even afterwards for years the events of that day merely proved the supposed truth that I am a bad person and cannot be trusted. And so, as soon as I could, I traded the sour ecstasy of that day for the imprisonment that had preceded it, and I determined once again to be "nice" from that day forward, ignoring my essential self-abandonment.

As I did, so do we all. A conditioned human being goes through life making misery out of nothing real, and then defending the world that this creates, no matter how it kills our authentic spirit. That is just what we do. That is what we do, that is, until we catch on to the manner in which this destroys our lives.

My rage was not exhausted on that day—far from it. Several times over the next years it exploded again, with similar unhappy consequences. I brought it with me to the monastery, in fact, as you have seen. I have told you already about the hot sauce episode. The letting go that happened then put the anger away for a time, but eventually it began to seethe again within my thoughts. Soon after I was made the work director it started to build in earnest.

My first act as the work director was to change the way everything was done. I rearranged the tool shed, I altered the system whereby we track our needs from town, I threw mountains of perfectly good stuff into the garbage—I even changed our basic communication structures—all without the knowledge of the Roshi. I somehow imagined she would be pleased when she found out. I determined secretly (so secretly I did not even know it myself) that this would be the occasion at last when I would prove the competence I doubted in myself. Sound familiar? It was the nice guy gone berserk. I rearranged, re-sorted, and purged for an entire month, creating all sorts of fancy systems and procedures, until there could be no doubt it was perfect and I had succeeded.

I had not. The result was a perfect disaster. The confusion and disorder that erupted out of my "improvements" were so extreme as to have been comical if I had not been so invested in them. As everything fell to pieces and the daily flow came to a grinding halt, my hysterical efforts did not escape the Roshi's notice—nor, to be truthful, my own. Before long the head monk pulled me aside and said, "The Roshi is…surprised…by the changes you have made. She requests that you put everything back the way it was, and that you consult her in the future before making any decisions, no matter how small." I knew it was coming, but even so those words pried the lid off of my repressed rage and there it was, with all of the intoxication and abandon of that moment years before in Bruce's living room. Once again, from my perspective within conditioned mind, I had given everything to receive nothing but criticism and shame. I felt the energy that threatened to erupt through my body and my mouth; I felt the old-time desire to destroy my life as it was, and I looked around for some violent means to take revenge.

But I did not do it—almost, but not quite. Something had changed: I had learned to cast a shadow of doubt over the story of my inadequacy. On some level I understood that what I experienced was not real. I still raged, but I did not act. I did not believe in it anymore. For days I felt the energy of that anger course through my body, and for days I just let it go where it would. I felt my feet in my shoes; I kept my eyes on the leaves in the trees and the light that played in their branches; and held on to the moment with all of my might. I gave myself the space

143

to feel that karmic wind blow through—but I remained the space and not the wind, and thereby gained a piece of the lost manhood that I longed for.

17

The Fragments of a Once Whole Life

In the aftermath of this victory the false world of my unhappiness fell to pieces, at least for a time. Without the need to be who I believed I was, I enjoyed an unaccustomed permission to explore who I might actually be. I did not get very far, however. No matter where I turned, every "me" I imagined I might be was assembled from the same stuff, essentially, as the nice guy I had been. Each was manufactured from my thoughts, and for this reason, empty of anything I could truly identify as myself.

One Sunday evening—it must have been two or three months after I had been made the work director—I found myself waiting in the dining hall for the Roshi. We had planned to meet to discuss a number of issues that had arisen so that I might receive her guidance. This was an exercise that we performed frequently together, but never before on a Sunday. Sunday evening is normally free time—"Holy Leisure" we call it. In fact, it is just about the only free time that we have. Because of this, that evening I very much did not want to meet with the Roshi. "This is my time!" the voices said, and I believed them.

Nevertheless, I made my way to the appointed place at the appointed time. A monk has no choice in these matters, you know, regardless of what the voices say. When I arrived, the Roshi was not there. I waited for what seemed a long time—it must have been at least two minutes—then I composed the following note:

Roshi,

You do not seem to be around, so I think I'll head back to my hermitage and figure we can get caught up tomorrow.

Gassho,

Dave

After I had finished writing I went to post the note on the board. As I did I noticed out of the corner of my eye—I really didn't mean to see it, but I accidentally did—the flash of headlights reflected in the windows of the dining hall, and I knew the Roshi was coming. For a moment I hesitated. For a moment I stood in the place of choice between freedom and suffering, with both experiences available to me. Then weakness overcame good sense and I posted the note anyway, then hurried off the back way into the darkness like an escaped convict, and made my way back to my hermitage.

Now, as a monk you don't go sneaking around to avoid your teacher. You just don't. The next morning, I found a note posted to me in her handwriting, folded together with the one I had written the evening before, which said:

Dave,

   Who wrote this note?

Gassho

I didn't get it. "What does she mean, 'Who wrote this note?'" I said to myself over and over. "I wrote this note!" I remember I left the dining hall and began to make my way towards the nearest outhouse, asking myself again and again, "What does she mean, 'Who wrote this note?'" I got it while I relieved myself. "Oh, my god!" I said aloud—and with the most awful sinking feeling I saw that who I was the evening before was not me at all, but was some conditioned imposter.

In the lingo of the practice that person who was not me but pretended to be was an "aspect of personality" or "subpersonality". Here was an unknown entity I called "I" just like the nice guy. Both of these "people" live inside of me. As a conditioned person the illusion I lived within said there was just one "I", but as I had begun to suspect and as now became evident, there was and is a host of different entities living within my mind, all competing for the privilege of being "me".

So it is with everyone. Within conditioned mind we relate to the world through a parade of points of view: the aspect of the personality who captures the body in any given moment determines our experience of life while he or she is there. The moment this "I" departs another seizes our perspective and the world reorganizes to reflect this new point of view. As conditioned beings we have any number of subpersonalities who may represent us both to ourselves and others. Each aspect of the personality arises in response to a particular type of internal or external circumstance. And so we go along through life with this crowd following close behind, each one primed to leap upon the stage as soon as her or his cue is given. As we do we suffer, because none of these "people" is who we truly are. None of them is real in and of itself, and so none can actually meet our needs.

Over time I began to see that each of these subpersonalities functions as an autonomous entity. Each one speaks in its own way to me; each believes what he believes, and many times the assumptions of one contradict the assumptions of another. Each projects from these beliefs and thus creates a world that magnifies its particular point of view. They really are different people. And yet, until I began to look I had no idea they were there. All along I thought I was just being "me". And so I remained trapped within an ever-altering sequence of fixed perspectives, responding to the world that each one perceived as if it were real. No matter how my perception changed from one moment to the next, I assumed that who I was in each instant was the "person" who at that moment dominated my ears, my eyes, and my mind.

I discovered this simply by attending to the voices, as the Roshi encouraged me to do. Each subpersonality talks in a particular way that expresses its unique viewpoint. If I could hear what was said, I saw, without believing it, then I could stand outside of the identity and could see who was there. The fellow I call "the rebel" was the next to be uncovered after the nice guy. He is the most dramatic, and so was the easiest to see. The moment I saw him—get this—he was giving the Roshi the middle finger over the telephone while she explained to me the importance of some guideline or other. "Aha!" I exclaimed, as soon as I hung up. "That was not me!" After that it was not long before I made the acquaintance of many of the others who live inside.

After that I figured I had this "subpersonality" thing licked. Alas, I did not know how wrong I was. My awareness of the different aspects of my personality was feeble as yet—and as yet I had not met Mr. Hyde.

I call him Mr. Hyde because, though he does not perfectly match the character in the novel—that guy acted from a place of evil that Mr. Hyde does not know—the resemblance is uncanny. Like the original he comes out when nobody is looking and does things that his daylight counterpart (Dr. Jekyll in R.L. Stevenson's story, me in mine) deeply regrets. When anybody else is around, Mr. Hyde, like the fellow in the book, is never to be seen, but at times when I find myself alone and vulnerable he sneaks out of his hiding place, assumes my body, and works his secret agendas upon the world.

So what does he do? Well, Mr. Hyde desires above all else to have control of everything, and to be right. It technically is not possible, of course, to be either right or in control, but this is something Mr. Hyde does not understand. And so he makes decisions that are not his to make. He does things that are not his to do. He says thing that are not his to say.

While I was the cook I was one hundred percent unaware of Mr. Hyde, so he was able to work freely outside of the light of my perception. Over time he completely redirected the way the monastery does food. I was told when I was first made the cook, for example, that we always buy three types of lettuce in equal proportion: green, red, and romaine. Well, Mr. Hyde despises romaine lettuce. It is inferior to the other types, in his opinion. So over time, without anyone noticing, he changed the guidance. Over the course of an entire year he bought less and less romaine until it was completely eliminated from our diet. Whenever he trained a new grocery shopper (and he trained them all—he saw to that) he always told them, "We don't buy romaine lettuce." Finally, he had so undone the original guidance that the other monks, even those who had been there the whole time, would have sworn that we had never bought romaine since the inception of the monastery. And Mr. Hyde remained undetected the whole time.

Ironically, after I left the cook's job and moved on to other things I began to pick up unpleasant notes from the message board, saying things like, "Dave, remember that we don't buy romaine lettuce." Mr. Hyde knew those guidelines were bogus, so he ignored them. By then, however, he was on to other things. When I became the work director, as we have seen, a whole new world opened up for Mr. Hyde: it would be his gleeful work for years to make all of our systems and procedures as he thought they should be, even after the disaster I described earlier. He felt he could reinvent the whole monastery without anyone noticing. He's a motivated chap, this Mr. Hyde.

Mr. Hyde went about this as he always did: he made lots of decisions without checking in with the appropriate people, he was right a lot and made others wrong, and he engaged in plenty of other nastiness. For a long time this went on undiscovered. You may wonder how this secrecy was possible given the incredible scrutiny a monk endures. For most it would not have been, but you see, Mr. Hyde is a master of deception. Even while he plotted to ruin my life and to destroy the peace and the ease of those around me, he feigned humility, and in this way he fooled everyone, including me. In addition, Mr. Hyde is wickedly smart, and in fact made the "right" decisions a lot of the time, so he left few clear tracks behind him that anyone could trace. In his own world he was so right he needed not fear discovery again—but if there is one thing I have learned about Mr. Hyde, it is this: he is not so clever as he thinks he is.

I had no idea all this was going on. As yet I had never seen Mr. Hyde full in the face. Looking back, I can recall glimpses here and there of his furtive profile, but as yet he remained a stranger to my awareness, so I did not recognize him even as he captured my own body. I just went along, unconsciously performing Mr. Hyde's secret tasks for him, creating the world in which he desired to live, and planting secret land-mines (his manifold bad decisions) everywhere I went.

One year in November the monastery asked me to travel to the East Coast to staff a retreat there for ten days. While I was gone another monk carried out my responsibilities. If you should ever find yourself in my position, having taken control of a Zen monastery all by yourself, take my advice: never leave your post undefended. Or if, like me, what you really want in your heart of hearts is to end your suffering, pray that somebody will pry the world of your invention from your hands if you cannot, and then pray for the strength to survive what must follow. What happened next was unavoidable: as people moved into Mr. Hyde's confidential areas, they began to trip the mines. I returned to California to find his fortifications breached and in ruins, and the enemy (the Roshi) seated amongst all his various smoldering deceptions, on a pile of questionable decisions, waiting for me with the cheeriest smile you've ever seen. It was awful.

It was at the same time, however, the best thing that could have happened. Even as painful as the aftermath was, I did not lose consciousness completely, and through the course of things, as the monastery erected structures to protect itself from my conditioning, I got a really close look at Mr. Hyde. I saw for the first time the impostor that he is, and I began to uncover the authority he wielded throughout my life, and all of the suffering that he caused. Even better, I began to glimpse the clarity that Mr. Hyde hid behind him. I began to detect my own self-confidence, which he had absconded for himself.

This is not, alas, the end of the story. Just a few short months later a similar fiasco went down, only on a smaller scale. Once again that pretender worked his sour intentions on the world through my innocent hands and mouth, and once again I found myself wrestling in a bomb crater with the dastardly Mr. Hyde. I had seen him, the rascal, but still his power was much greater than mine, and as soon as the smoke cleared he was at it again. Then it happened again, and again, and again. Even a year later I still could barely see him.

And yet, over time something changed. Along the way, through the pain of all those misadventures, I found the willingness to align myself with my heart against Mr. Hyde and to risk going through life without him. I finally grew tired of suffering for his benefit. I wished instead to be a part of the human experiment, working for its good. I longed to become the person I knew myself to be in his absence, and from this came finally the willingness to walk away from Mr. Hyde.

Time went by and I got pretty good, in my estimation, at this subpersonality thing. I figured I had it licked. Once again, I did not know how wrong I was.

One evening after our schedule had ended for the day I was asked if I would help move a piece of furniture into a neighbor's house up the road. I said that of course I would, and so I found myself before long grunting and groaning along with a few other folks beneath a large cabinet. We had to carry it from the driveway up some stairs and into the hallway beyond the front door. We worked in silence apart for some laughter and a bit of complaining (the folks I assisted were not monks), and I enjoyed the quiet as I always do. At last, after lots of shoving and heaving, we deposited our burden in its new resting place—and then, as we stood up to celebrate our achievement, unexpectedly and to my complete surprise, everyone began talking.

Now, I had already lived by then several years as a silent monk, and over that time had been handed innumerable opportunities to practice in social situations. Every time I went to the hardware store, or to buy gas, or, more rarely, to visit family, I practiced being present and aware during my interactions with people. I would not have imagined the sudden conversation to be a difficulty for me, but it was. The change was just so immediate, I think, that self-consciousness could not keep up, and I found myself all at once exposed to my companions in a way that I never allowed, and without any of my usual defenses.

What happened next has fascinated me ever since. Somebody said, "So, Dave…" and asked me some question (heaven knows what it was—I never heard it), and as the attention of the group turned to me—it happened in slow motion, as if it were a car accident—I watched as awareness abandoned my body, leaving an empty shell behind, pretending to be me. It was such a dramatic desertion that I could not avoid seeing it, and the experience is burned forever upon my memory. I heard my voice respond to the question with some sort of gibberish, but as I did I was most painfully aware that the person who did the talking was not me. I felt as if I were ten thousand miles away, watching what happened through the wrong end of a telescope.

That was the first time, I think, that I understood what is meant by the expression "Cardboard Henry". I doubt anybody remembers where that phrase came from, but I have loved it ever since I first heard it. Your Cardboard Henry is the façade you present to the world. It is also, you might say, who you pretend to be most fundamentally when you are not who you are. I had seen many times before this day how the various actors in my internal fantasy take the stage to perform for some outside person, and how I hide behind them with my secret thoughts and feelings. But I had never seen how, in exactly the same way, I was excluded from the experience of myself. I realized suddenly as I stood there by the cabinet, and as I reeled from self-abandonment, that on a level I could not see I believed my own pretense. In effect I stood in relationship to myself as an outsider, divided from my authentic nature by my own Cardboard Henry in the way that others are, like them with no power to see what lies behind the deception. Then, suddenly, there he was, right in front of me. I watched him in amazement as he babbled on and on about nothing. He had no heart, I saw, or any real intelligence: he was a non-person, just a reflection of the life he did not possess. For perhaps the first time in my life I stepped far enough away from him to see him, and without my support he collapsed like a pricked balloon. All that remained was an empty confusion pretending to be Dave.

Before long the conversation turned and I pulled myself together. That is, "I" pulled my separate self together in the way it had been before, but I was not deceived, at least for a time. For the longest while I stood behind the scenery of the "I" that I pretended to myself to be. From there I could see what it was made of: just some old cardboard and a bit of paint. It was stunning. Until that day I had felt myself to live behind the wall of conditioned mind, trapped by my beliefs and my projections in a place of separation from what is. And so I was, but I had never questioned the reality of the "me" that experienced this. Even this, I saw, was an illusion. There is no "I" having my experience. There is no "my experience", even. There just is what is in the experience of this moment, belonging to no one. The function of the wall, I saw, was not so much to isolate me from my perception of the outside world, though it effected this perfectly as well, but to separate awareness from what within me just is.

In the collision of my spirit with the conditioned world I had lost my way within the illusion of a self that forever shifts and changes, always seemingly complete but always separate from Life. And yet, I never lost touch with my authentic nature. On some level, I saw, the suffering I endured never completely erased the experience of the vast intelligence, whatever that may be, which animates me. Something of what I once had been when I emerged as a mortal being upon this earth persisted through all of that endless trouble and confusion, all of that

153

misery and doubt, and it was this that saved me. Even at the times when I was the closest to despair and exhaustion my heart still stirred at the sight of a yellow autumn leaf tumbling slowly to the ground, or at the sound of rushing water, or at the feeling of my feet as they walked upon the earth, or at the naked innocence of Rhea as she lay sleeping in the night. Something underneath the illusion named "me" called me to the unity I had forgotten.

Nothing really happened. I can say this despite the agony of it: I only dreamed for a time instead of following my natural waking life.

The shattering of our essential unity is an illusion. This is what the Buddha taught, at least so far as I understand it. The oneness we are born with breaks, it is true, as we are socialized, and we truly suffer in our grief for it, but this breakage occurs only in our perception. In order to survive we must yield to the belief that the wholeness of our hearts is gone—but it is not gone. It is only that an illusion separates us from it. Ending suffering is the discovery that our original unity was never destroyed; that rather it lives through us in every moment, and that as we let go of the need for our personality to endure we may reunite ourselves with that unity once again and be free. Nothing that claims to be my self is me. Each is merely the fragment of a once whole life.

18

Self-Hatred

For some time I basked in the understanding that had come from the insight just described. I had glimpsed the ineffable presence that lay behind the illusion I had believed in all my life, and it moved me. Here was an experience I might call "me" that was full of gladness and harmony rather than scarcity and defeat; in a way I knew this place within me more intimately than the world that filled my senses—it is who I am—but in another way I knew it not at all, and I was filled with awe and gratitude to experience it in my waking life.

The question that arose next was this: how is it that I do not naturally live from that place of authenticity? The feeling of reality and depth that accompanied it contrasted radically with my habitual state. It was like the difference between my face and a reflection of my face in a murky pool of water: until then I had only seen the reflection. Given that, how could it be that the ease and grace which—I could now see—are an aspect of who or what I truly am, did not effortlessly guide me through every day?

I puzzled over this question for a number of weeks. Then, as always happens sooner or later, Life provided me with an experience that began to answer it for me.

A stray dog showed up on the property one evening. She was obviously destitute, so we took her in until we could find her a home. We decided while we waited that we should have her spayed, and so one day we did. I brought her home from the vet myself, all woozy and sore as she was from the surgery, and made a nice place for her to rest and recover on the back porch.

One of the monks had made a habit of taking the dog with her for a romp after lunch for some exercise. I knew this, of course, and, at just the wrong moment, while I was stranded in the car without paper or pen, it occurred to me that as the work director I should inform that monk of the surgery so that she would not take the dog running that afternoon. The vet was clear with me that the dog should do nothing vigorous for several days at least, or risk bursting her stitches and getting infected. "Right!" I told myself, "I'll do it as soon as I get back!" But I did not. I was distracted by other things after my return to the monastery, and the window of time passed in which it needed to be done. I remembered thirty seconds too late, in time to see the monk vanish up the road with the poor dog in tow behind her on a leash.

Imagine my horror when I realized what had happened. I bludgeoned myself mercilessly for it. It seemed unforgivable— and yet, even as I suffered over my incompetence, as I judged it, I managed to glimpse the manipulating influence of conditioned mind behind the event. It was so typical and inevitable—so like everything that had happened to humiliate and punish me since I was a boy. As I pondered that obvious fact I began to realize that something that was not me had possessed me and caused the disaster to happen. I did not do it: something, some other force, had done it through my body, mouth, and mind. It could be said that I was innocent. That fascinated me in a horrible sort of way.

I looked forward to my next appointment with the Roshi in order to describe what had occurred. "As you know very well," she said when I was finished, "there is something larger than the various aspects of personality that you've been working on which holds them all together. They are supported and maintained, we might say, in a single drama. This something has no interest in unconditional love or acceptance; it only wants you to suffer."

"Why do I persist in believing in it? The experience of authenticity is so much more real and happy."

"There is a barrier," she replied, "that we must get past before we can live from our authentic nature. We cannot end the illusion until we remove the assumption at the center of it. Do you know what I'm referring to?"

"Self-hatred?" I asked.

She nodded. Self-hate! I knew at some point it would come down to that.

We each know somewhere deep within that everything our heart longs and waits for lies just beyond our reach. We can sense it; it seems it should be so easy to just open our arms and receive the joy that is natural to us as existing beings. Almost no one can do that, however. Instead, we sacrifice our capacity to enjoy this beautiful life to fear and deprivation. This is the most tragic and confused act imaginable, but to a person we all do it. We do it because we have been trained to hate ourselves.

To experience happiness, or peace, or joy, or well-being, is actually very simple: just be happy, or peaceful, or joyful, or content. That is all it takes. Why, then, do we choose otherwise? We choose to suffer because we believe we do not deserve to receive the goodness that Life offers. Deep beneath the level of our awareness we assume that there is something wrong with us, that we must correct or compensate for a fundamental flaw in our being before we may receive our natural happiness. We believe that because of this defect we are unworthy to be accepted and loved; unfit to just live in peace and gratitude. This belief underpins the device called "self-hatred." Self-hatred is the mechanism through which we deny ourselves our natural happiness and joy.

Self-hatred is not a passing emotion, like sadness or jealousy; rather, it is a core piece of ego's machinery that persists, for every conditioned person, through each waking moment. It functions to keep the deception alive that we are separate from the life that animates us. Without self-hatred we would pretty quickly drop this confusion and just be. Without some internal motivation to keep the illusion intact it would dissolve, if for no other reason than it is just too exhausting to keep it going. Self-hate provides this motivation—it tells us we must fix the flawed

157

person that we are before we can be happy or receive love—and thereby keeps the system of our suffering alive and functioning.

It used to be that the monastery kept peacocks. At one time we had several, and one spring, much to the monks' delight, one of the hens hatched a handsome chick for all of us to admire. He was the most adorable little critter I had ever seen, and he became instantly our common pride and joy. Mamma peacock would have nothing of our fondness for her little one, however. She would not let any of us near, no matter how we soothed and flattered her. She bristled and squawked whenever we came by until we finally gave up and resigned ourselves to a distant love for that tiny being.

One day, as Rhea and I hurried down the path on the west side of the main buildings, we suddenly came across the mamma peacock and her youngster. I stopped for a moment to take in the little guy's cuteness. Unexpectedly, Rhea lunged. I couldn't believe it—she had never shown any aggression towards the birds before. Mamma peacock shrieked and attacked Rhea with a power and a ferocity that I could never have predicted. She would have torn Rhea's eyes out, I feel certain, if she could have. Rhea, who is just a speck of a dog and a confirmed coward, freaked and began to bawl. Something needed to be done—and I froze. It was the strangest thing: for a few moments I just could not move. Another monk stood nearby; he said softly but urgently several times, "Move on, Dave, move on!" But for those few panicked seconds my feet were rooted in the ground, my brain misfired, and I could do nothing.

As soon as I awoke from my astonishment I tore Rhea away from the infuriated peacock. It was over in an instant, and everything, as it turned out, was fine: Rhea suffered some minor scratches only, and the chick was untouched. Everything was fine except for the tirade of abuse that poured onto my head from within my own mind for freezing up the way I did. I could not believe the viciousness of it. From the punishment that I endured for those two confused seconds, you would have thought I had killed the chick myself. I was called every degrading name in

158

the book, and threatened with every imaginable punishment: it was awful. "I see," I said to myself as I listened. "This must be what they mean by 'self-hate'."

I did not know that I believed there was something wrong with me. Or, rather, I knew it but could not see where the belief resided. I could not see this supposed wrong thing that was the obstacle I could not pass into the enjoyment of my life.

As the years passed I chipped away at the self-hatred that orchestrated my unhappiness, with good success. As with all of us, however, the belief that I am not okay, that I am inadequate to my life, ran deep—it is the fundamental belief that holds identity together—and it remained unaffected at the core. This was the barrier that the Roshi referred to. Self-hatred was more real to me than the authenticity I had experienced here and there.

"There is a part of you, a small child," the Roshi told me, "who absolutely believes there is something wrong with him."

"A small child?"

"Yes," she replied, and smiled with the most exquisite compassion imaginable. "A boy. You must teach him that this is not true."

"How do I do that?" I asked her.

"This will sound familiar," she answered, laughing. "You must be here, present and in this moment, because here is where that boy is. He is here right now, trapped in a place that you are conditioned to ignore. The compassion and the unconditional acceptance that he needs is here, in this moment, also. If you will practice being here, then eventually you will discover how to bring that boy and that compassion together.

"Without the understanding that he is here, however, and without the experience within you of what he is waiting for, this could take a long time. So here is what I would suggest: watch for him as you go through the day. You might think of him as the entity that is underneath or inside each of the aspects of personality that you are working on. It is he that suffers through them, you might say. See if you can learn to recognize his suffering within you, and when you see it, when you feel him, hold him in your attention as compassionately as you are able. That is what he needs.

"The entire function of conditioned mind," she continued, "is to manage our attention so that our natural compassion is never united with the being inside who needs it. This separation is only possible outside of the present moment, so our attention must be continually forced through threats and promises into the past and future. Here, in this moment, following the breath, coming back to our senses, the power that conditioned mind has to enforce the separation ends. It ceases to exist when we are here, where we actually are.

"Now, it is true," she added, her eyes narrowing, "that you will need to let go of self-hate in order to end that separation. You will need to completely and absolutely let go of the idea that there is something wrong with that boy that he needs to be punished for. That is your piece of the work. You must realize that you are not that boy; that you are the unconditionally loving parent that he needs. His work is to wait for you to find the heart to finally save him from the misery he has endured for so long."

"Wow." I said. "That's big."

"It is. And one more thing. I think I can guarantee that you will be required to face the reaction that conditioned mind will have to this. The suffering of that child is the glue that holds the whole illusion in place. If you attempt to interfere, conditioned mind will stop at nothing to scare you away from that possibility, or to drag you someplace far enough away that you lose touch with it and forget that this is what you are here to do."

"Yikes!"

"I'm not trying to set you up. Nothing would please me more than to find out that I am wrong about this—but it is not likely. When it happens just remember what *is* happening: it is ego's attempt to get you back."

I will admit that this admonition rattled me a bit. I could see to some extent the tremendous hold that self-hate had on me. In many ways it was the largest single power in my life—after the power of the awareness practice I had been called to. I could not imagine actually ending the relationship. All I could do was take it on faith that if Life presented me with that opportunity it was because the wherewithal to accomplish it lay within my grasp. In the meantime, I decided, I would practice being as present as I could and hope that somehow the miracle would happen.

Sometime afterwards, on a clear summer morning, I went to work with a gang of monks at the far end of the property. We were building a new hermitage. I felt nervous, as I was still somewhat new to the world of saws and levels, nails and two-by-fours. I even felt a little sick to my stomach as I pulled on my overalls and tied on my boots. I doubt I was aware how much conditioned mind had staked upon my performance that day, or how leery I was of the outcome. It was a self-hate opportunity, to be sure.

To make things worse, the Roshi put me in charge of the project. There you have monastic practice in a nutshell: find the guy who most does not want the job, and give it to him. I felt the adrenalin course through my body as I heard the news. "Heaven help me," I muttered to myself.

I went to work in a fever of anxiety. To my surprise, things worked, more or less. I even sort of knew what I was doing. Together the other monks and I measured and sawed and nailed, and in just a couple of hours had framed the first wall.

Then something regrettable happened. Our success intoxicated my stumbling sense of adequacy, and it carried me, alas, without notice beyond the bounds of compassionate self-awareness. Before I had only been afraid of failing, which left me suffering but humble and easy to get along with. Now that I had glimpsed the possibility that I might succeed, I felt I must, and everything other than this desire went out the window. Insensibly self-hatred seized my thoughts and projected itself through my eyes onto the world around me. Invisibly I crossed into the world of right and wrong.

One of the monks in particular caught my attention. She moved sluggishly, with obviously no enthusiasm for the work that threatened and inspired her supervisor. Gradually I began to resent her for this. At first, as we laid out the framing for the second wall, I pushed my irritation aside to make room for my eagerness. Over time, however, as we worked and as she shuffled here and there, accomplishing nothing, indignation obscured good sense, and I felt an urge arise to act. Somehow I decided it was my job to steer her the way I wished her to go. Finally I pulled her aside. I do not remember what I said to her, only that my words were steeped in the heartless convictions and the aggression of conditioned mind. I did to her what I did to myself—what self-hatred did to me in its abuse of my innocence.

I will never forget her eyes as I spoke to her—so open they were as she turned to me, and startled, too astonished to hide her injury. I watched as the innocence within them drained away until only hurt remained. Then I saw how I had wounded her. It was not even in the words that the hurt was done: it was in the assumptions of self-hatred. Ordinarily there is no right and wrong in the monastic environment; over time one forgets the need to huddle in defense against it, and learns to live with the heart exposed. My identification with self-hatred had blinded me to her vulnerability that morning, and to the tender opportunity, whatever it was, that she struggled with as she worked. I saw in her eyes how I had blundered.

Before I could mend the breach she turned and ran away. I followed, and I found her by the garden, staring blankly before her at the ground in obvious dismay. The shame and the impotence I felt in that moment cannot be described. With a heavy heart I walked away. Knowing I could only do more damage on my own, I called the Roshi to confess what I had done and asked for her intervention.

The rest of the afternoon the monastery suffered the rippling effects of my unconsciousness. Another monk was called in to council the young woman, and after some hours all was well again with everyone but me. In the evening the Roshi showed up. I most desperately did not want to see her—I felt so unworthy of the opportunity she provided me, and so wretched for violating her trust. She asked for me, and though I expected punishment I gave her my unhappy obedience, anticipating the worse.

She said, "Are you okay?" I stared at her in disbelief. I had not expected kindness.

A sudden breeze ruffled her hair. She frowned with divine concern upon my aching heart, and all of my self-hatred dissolved. The compassion in her words moved me to tears and transported me to a world I had only guessed at until then: a world without the assumption that I am not okay. I understood in that moment that she did not see through the illusion of self-hatred, but with the clarity of compassion. She perceived the hurt in me that had harmed, and because of this could offer me what I could not offer that struggling monk earlier in the day: an understanding that transcends conditioned mind. Her kindness invited my own, lifted me from my despair, and taught me to look within myself for a way of seeing beyond the taint of the self-hatred. If she can do it, I told myself, then so can I.

For a long while afterwards the power of self-hatred amazed me. I saw that more important to me as a conditioned being than anything else—more than my own happiness, more than peace, more than joy, more than enjoyment and relaxation, more important even than the survival of the angelic spirit that inhabits my body—was the preservation of self-hatred. The truth of this could be seen everywhere in my self-sabotage. I said that I wanted to be happy, but I did not—not when I was identified with the conditioned machine. Within that illusion I would dismiss or destroy anything that threatened self-hatred, because I looked to self-hatred to preserve and protect me in a world that seemed to care nothing for my needs, despite the vast evidence to the contrary.

Living within the prison of self-hatred, I saw, I was actually safe only from my own happiness. The only real danger to me as an adult survivor of the process of social conditioning was self-hatred itself. True safety would come only when I could shut self-hatred out of my consciousness forever.

All this while Rhea's training proceeded nicely. She did not struggle with self-hatred, as far as I could tell, but she did have her own piece of work to do. As she did that work, I like to think, she showed me how to do my own, and modeled for me how to live without the constant judgment and punishment of ego.

The reader will no doubt recall how I was guided to train her towards a peaceful relationship with the cats, and how she had lost her liberty until the time when she no longer chased the little buggers. True to that guidance, we practiced for a year and a half, every day. That's how long it took. There were times when I despaired, but my longing for her freedom drove us on. Finally the day came when a cat walked by in front of Rhea, tempting her as only a cat can do, and Rhea did nothing but wag her tail. I was amazed. Her willingness and her love for me, I realized, was stronger than the nature she was born with. We continued to practice until she no longer would chase deer, squirrels, or even—and this was the hardest of all—gophers. I never would have believed it to be possible, and yet there it was. When I finally felt sure of her I went to the Roshi in triumph. Her ironic smile said everything. "Turn her loose," she said.

Everything that occurs inside and around us is a gift from Life towards our happiness; if we just get out of the way, we can see how this is so. By the time Rhea again ran free, I understood spiritual training—and not Rhea's so much as mine. The process taught me how to experience myself in alignment with the simple compassion that makes transformation possible. How I was with Rhea as I trained her was how I aspired to be with myself: firm and forever unyielding, but kind. The experience taught me how to return again and again to the place in my heart from which I can see the tremendous power that resides within me, and from which I feel strong enough to make a stand for my own true life. I wanted more than anything for Rhea to be free—it broke my heart to see her without her liberty. I saw my own imprisonment less clearly, but in my heart I wished the same for me. I saw that I wanted for myself the same opportunity to experience myself upon the earth in freedom.

Time passed. The self-acceptance that had sprouted way back when I had first discovered practice began to grow in earnest. It was a wonderful time, full of the magic of self-love. Along the way, as has always been the case in my monastic career, Life assisted me in the work of self-compassion with the many challenges it offered. On a daily basis the tasks required of me as the work director triggered my lifelong belief in my inadequacy and threatened to crush me under self-judgment. Oftentimes I gave in to it, but sometimes I did not. Over time I learned to hold myself instead of hate myself when faced with something I imagined I could not do, or when things did not go as I had hoped. I came to see that every time I was asked to do what threatened me, it was as if Life was saying, "Can you love yourself even now?"

Then came the day when I was asked to facilitate my first retreat.

As usual, I reacted to this news with horror. I had facilitated a great many Sunday morning and Tuesday evening groups by that time, which was bad enough, but these were nothing compared to this. An entire retreat! I was being asked to offer to eight innocent and unsuspecting people their best opportunity to experience compassion in their lives—me! This was not something I believed I could ever do: I am just not the kind of person (self-hate said to me in my voice) that can access the compassion and clarity required. "They have made a terrible mistake," I told myself—and then, after some hesitation, I told the Roshi also.

She did not agree, so I took a different tact. "But I don't *want* to facilitate," I said.

"Look, Dave," she replied. She has a way of scrunching up her eyes at you to make a point that is quite effective. "You *do* want to. If you didn't you would not be here. It is time for you to take this step."

So there I was, stuck from Wednesday (when I was told) to Saturday (when the retreat began) with the terror of being commanded to do what I absolutely could not do.

And yet, to my astonishment, I did it. We had group three times a day, for two hours at a shot, and during those times I was okay. The workshop required every bit of my attention, with none left over for self-hatred. In between groups, however, and all those endless hours through the night, conditioning flogged me for daring to believe, which somewhere in my heart I must have done, that this was something I could do. Self-hate revenged itself upon me in every imaginable way during every unconscious moment I spent outside of the meditation hall. Still, three times a day for a week I felt my adequacy to the task before me, and more than this: I experienced my competence, my understanding, my delicious humor, my kindness, and everything else self-hatred would keep from me—with all those people as witnesses. The experience devastated conditioning. Nothing has so undermined its authority in my life, and nothing has so assisted me to grow within myself to become my own authority, than this. I have facilitated dozens of those same workshops now, and the result is always the same: I win. I win, and I discover myself to be again the compassion that I am, while self-hatred loses a little more of my life.

As it is with me, so it is with everyone. When we look without self-judgment beyond the door to our authentic being, when our love uncovers the person it conceals, instead of the bad or wrong thing that self-hatred has promised we will find there, we discover ourselves to possess all of the beauty, and innocence, and wisdom that we could ever imagine. All this time conditioned mind has stuffed the miracle of our authentic nature behind an illusion of our imperfection, where we would not find it. Who we are is peace, and love, and joy, and well-being—who we are is everything that we have always known in our hearts that we are. Self-hatred is the mechanism created by conditioned mind to prevent us from being ourselves. The possibility available through practice is to annihilate self-hatred by realizing the perfect beings that we actually are.

How glorious life would be if we loved ourselves so much as this! This is what we practice for. We practice in order to find in ourselves the love that opens the way beyond conditioned mind. We practice to go beyond self-hatred that we may be free to explore this life that has been given us, and in that exploration to become for ourselves the compassion we have always wanted.

19

The Opportunity

One of the things that attracted me most to Buddhism in the beginning was the understanding that the possibility the Buddha offered was not something I was required to believe in and helplessly hope would come to pass, but something I could experience in my own life and practice every day. There is a path that lies before every human being, said the Buddha, that will carry us beyond suffering if we will go. There is a way to find the clarity and peace that we long for. As our morning ritual says:

Here in my hand is the opportunity,
And the way is clear beyond the gate of thought and desire.
There is no self and other
As the awareness of pure, undisturbed consciousness
Slips into all consciousness.

The way is clear, he said. If we will follow the path he prescribed then the transformation will happen inevitably. In my own case, it has always seemed to occur as if apart from my own will, in a place where I could only catch glimpses of it, and has remained a mystery even to me. And yet, I have witnessed the change; I have felt the exquisite revolution and seen it reflected in my response to life, which has a certain quiet gladness in it, and a certain eagerness, which it never had before. I know that the awakening the Buddha experienced is possible in me and in all people because I have experienced it and have seen how it works.

The end of practice is not bliss, or unbroken contentment, or any other state, at least in my experience—not even the state of awe that results from our transformation. The end of practice is the process through which the metamorphosis occurs. As is often said, the journey and the end of the journey are the same.

This way that the Buddha taught is nothing like I anticipated. When I set out upon the path I imagined it would entail a gradual and relatively easy letting go into a state of peace. To a certain extent I was right. This is a path of letting go and "peace" is one word that describes the experience of travelling it. I was a bit off on the "relatively easy" part, however. I did not anticipate at that time either the existence of egocentric, karmic conditioning or the war it would wage every moment of every day to keep me within its power. Who would have dreamed that life would turn out to be a violent daily contest with a force that desires my suffering and feeds off of my life energy—a force that, if permitted, would dominate my every thought and feeling, even though it is not real? I am grateful I did not foresee the pain I would undergo as I submitted myself to that contest, because I doubt I would have ever begun. Taught to believe in a happiness based on outward things, and weakened by this fantasy, had I understood the reality of spiritual practice before I was irreversibly committed I would have balked at the moment by moment effort and dedication required to live beyond conditioned mind.

There is a sort of compassion and even kindness in this that is difficult to see at first. The suffering contained within my body, emotions, and mind asks me to rise within myself to a place of clarity and self-acceptance that I never would have sought without it. If there is intentionality behind the way things are—if there is a point, in other words—I suspect this is it. We suffer, we are given the intelligence to see that suffering, we are offered a way to go beyond it, and we must choose. If we choose to follow the path that ends suffering, then we are also given, in my experience, everything we will need along the way.

I arrived at the monastery a month before my thirtieth birthday. My hair was brown and curly and it stuck out in every direction. My skin fit tightly over my muscles and bones. Now my hair is grey, what remains of it, and my skin bears the signs of middle age. There can be no going back for me now. Other than my immediate family and a handful of others—including my dear friends Lisa and Janey, referred to elsewhere in these pages—I have let go of every other relationship I maintained before I became a monk. All I have at this point, and all I want, is the opportunity to go beyond ego and live free from suffering in this lifetime.

The contest with conditioned mind continues to this very hour. Every day I wake up with the determination to live as fully as I am able, to be as present as I can to each moment as it passes, and to cultivate compassion and clarity as I do. Each day egocentric, karmic conditioning arises with me, determined to thwart me at every turn. We each give it our best shot all day long. Some days I win, some days it does—but I win more. Even when ego wins, if I watch it do what it does, if I go to sleep that night with the determination to fight the good fight again the next day—even if I just keep my feet on the monastery property—then the win is mine. So long as I do not abandon the path I am on I cannot lose.

When I look back over my wandering journey I wonder at the guidance that led me along the way. I often forgot that it was there, that guidance, and yet I was never without it. Even those years while I resisted my transformation with all my might, I walked along the road towards myself. There was no wrong way to go, because every way led to where I now stand, and towards the further opportunity that as yet I do not know.

This past weekend we hosted our annual "Kid's Retreat" here at the monastery. Blessedly, I spent the entire time with the most adorable and happy five-year-old boy you have ever seen. I immediately fell in love with the little rascal. It astonished me, in fact, how completely his toothy smile and his little hands and feet captured my heart. I wanted very much to give him some special experience—I wanted him to feel the love and the joy that I felt in him—but I didn't know how, and so I waited and hoped that I would see the way. Then on Saturday evening while we sat there, he and I, eating fake hot-dogs and real corn-on-the-cob, suddenly I realized that all he needed and wanted from me was me. All he needed from me was to just be. And all I needed from me, I realized, was the same. I could simply enjoy him and enjoy myself with him. And so I did.

It was wonderful—wonderful enough, in fact, to make perfect sense of the bizarre and difficult life that I lead, even just that one tiny awareness. My little friend, I realized, reflected for me the innocence that resides within my own heart, calling for my loving attention. In giving myself to him, I gave also to the little boy within me that needs that same love. What more could I ask for? This is the opportunity that life gives to each of us in our existence on this earth, that we may learn to hold ourselves in unconditional love. That evening, as I made my way to my hermitage, I dedicated my life once again to the pursuit of this practice and this opportunity. A way exists beyond fear, doubt, and isolation, and it waits for our discovery. There is a life that we are here to save—just one. This is the gift of our lives to us; it is the work that each of us is here to do. This gift is our endowment as human beings, and is, at least for me, worth giving a life for in return.

20

A Fork in the Road

A few narrow spotlights pierced the darkness of the cabin. Here and there one of my fellow travelers stirred sleepily in their seats, but otherwise all around me was strangely still, even as we hurtled fifty thousand feet above the earth. The muffled roar of the engines, the artificial twilight, and my own fascination with this scene gave it a mystical quality in my imagination, as if all of us who participated had stepped somehow out of time, or as if we had all fallen into the same fantasy. I curled myself against the wall below the windows, relaxing into the vibration emanating from the fuselage of the plane. A stranger in this place, but a friend within myself, I gazed down towards the lights dotting the eastern coast of Africa.

Eight years had passed since I first set foot upon the monastery grounds. How much had changed since then! When I first began my training the monastery was mostly invisible to the world. We lived in seclusion from society; even in the adjacent town few knew that they had a group of Buddhist monks as their neighbors. We flitted in and out of the outer world like ghosts, procuring the goods we needed for our maintenance without intimating to the people there the purpose that had gathered us together.

Then, gradually, a shift occurred. The Roshi's own practice, I dare say, carried her into a larger vision of her life's work, and this vision carried us with it. On her own, the Roshi had been visible in the world for some time, shining like a lighthouse as she travelled and taught throughout the country and in other countries as well. A time came when she desired the rest of us to show ourselves as she did, that we might offer the world the fruits of our silent work and build a foundation for practice that would survive her eventual death and prosper when she was gone.

Among the many good works that the Roshi envisioned during that time, the most startling was a service project in Africa. For a great while, I think, she had been aware of the suffering on that continent and had longed to assist. One day the means appeared in the form of a Catholic nun with a big heart and connections in Zimbabwe. The Roshi leapt at this chance to make a difference in one of the poorest places on earth. Particularly, she wished to feed and educate children who had been orphaned by the African AIDS pandemic. Inspired by this possibility she went to work, first in Zimbabwe and then, as the political situation deteriorated there, in Zambia.

For some time—almost three years—this project took form mostly in the periphery of my awareness. Little changed at the monastery itself: as we always had, the monks practiced together day after day in silence, mostly untouched, though not unmoved, by the steps the Roshi was taking. All the while, however, the Roshi slowly dismantled the barriers she had erected earlier between the monastery and the world at large. I did not understand this at the time, or even notice it, really—until the day she asked me if I would like to take a trip to Africa.

It was a Sunday in April, I remember, when I received her message. In my mind's eye I can still see the shimmering spring wildflowers that kept me company that breathless afternoon. The thought dazzled me. I had not been more than twenty miles from the monastery grounds in two months. To go to Africa! I had never dreamed I would have such an opportunity. I said "yes" without knowing more, and little guessing that the man who I was when I departed for that distant land would not return.

That July, after many hours of planning and preparation, four of us, all monks, left together for Ndola, a small city in Zambia. We spent three weeks there working, forming relationships with the people we met, and watching our hearts open. I had never seen hunger, nor the courage required to face a life in which there is not enough food. I had never seen such beautiful

173

people—or, more accurately, I had never before allowed myself to see just how beautiful people are. As the days passed I found within myself a love I had not experienced before.

Strangely, against the African backdrop I could not see the change that occurred. I sensed the compassion that those days stirred up within me, more profound than anything I had yet known, but I could not see the alteration that it caused in me. This only became apparent as we finished our work and began our journey home.

This is how I came to be fifty thousand feet above the mysterious African continent, gazing down upon the lights sprinkled here and there over that dark mass, and longing to remain. Longing to remain? Yes. I had been happier than ever before those three weeks, and I wished to stay in the place where, it seemed, that happiness dwelled. As long as I remained within the African landscape and experienced the wide sky, the smoke, the earthen houses, and the throngs of people always along the road, wandering aimlessly in search of work, my life at the monastery seemed a dream, but once we said good-bye and stepped onto the airplane, the fact of the life I returned to came back to me. It seemed suddenly that I could not go.

On one level, I am sure, I knew the expansion could not last, and I dreaded the contraction that must follow my return to America. Looking back I can see, however, that there were other influences than this. Most fundamentally, my commitment to this our world and to the vocation of service that Life offered me within it had deepened dramatically in recent times. This was the result not just of the experiences in Ndola, but of all the sincere practice that had preceded it. Eight years is a long time to live in silence. A change had occurred that could not easily be undone. The illusion had faded that I merely followed a Zen dream that would at some point be over. The dream had become my life, and little remained of what was there before.

In addition, my relationship with self-hatred, the primary and largest obstacle to union with life and real happiness, was threatened as it never had been before. Self-hate could not ultimately survive in the world of possibility and compassion that my life as a monk offered to me, and so it worked ceaselessly to undermine my efforts and to inject uncertainty into my mind. I experienced myself without self-hatred while in Africa—the joy I found there was just too much for it. The contrast showed me that in my usual state I was drunk with self-hate, and I glimpsed what life could be without it. More than anything else, I suspect, it was this that conditioned mind reacted to in what followed.

The primary difficulty at this time was that I did not yet make a free choice in being a monk. There was still a "should" in it—I still felt as if I were required to live this hard life by some entity, call it "God" or "Life", that wielded a power over me that I could not dispute. When I first discovered practice, it seemed to me, I was taken by surprise and swept off my feet before I had the opportunity to say, "Yes, this is the life that I choose." It appeared as if I had never consciously aligned myself with whatever force it was that made this choice for me. This imagined omission had become an obstacle in my journey and an opening for the resistance of conditioned mind. Finally the time had come for me to choose my life of my own accord.

Instinctively I sensed that for this choice to be free everything within me that argued against it would need to be put upon the table. I would need to bring to the surface everything I believed I wanted instead of my monastic life in order to examine each piece to see what was authentic and what was merely an objection of conditioned mind. It could be, I understood, that I would find something there that would make the life of a monk impossible for me. If so, then I would know it was not my true life and I could go in peace. If I did manage to bring it all into my awareness, however, and if I did not find any real indication of a truer life that awaited me in another form, this would give me the power to commit with my whole heart and turn away from the question, perhaps forever.

The opportunity arose during those weeks in Africa. In that strange and wonderful land, so different from all I had known before, the constraints fell away that had fixed me as one who has a foot in two worlds: the world my heart wanted, and the world full of the desires of a separate self. During that time the world became one place, and I became one united man with just one desire: to love. The opening I felt inside and the immense possibility that arose in response thrilled me in a way that was beyond words and understanding.

The reaction from conditioned mind to all of this, could I have seen it, would have appalled me. It managed to poison the experience, as it always attempts to do. I can see now what I could not then, that "I" had gradually crept into the freedom of those weeks in Africa. The opening that occurred allowed to pass both the compassion that moved me and the identification that made that compassion "mine". I became "I"; "I" loved what had happened to "me"; and "I" dreaded the extinction of "myself" when I returned to the monastic environment, where the deception would be reflected in a way I could not fail to see. I chose to live at the monastery expressly in order to have that reflection, of course, that I may remember who I am. I thought I was "I", however, and so imagined I would lose myself when I returned.

It is strange, isn't it, how easily we forget what is so? The life of a monk that I had followed for years, and the spiritual practice embedded within it, was the direct cause of the opening I felt occurring within me in Africa and the source of all the beauty and compassion I perceived inside and out. I loved that life, even as hard as it was, with all of my heart. I needed it as well, because without the support of the monastic environment I would inevitably fall prey to the snares of conditioned mind, as had just occurred. If I could have seen then how much I needed it, and if I could have recognized the conditioning that infected me, it would have saved me all sorts of heartache, but that's never the way it goes. We suffer until we just can't and won't suffer any more. And so, as the airliner taxied out onto the runway, as the engines roared, and as we lifted off towards the American continent, I began to question the fundamental life choice I had made eight years earlier to relinquish the world of pleasure and dissipation, of ambition and despair, in order to live in silence and turn my gaze inward. I longed to never leave that little slum in Africa that had so caused my heart to open, and to never return to the life where my next challenges, whatever they may be, lay waiting.

I was little aware of these things as I huddled against the window of the plane on the journey home. It all boiled just beneath the surface. I was physically exhausted from our journey, but sleep was impossible, and so I sat and breathed, wondering at the revolution that occurred inside of me, until the small hours of the night.

What happened next is difficult to describe.

All my life I had travelled along the way that conditioned mind had prescribed for me. This way involved the fundamental bargain that we have all made in order to survive, that we will relinquish, even avoid, what we want for ourselves and our lives in order to have a "safe" place within conditioned mind to live.

In a certain place along the way, there had always been a fork in the road. One half of the fork, the one I always pursued, led towards deprivation, loneliness and the other things that follow from that bargain—but there was another I had never tried. This fork led towards what I believed I wanted, towards the things and experiences I would give myself (relationship, friendship, sex, freedom of movement...) if I had the power. Periodically as I traveled along I would pass by this fork in the road. In the beginning I did not even see it, as foggy and confused as it was along that way. After I began to practice I started to sense that other way, and even, as I progressed, to test it sometimes in situations that appeared safe. At the bottom, however, remained the belief that I must renounce what I want in order to live and so, whenever I came to that fork in the road I always hurried past, towards unhappiness.

Even as a monk this was so, despite the radical choices I had already made, and despite the rebellion I had accomplished against the life I was programmed to live. At a certain level I

177

still practiced the same deprivation: I still could not allow myself to want. This structure had steadily given ground over the years, but I still yielded to the final will of ego and ignored what I believed I wanted in order to preserve its existence and my identity. The unhappiness that resulted, it had always seemed, was my destiny—and yet, it could not be. I knew it could not be because I had just spent three weeks without it in a state of joy.

Racing through the night in that giant airliner, with my heart full of love for myself and the people I had served in Africa, I found myself suddenly and unexpectedly at the fork in the road. What happened next was simply this: I chose the way I never had before. I did not think it, I just chose. I allowed myself to want. Granted, what I believed I wanted at that time was not what I truly want, yet it was a tremendous act of courage even so to allow that wanting. There had never been a real choice before. "No" is not a choice. In that moment I said "Yes", ignorant of the upheaval that would follow that simple act of faith. I needed almost two years to recover my balance afterwards.

Years ago, during my brief career as a whitewater river guide, I travelled to West Virginia one autumn to paddle the Gauley. The whitewater section of the Gauley River begins below a gigantic reservoir. The put-in lies at the foot of an immense dam, hundreds of feet high, as I remember it. Through the base of the dam protrude three immense circular pipes, each the size of four school-buses. When the floodgates open the water roars through those pipes with a power, a violence, and a sound that is nearly inconceivable. The water is under so much pressure that it roars through the air for a hundred feet or more before finally crashing into the riverbed.

With less noise but all that power, the wanting I had suppressed my whole life rushed through the opening that sudden choice had made. How much pain had accumulated there! How it thrilled me to want finally and to not be punished for it! A feeling of immense power rushed through me. Suddenly I no longer needed to sacrifice myself in order to be "good" or any other illusory thing. Suddenly I could just want. For a few precious moments I was free.

Quickly, as we are wont to do, I leapt from that place of clarity directly into confusion. I began to imagine that I wanted something in particular rather than simply that freedom. The openness I felt closed around images of the things I had wanted but never had, and the imagined feelings that would come with having them. This is what, I thought, I had been waiting for all my life: permission to possess and consume, and the power—sprung, ironically, from all the years of practice behind me—to acquire what it was that I believed I wished for.

I have often marveled at what occurred during that long journey back to America. Did I believe the voices? Everything that followed from that moment—the turmoil, the desperation, the immense suffering, the tears—suggests that I did. And it cannot be doubted that, on a certain level, this was so. On a deeper level, however, something remained of the inspiration that had guided me until that moment through the demanding life of a monk, supporting me as, against all appearances, I took this tremendous step towards freedom.

My delusion was not complete, in other words—or, at least, not yet. Something genuine remained. At the center of the revolution within me was the boy who had been sacrificed for years to deprivation. I saw him and accepted him, and the relief of this moved me for days. I just became confused about the means of saving him, thinking he needed to be given what he had not had before. Unfortunately, I believed I remained clear, and so could see nothing of the way conditioned mind swindled me with this idea. I cringe at the thought of the chaos that followed.

The flight from South Africa to the East Coast of the United States was eighteen hours long. The whole time my mind boiled with all the opportunities that lay before me—all the forms my life might take with my new freedom—and the unavoidable recognition of the one obstacle that lay before me: the fact that I remained a monk.

179

Once I met my fellow-monks by chance in the back of the plane as I attempted to walk off my restlessness in the aisles. "How are we now?" someone asked. This was a game we had played throughout the trip as a way of remaining aware of ourselves and communicating our state of mind to the others on the team. The response from each of us was to be one word.

"Open," one of the monks replied.

"In love," said another.

"At peace," said the third.

"Tense," I said. At this point we were only two hours out of Washington and the step I contemplated taking there or soon afterwards.

Something had changed inside of me, it seemed, forever. I could not return to the life I had led before. Knowing this, one simple act was required of me. By the time we landed I had resolved upon it: I would tell my teacher that I could not go on, and that I must leave the monastery to find my own way.

21

Confession

"Who am I?" This is the question that has perplexed the curious and the inspired since humanity first began to peer upon the world with the eyes of God.

This is also the question, essentially, that awoke my spirit and brought me to spiritual practice. I sensed that I was neither who I was taught to be nor who I believed myself to be, and I longed to grasp who or what I might be instead. As I have described, I sought my essence in the harmonies of nature, in the eyes of other people, and, to the extent I was able at the time, in the still depths of my own heart, but as much as I tried I could not find it. The trouble was not so much in the places where I looked, as these could have taught me wonderfully of my true self if I allowed it; the trouble was that it was not I who did the looking. It was "I" who looked, and so all that I saw was "I."

Conditioned mind cannot see what is. It can only see itself. This is why the discovery of one's original nature is so difficult: in order to see who we are we must be who we are, and this is the last thing in the world conditioned mind will allow. Within conditioned mind the only way to see something is to stand outside of it, a subject that perceives the thing as an object. It is not possible to see our authentic nature in this way because who we are cannot be objectified: who we are is the process of life manifesting through our unique form, and there is no getting outside of that. In order to experience who we are we must go beyond subject and object: we must see without separation, even if this separation seems to be our most personal experience of ourselves.

To say it another way, in order to experience what is we must simply be, residing in the awareness that is our most fundamental aspect. I see a difference here between me and Rhea the dog. She just is who or what she is, at least as far as I can tell. I am just who or what I am also, but I am also aware—when I am aligned with Life rather than "I"—of who or what I am. This awareness is not the same as intellectual understanding. Thoughts may arise to describe the experience of what is, but within the experience itself there is no thinking; there is only being and awareness. There is no separation between that which perceives and that which is perceived. I am all that is, and it is all of me.

From the perspective of conditioned mind this is bizarre and impossible. Conditioned mind structures itself around its separation from Life, which excludes the perception of unity. Ego only knows the two extremes: identification with experience, and isolation from experience. It does not experience awareness. To be aware of what is, of the experience of life manifesting through our senses and perception in this moment, untainted by conditioned mind, it is necessary to drop the illusion of separation and experience the unity instead. This is talked about sometimes as "the practice of pure attention." When our attention is here, in this moment, rather than directed by ego, we are able to see what lies beyond the human fantasy.

Who we are without conditioned mind is pure joy—but we are deeply conditioned to believe otherwise. This is the reason why so much courage is required on the path of awakening. In order to live from our authentic nature, we are required to let that belief go and accept the fact that is the most difficult for a conditioned human, that life is perfect just as it is and we have no reason to be unhappy.

After our flight across the Atlantic my fellow-travelers and I spent five hours in Washington, then boarded another plane and made the final leg of our journey to San Francisco. Exhausted, but pleased with our success and fascinated by the American world as we saw it through our African eyes, we made our way to the monastery's urban center south of the airport. Soon weariness overcame us and we settled down to rest. Unlike the others, however, I did not drift off to sleep within the glow of our perfect adventure. I could not predict what form it would take, but I recognized that a more difficult and less happy adventure awaited me.

The next morning we parted company. The other monks returned to the monastery while I headed further south to staff a retreat on the coast that was to begin that evening. A kind friend of ours drove me down. He was accustomed to silence, luckily, and so gave me the space to study the strange upheaval occurring within me. My stomach was a mess, my head hurt, and my heart pounded as if I were exposed to some terrible danger—but my imagination soared with new freedom. My sudden resolve to leave the monastery had survived both a night of sleep and the reflection of western society. If anything it had grown stronger. My life as I had known it these past eight years, I told myself, was done: I was a free man, with a world of experience waiting for me and an eagerness to embrace it that I had never known before. All that stood in my way was the hard task of finding an honorable way to say goodbye.

As I arrived at the retreat center and went to work, I fought for the courage to let the Roshi know about my change of heart. This was a most painful thing to imagine: I feared the exposure the act would require and the humiliation I imagined would surely follow. In addition, I worried I would not succeed in accomplishing it in a way that I could live with afterwards. Once, in the first months of my training, the Roshi had compared the relationship of a monk to the monastery to a marriage. "It cannot be treated lightly," she had said. "The agreement must be held in an environment of mutual respect no matter what happens." These words came back to me as I contemplated what I must do. I resolved that I would leave the practice in a way that honored all that it had given me. Otherwise, I knew, remorse would dog me for the rest of my days.

At a short walk from the retreat center lay a park with broad fields and a wooded brook. Whenever I could manage it over the

183

next several days I made my way there. Protected by the silence of that place and nurtured by the solitude, I spent many a tearful hour watching the wind toy with the blades of grass and the water gently flowing over the stones in the creek bed. As the days passed I resolved to reveal my intentions from that place. Finally the time came to speak. I chose a moment when I knew the Roshi would be occupied and would not answer her phone. Sick with dread and inflamed with passion, I called.

"Roshi, it's Dave," I said into her voicemail. "I need to tell you something."

A frog began chirping just then. The water burbled in the creek, the blue sky whirled through the trees over my head, and time stood still. I felt as if I touched eternity in that moment. I saw myself as if from a great height: there he stood, that terrified, ecstatic young man that I was, with a phone in his hand and his life in upheaval all around him. I was moved by his innocence. There was nothing bad or wrong within him, that sincere young man. There was only a deep well of emotion, an inexperienced mind, and all that had gone into producing him and the scene he inhabited from the beginning of time.

Several moments passed in silence, and then I remembered myself as I believed myself to be. I reached back through time to the words that I had rehearsed in the previous days. "Roshi, I have had a change of heart," I said. "Something has happened inside of me—something big."

The trees danced ecstatically around me, playing with sunlight and shadow. I could not believe that I was here at last, at the end of my monastic journey.

"I do not feel myself to be a monk anymore," I continued. "I want something more. I want to explore the world, to see what it is to be a man in this time and in this place. I want to have human friendship. I want a place that is my own, a work that is my own, and someone to share this with me."

Tears welled up in my eyes, and my emotion threatened to choke the flow of words. Quickly I gathered myself together for the essential point.

"I want a different life," I said. "And so I humbly and respectfully ask for your permission to leave the monastery and to take my practice into the world on my own."

There—it was done. I stopped speaking, ended the call, and just stood there for a moment, perfectly still. The woods around me seemed to echo the sound of my voice. All of nature seemed to wonder at this strange young man and his audacity. For a while more I studied myself in the ripples and eddies of the creek, then slowly I turned away and walked off towards the consequences of my act, whatever they might be.

In the language of practice, we use the word "center" to name the place where we are not identified with conditioned mind and are aligned with the Life that animates us.

This place that we call "center" cannot be easily described. This is because it lies beyond the grasp of conceptual thought; it cannot be understood by conditioned mind, in other words. What center is not, however, may be easily said. Luckily, I have vast experience in this area.

Center is not the same as an emptiness of the mind, in the sense of an absence of thought, or an end of subjective perception. Often the word "emptiness" is used to describe center, but the emptiness that the Buddha spoke of, at least from my point of view, is not the same as the eradication of human experience. This emptiness is full of experience, even the experience of having a mind that thinks and breaks things down into concepts. Center is the experience of Life, not death. It is only that at center we do not identify with thought and the delusional realities we create to reflect an "I".

Center is also not the same as a feeling. Even feelings we might describe as "peace", "love", "contentment", or "happiness", are particular contents of experience as opposed to the experience of Life moving through us; they are "things," but center is no thing. This is important to remember, because if we can be convinced, for example, that being centered is the same as being happy, then we will need to make ourselves feel happy in order to be centered, which cannot possibly work. In my experience, center is that which contains all feelings, even the hard ones, and which accepts each emotion as it arises in unconditional love and acceptance. There is a happiness in this which is more than mere feeling and cannot be compared to the conditional sort. This unconditional happiness may absolutely be achieved because center is who we are. Center is what is here when we are not doing anything else.

Most especially center is not the same as getting what we want. When we are centered we do get what we want, it is true— on a process level rather than in the stuff of life and in our circumstances—but that comes as an effect, not a cause. Most everyone organizes their life around this misunderstanding, spending their precious days in a wrestling match with the content of life in an attempt to induce the fulfillment of center. This can only lead to disappointment, as center cannot be bought through a relationship with things. Center is the process through which we live in cooperation with the energy that enlivens us. As long as we believe that center lies mysteriously in something "out there," it will remain out there, and we will never experience it.

When I began to practice, the experience we call "center" was a rare accident: once in a long while it just fell out of the sky to amaze me, then departed just as suddenly. I could not understand how it came to me when it did, or where it disappeared to afterwards. Over time as I practiced, and as I learned how to direct my attention, I gained the power to disentangle myself from my thoughts and feelings, carving out a place to be inside where I was untroubled, and where, sometimes, I experienced a sort of spiritual ecstasy. As I did, however, I made an unexpected discovery. This sometimes experience of bliss was not what practice carried me towards, and was not center. It was marvelous, but it could not on its own make a real difference for me. What my transformation requires is the willingness to allow Life to explore itself through my eyes and ears and hands. I am asked, as we all are, to hold on to nothing, even my own redemption.

In the days following my confession by the creek I held my breath, waiting for something to happen. Nothing did. I spoke with the Roshi any number of times, seeking her guidance on various aspects of the retreat I was managing, but she never once made any reference to my voice message. I began to wonder if she had received it. Eventually the retreat ended and I returned to the monastery. A week passed there, and then another, but still nothing. The state of suspense I endured during that time was nearly unbearable. All of my life was thrown into confusion and I could do nothing but wait.

I can see now that the Roshi was giving me a chance to allow things to settle a bit. After a gigantic upheaval such as I had experienced, it often takes time for clarity to arise out of the chaos. In my own case it would be two more years before I experienced anything like clarity, but those long days of doubt were my first steps along the way. Finally, one day from out of nowhere the Roshi brought it up. "So you are thinking you would like to leave the monastery?" she asked.

"Yes," I replied, breathless with horror and excitement.

"Hmmm...." she murmured, then paused, as if she were considering it for the first time. "Well," she continued, "Who knows? You've been living out here at the end of a dirt road for a long time now. Perhaps it's time to see yourself reflected in a new way. It will be interesting to see where this goes."

I heard her with a mixture of elation and dismay. It moved me that she would take my desires seriously, but the question in her words shook me deeply. I understood instantly what she communicated: she was not willing to decide. She would require me to decide for myself, and to wait until I could make the decision from center. I could have predicted this had I not been so intoxicated by the fantasies that surrounded me during those days—her response perfectly demonstrated the compassion that had drawn me to her originally and had led me to choose her as my teacher—but I did not. In my mind the decision had been made. Now I found myself in the hardest of all possible places: I must either follow my teacher's guidance and wait for clarity, or ignore it and wonder all the rest of my life what I had done.

22

Integrity

At the center of a life that works—that expands against the constraints of ego, that embraces kindness and clear seeing, and that touches the divine—is an integrity that does not yield. This integrity does not accept any course that is not in keeping with the highest understanding available at any given time. No matter how violently the storm of resistance that beats against the call to awakening, this integrity can anchor us until the temptation passes and the mind clears again.

To my surprise, I was born with this integrity—or, at least, with the seed of it and the courage to give it space to manifest. Perhaps this is something we all begin with, I don't know. In my life so far and during my career at the monastery, I have done countless things that were unskillful, ignorant, or mean, and doubtless will continue to do so, but even so, this integrity has remained. It simply requires me to recognize the conditioning that acts through me on those occasions and to re-commit each time to living from center. Over the years of monastic training my integrity has been tested mightily, and there have been more occasions than I care to admit when it seemed I would give in to ego at last and quit, but so far it has held firm. It has seemed to me at various times both my greatest ally and my worst enemy; it is that which has said that I must go on, no matter what, and that which has given me the wherewithal to do it.

It was this integrity that responded to the challenge that my teacher put before me, despite appearances. It would not allow me to abandon myself in my confusion, but required me instead to hold fast and look—to really look at the thoughts and feelings that captivated me, and see—until there was no longer any doubt about what occurred. As you can imagine, conditioned mind rebelled against this with all of the violence it possessed. It shouted at me all day and night, saying that my life was mine to spend as I wished, that I deserved to have what I wanted, that the course I chose would only lead to more suffering and deprivation, and other similar things. But the integrity said, "I want to know," and this is what prevailed.

Here was the beginning of all the hell that followed. To choose ego is fairly simple and easy. This is what almost everyone has done and does all day long, every day. The suffering that results from this choice is hideous, but it is quiet, mostly, and lives in a place where it is rarely seen. To choose against ego is quite another thing. This brings ego to the surface to war openly until it either wins or dies. Compared to my beginnings I was fairly strong within myself after eight years of training, but compared to the force of suffering that has rolled over eons through countless human lives, I was like one man facing an army. For a short while I struggled bravely and held my own, but soon I was overwhelmed.

Gradually I began to oppose myself to the Roshi. That is, gradually conditioned mind began to oppose the Roshi through my body, mouth, and mind. First I questioned her, then I distrusted her, then, as time passed, I detested her. I came to see her as the one thing that stood between me and the happiness I was looking for. Over the next several weeks I tumbled into a state of resistance towards her, the monastery, and the other monks. As you might suppose, the more I combatted my life as it lay before me, the more miserable I became. Misery had been my companion countless times before during my monastic career, as I have described, but this was different. Before I had always cheered on the sidelines for my awakening; now, at least on the surface, I rooted for the other cause. Of course, I could have simply packed my things and departed. Others had done it. I could have left silently in the night, turning my back forever on the monastery, and never have suffered a word or glance from anyone who knew me there. I just could not do it. I knew, I think, that I would suffer my own questioning look, and this was more than I could bear. And so I steeled myself against the onslaught I endured and waited for a way to clear before me towards the new life I believed I wanted.

After about eight weeks of this, which seemed an absolute eternity, a time came for the monks to travel down out of the hills to the monastery's urban center, to attend an event down there. We all piled into the monastery van, as we often had before, and set off one Friday afternoon. I was chosen to drive. I accepted the job without complaint, but I drove in silence those three hours, grimly staring down the road, while the others discussed monastery business. Typically, the monks travel together without speaking, but whenever the Roshi is included we use the opportunity to receive her guidance. I wanted none of it. I only wished to be left alone in my defiance of the life that imprisoned me, and to not have my unhappiness interfered with.

We arrived at our destination as the day ended and unloaded the van in the fading light. When we finished the others began preparing the evening meal while I busied myself outside, dreading the moment when I would run out of useful things to do and would be forced to participate with the others. Looking back, I am amazed at how completely the turmoil inside of me had transfigured the determined monk that I had been not long before. The road to hell is quickly travelled when we take it as eagerly as I did.

When the Roshi found me there in the parking lot I was no longer even pretending to work. "Care to take a walk with me?" she said. I assented silently, then trudged behind her across the street and into the small park that lay there. By this time the daylight had completely vanished. The park's paths were lit by lamps here and there, and the light from neighboring houses cast faint shadows over the grass, but otherwise we were surrounded by darkness, and alone.

"Would you like to tell me what is going on?" the Roshi asked as we walked slowly together.

"Yes," I said, and I meant it, to my surprise. The love I felt and feel for the Roshi is something profound and stable, like the

191

earth that supports the trees or the air that supports the clouds that drift across the sky. I have resisted that woman over the years in ten thousand different ways, but even so my love for her has never failed me. Sometimes, as on this occasion, I need to see my suffering reflected in her gentle eyes, to feel her loving acceptance, and to be held by her voice as she speaks before I can remember my love, but I always do. "I cannot do this anymore," I said.

"You cannot suffer in this way, you mean?" she asked innocently, knowing as well as I that this is not what I meant.

"No, I cannot continue to follow the life I am leading."

"What do you want instead?"

"I want to have a human life," I replied, embarrassed by my earnestness, but determined to say what needed to be said. "I want what others have. I want a life that is mine to take where I choose. I want human friendship. And I want..." I hesitated a moment while I summoned the courage to reveal all that was on my mind. "I want someone to hold me and call me by my name."

I could not see the Roshi's face as she responded, but I could hear the seriousness in her voice and the care with which she chose her words. "It is certainly possible that a man at your age, after the training you have done, would discover that he is called to practice in the world. This should be carefully considered...." She paused to allow the words to sink in. During the next moments of silence we emerged together from the shadows of a gigantic cedar tree into the pale light of a streetlamp, then stopped walking. "And yet, I am afraid for you, Dave," she continued. "I am afraid that your motivations are not pure, and that they are invisible to you. I am afraid that you are in danger of making a decision that will erase the opportunity you have to find real freedom. It is a precious gift, this opportunity. To waste it would be tragic."

I was moved by her compassion, but not by her argument. "But how do you know that the way to freedom for me is monastic? How do you know it is not through relationship, for example?"

"I do not know that. It very well could be. This is why we must take great care. However, I do know you, Dave." I was glad that my face remained in darkness and she could not see me blush at those words. "Personal intimacy with another would be difficult for you. It would be a hard path." I attempted to protest, saying that difficulty is a part of any path, and that I accepted it eagerly, but the Roshi persevered. "I also know conditioned mind," she continued. "I know how things are made to seem as they are not, how we give ourselves and our lives to illusion and so miss our opportunity for real peace, love, and joy.

"Here, let me tell you a story while you consider this," she said, and we resumed our stroll. "I heard it from my grandson the other day. It's from a piece of fiction he read for school. It goes like this:

"The main character in the story is married and in love with his wife. One day he notices she is being deceptive—he can sense that she is hiding something from him. He starts to pay attention, and over the next few days finds evidence that she is secretly spending time with his best friend. The days pass and he sees more and more deception in her. He detects secrecy on the part of his friend, also, and concludes, to his anguish and dismay, that they are having an affair. More days go by, and he becomes certain he is right. Gradually he decides to kill her out of revenge. He decides to do it on the night of his birthday, which is just a few days away. When the day finally comes, he returns home as usual after dark, but instead of going inside the house he calls his wife out, saying he needs her help with something. When she comes out he strangles her and puts her in the trunk of his car. He then goes inside to get the things he needs to deal with the body. As he steps through the door all the lights come on. Everyone he knows is there. They all shout, 'Surprise!' It is his birthday party. His wife and his best friend had been planning it in secret."

The Roshi paused as she concluded her narrative. I could see a portion of her shadowed face. There was no earnestness in it, no need for me to hear or agree—only compassion. "Do you see why I tell you this?" she asked.

"Yes," I answered. "You suspect I am being set up in a similar way."

"I do. As we both know, it is in the nature of suffering to present as true that which will most damage our opportunity for real freedom. It is in the nature of the possibility of ending suffering to ask us to go against everything that seems true and right so that we may access our hearts. I worry for you, Dave..." Here her voice dropped in volume and in tone. She spoke more slowly, and with great precision. "I worry that you are about to throw away all that you have accomplished these past years."

I could not remain unaffected by her attention to me and the sound of my name as she spoke. I loved her probably in that moment as much as I ever had before. "I'll think about it," I said.

The thing is, there was something true running beneath all that happened that evening and all the troubled months that followed. I suspect that the Roshi understood this as much as I, though it could not be said at the time. There was more to the struggle I was engaged in than just conditioned mind. This is what moves me most about this period of my life: there was a wisdom beneath all of my insanity that said, "I have to know." I had to find out what was so about the revolution that had occurred within me during the time in Africa. I could not just say "No" to the vast desire that I experienced, suppress it, and go on being "good", being the "right" person and doing the "right" thing, but feeling deprived. This is what I told myself over and over later that night as I walked furiously through the half-lit streets, too wound up to face my fellow monks, or to sleep: "I want to find out. I will not be satisfied by an idea. I need to know what is true about this for me." I imagine that both the Roshi and I understood on some level that this was the need that

I actually had—for the truth—and that we both trusted that I would stick to the path until I found it, come what may.

A long pause followed. Unexpectedly, my heart spoke for a moment. "I admire how you have handled this," I said meekly. "The slightest taint of judgment from you, and I would have torn the place apart. Forgive me what I've done, and what I will likely do after this."

Then the Roshi did the most astounding thing. She hugged me. I had trained with her for years at this point, and this was the first time that she had ever voluntarily touched me. "I love you, and I only want what is best for you," she whispered to me over my shoulder. My heart melted inside me. She had never told me she loved me before.

With this, the Roshi turned and departed the way we had come, leaving me alone with my conflicting feelings. Her love had gotten through.

Conditioned mind was shaken—but not for long. Gradually, as I continued to walk through the night shadows, listening to the sound of my footsteps on the pavement, glancing at the stars through the branches overhead, I gathered together the pieces of the man I had become—driven, fixated, and alone—and patched him back into something I could believe in. Somehow I managed to close my heart to her again. As I did, I realized with glee that my resolution to follow the way I had chosen was not undone. Even the Roshi could not destroy it. A drunken ecstasy sprang up inside of me. I was on my own at last.

I could not go back and face my fellow monks—not after that. I feared they would see my hysteria, and so I headed off into the night. In a short while I became intoxicated by my power, as it seemed to me, to stand fast against my teacher, and by the immense feeling of freedom that came as the world of my desires opened up in front of me. It was not actual freedom, of course. It was the delight of conditioned mind at having me at last to itself. On some level, perhaps, I understood this even then. But it was delicious, rapturous, that feeling. That feeling said: finally, after all this time and trouble, I will have what I

195

want. I will gather to myself everything that is rightfully mine, and nobody on earth can stop me.

23

How to Get Expelled from a Zen Monastery

Over the days and weeks that followed that tumultuous walk through the night streets, a further change occurred. I lost the ability to feign willingness. Somehow, my practice survived—I know this only because it was practice that saved me in the end—but just barely, and it existed in a place beneath and out of the reach of my awareness. I began to actively reject the Roshi as my teacher and to disregard her guidance. I began to court eviction from the monastery.

When the revolution had first occurred within me, some two months past at this point, it had been immediately obvious that if I were to change the direction of my life, it must be with the support and approval of my teacher. Without this I would have no authority to offer spiritual practice to others. This is the tradition in Buddhist practice, that a student does not become a teacher until his or her teacher gives the nod. Were I to leave the monastery under my own impetus, without the Roshi's backing, all the labor I had put into learning the deep skill required of one who offers practice to others would have been lost. I would have forfeited my power to give what I have to give—and even in those darkest days I truly wanted to give it, if I could.

As time passed, however, and as I became more and more embroiled in the desires that tormented me, I began to lose even this. Without understanding it I conspired with conditioned mind to sabotage all of the work I had done. If I could get myself kicked out of the monastery, and if I could accomplish this in a way that left me feeling justified and misused, then I could leave the entire path I had followed those eight years behind me. In my confusion, this is what I believed I wanted. Of course, in my heart I did not want this at all, but my heart was little to be found in those days.

And so I began to push the limits of what I knew to be acceptable behavior in a monk. A monk is freely permitted to think or feel anything; the one requirement is that the monk remains willing to follow the guidance of the monastery and the teacher who anchors it. First I began to ignore the monastic guidelines, then to defy them, but always masked by a pretended humility. This is one advantage of being perceived as obviously confused: people assumed that my actions were guided by my confusion rather than by intentional disobedience. I pushed and pushed, savoring the pandemonium that my disobedience caused and the scrambling I could sense behind the scenes as the Roshi and the other monks attempted to contain me. I remember one fall morning, hanging my laundry on the lines while Rhea looked on. "Would you still love me if I got myself kicked out of here?" I asked her. She just looked at me, without so much as wagging her tail. I think even little Rhea knew that I was troubled.

The Roshi attempted to save me from myself many times. She asked me once, "What of your life here would you really trade for what you think you want?"

I lied to her when I replied. "Nothing," I said. In reality, there was nothing I would not trade for even a taste of the life I imagined waited for me beyond the monastery gates.

Several more weeks passed in this unhappy game, and I grew even bolder. It seemed that I had nothing to lose but a life I did not want. I pushed against the Roshi's authority in a hundred ways. Strangely, I dreamed I was stronger than her and could see more clearly. If I proved myself to be the stronger in the end, it seemed, then I could have it all: I could retain the status I had achieved and have what I wanted at the same time.

This could only go on for so long. I was not the stronger, of course, at all. In my confusion I was weaker, possibly, than I had ever been before. It was only the Roshi's own great strength and understanding that gave me the space to struggle and, hopefully, to find my way through my confusion to the other side. A lesser teacher would have sent me packing—would have sent me off into a life of suffering made all the more horrible by the opportunity I had forsworn—long before. The time came, however, when something had to be done. My actions began to threaten the very structure of the monastery, and to interfere with the training of the other monks. Things had to come to a head; even I wanted this, and I kept pushing until my unwillingness simply had to be addressed.

Friend, I am not going to tell you what I finally did to bring this game to a climax. Everywhere else in this book I have attempted to be as transparent as possible, but I will bury this one act in oblivion. What I did was not worthy of the monk that I am, or the training I had received. It was the act of a young man over his head in a sea of confusion that stretched far into the past and beyond the beginning of his own life. Let us just say that the thing that I did was something that could not be ignored.

The next day the Roshi showed up for lunch. This was not unexpected, as we had a group project planned for the afternoon that she was a part of. Still, she was early, and when I saw her my heart beat hard with fear and dread. A few minutes later, as I was finishing my meal on the west porch, she came and sat down beside me. I will never forget that moment: the scraps of lasagna that remained on the plate in my lap, the way the sun filled the cool autumn air and lit up the porch tiles around us, the gentle energy of my teacher, and the feeling of humiliation that crept through my body as I understood why she had come. She did not refer to my act in any way—she did not have to. There was no tone of judgment in her voice, or sympathy, or concern. She spoke in the same manner as she might have in order to describe an idea about a project we might do, or to inform me of a concern she had about someone else.

"Dave," she said, "perhaps it would be a good thing for you to spend some time away from here, considering what you want for your life and your commitment to practice." I lowered my gaze and stared at my shoes while she spoke. It was the lowest moment of my life so far, which I hope will never be surpassed in sorrow and shame. "We need for you to decide if you really want to train," she continued. "Perhaps you might take a month or two to see what life is like beyond the gates, and to see if you can get in touch again with your heart. At the end of that time, if you decide you would like to continue your training, then you can come back and we can resume. What do you think?"

I could not speak. I only nodded in reply.

"Why don't you take the afternoon to consider the idea," she added.

"May I be excused from the project?"

"Yes. Perhaps you could go for a walk instead. Then, whenever you decide you can let me know." With that the Roshi left me and joined the others, who were gathering to begin work. In the most solemn state of mind imaginable I rose, walked into the kitchen to wash my dishes, and then wandered off into the afternoon with my hands in my pockets.

There—it had happened at last. I had gotten what I wanted, what I had pushed for those past weeks. I was free to go; there in front of me was a wide open door to any life that I might chose, but I felt no euphoria, as I had anticipated. Instead, I felt only grief.

As I trudged down the hill away from the main buildings, I recalled the first time I had witnessed an expulsion from the monastery. Every once in a while it happens that, like me, a monk reaches what is called "a place of unwillingness," refusing to take responsibility for himself or herself in the way that the monastery, representing Life, demands. At this point, invariably, the monk is asked to seek their salvation in another place. The first time I saw this happen it completely rattled me. One of the monks, after a string of unskillful choices and behaviors that went back for years, did something that demonstrated a dramatic unwillingness to practice. I happened to be there, meditating in the evening darkness, when it all went down, and when the Roshi emerged from the hall after the (I would imagine) energetic meeting that followed. I heard her car door open and the motor

200

fire, but I did not hear her pull away. Instead, I heard her footsteps as she returned, as she entered the dining hall for a moment (to write a note, I concluded later) and as she then strode back out to her car once more and departed. I did not make any particular significance out of those sounds at the time, but I recalled them instantly the next morning when I arrived at the main buildings to learn that the monk in question was gone.

The whole thing shook me up—it shook us all up. I struggled for days to find the wisdom in that action before I did, but once I understood it, my mind opened to a vast new realm of practice. The monk had chosen suffering, I realized. Even at the monastery, with all the support that was available, her choice was to suffer, and the ruthless compassion of our practice refused to accept this choice. The monastery's commitment is to the monk's transformation—that he or she let go of the habits of self-destruction and learn to take responsibility for his or her life. The monk's commitment is to accept this guidance. If a monk has stopped practicing, he cannot be allowed to believe that he is. He needs to be woken up to this fact, which is exactly what happened in this case. The gift I received from that monk's departure was this glimpse of the stand that real compassion makes for freedom, and the opportunity I have to offer this same unyielding support to myself.

Now it was my turn. Who would have thought it would come to this? Who would have thought that all of the effort and all of the outrageous hope that preceded this unhappy day would have resulted in such a shameful and disappointing end? I had imagined that I would walk for a few hours, as the Roshi had suggested, to consider the change in my life that lay before me, but I could not do it. I headed to my hermitage instead and lay down on the bed. For a long while I stared out the window, unsure of anything other than the fact that my heart was broken and I wanted no more to live.

As I lay there, suddenly I realized what I must do. I could not allow my training to end like this. To be sent away for unwillingness was not worthy of me or of the sincere practice I had followed all those years. I could not allow myself to fail, even to get what I believed I wanted: it was too great a price. With sudden conviction I leapt up, put on my shoes, and strode back to the main buildings. I knew I had to act while I still could.

The others were working in the meditation hall. The Roshi spied me outside and came out to meet me. "Forgive me," I said. "I am confused. May I please stay?"

The Roshi nodded simply in reply.

"I cannot promise that I will not cause more trouble as I go through this," I continued. "I cannot put this thing down. I need to see it through. I am sorry for the impact this is having."

The Roshi shrugged and smiled as only she can do. "Think nothing of it," she said. "It's why we're here."

Tears filled my eyes. "Thank you for your kindness," I said. "May I please join the group?"

She nodded again, then together we entered the hall to join the others.

This was the end of the turmoil of that day, but nothing near the end of my insanity. I could not help but see how I had fallen out of integrity, but the questions that plagued me were still unresolved: What do I really want? What is true for me? Who am I, really? What is the life that I am here to live? In no way that I was conscious of or could have articulated, it was the answers to these questions that I sought through all those difficult times. What I did understand was that there was no way out but through the confusion to the other side.

Later that afternoon, when the upheaval of my mind and heart was too much to bear in company, I left the group for a while to walk it off. As I did, something amazing happened. As my thoughts churned and my heart raced and ached with the agony of my situation, as conditioned mind fought to repossess me after the willingness that had broken through earlier in the day, and while I was still moved by the courage of my resolve to stay and the Roshi's acceptance of it, I rounded the corner of the building by the pump house, and the sweetest voice in the world said, "You know, you don't have to do this."

My feet immediately grew roots in that spot. I hardly dared to breathe. "What?" I said out loud.

"You don't have to do this," the voice repeated, just as miraculously as before. I looked around carefully: mine was the only body in sight. Then the voice added: "You don't have to suffer in this way. You are okay just the way you are. Why don't you just relax for a while? Everything is going to be fine."

The words sank all the way down into the bottom of my heart. I begged for more without success, yet what I had heard already was enough to absolutely reverse my experience of that day. I was moved by the compassion in them, and I felt suddenly safe even in the midst of all the trouble that had befallen me. I sensed from those few soothing words that the presence behind them knew me as no one ever has, and that I was seen. Even my own mother, bless her, cannot see me; like everyone else she sees the person she believes that I am—but the voice, whoever or whatever he or she or it might be, possessed a clarity that pierced through the mirage to the authenticity behind it. I knew this not from the words, but from my heart's reception of them: they touched me in a place nobody else on earth besides myself has ever perceived. It was as if my true parent suddenly came back home, bearing the unconditional love that I had spent my life until that moment missing, and offered it to me.

This voice was nothing like the other internal voices that I had learned to be suspicious of: it spoke from a place of love they do not possess. It did arise from within me, however; that was clear, but just as clearly it came from some place outside of what I was accustomed to think of as myself. "I" had nothing to do with it. This was not the first time, of course, that I had experienced the voice of compassion. Over the time since my arrival at the monastery, I had gradually found within myself a capacity for kindness, and had learned to practice offering that to myself, but I had rarely experienced this as something apart from my own will, and it had never touched me so deeply before.

I became as simple as a child. Inside of me everything changed. I relaxed, I let go of all that troubled me, I breathed, and I realized that there was nothing wrong—that nothing in the world inside or outside of me was wrong in any way, even right there in the midst of that painful trial. I stood still for a long time, just experiencing the beauty of this insight. Everything that is, I saw, just is, and it is all okay.

As soon as my feet began to move again, so did conditioned mind. Immediately I plunged back into suffering and set about surviving my life once again—but my experience by the well puzzled and touched me in a way I could not forget. Even as I threw myself back into misery my delusions appeared translucent to me, as if in any moment they might dispel like fog in the heat of the day and I might find myself reunited with that voice. My heart yearned for this, and for the great peace it brought to me. It would be a long while before I would experience compassion again in that form, but the memory of it guided me until the point when I had the courage to let go of the suffering of that time and allow it to speak to me again. Over time I would learn that the compassion within the voice I heard that day is who I actually am; that, in fact, it is more "me" than the me who longs to hear it. Who I am, I was to see—who we all are—is that which can save us from the hell of conditioned mind.

24

The Answer

Three more weeks passed and I behaved myself for the most part. During that time I looked about for some way to claim the new life I believed I wanted without sacrificing my integrity for it. I agonized over this night and day, until finally I came to a resolution: I must leave the monastery under my own volition, with or without the Roshi's approval. What I would do, I decided, was appeal to the community. The other monks clearly knew I had fallen on hard times, but only the Roshi knew the circumstances. I would call a meeting, I decided, to describe to the monks what was happening within me, to inform them of my decision to leave, and to ask them to make a place for me in the organization in a new role. I would suggest that I might find some way to live outside the monastery gates and participate from there, if they were willing for it. If the community did not accept my proposal, I would take this as a sign that I was finished with the practice forever, and would seek my fortune in another place.

As far as I was aware, there had never been an appeal to the community of this sort in the history of the monastery. It would be a rather dramatic act. In a sense it would be an attempt to go over the Roshi's head. An understanding that binds us as monks is that the only thing that truly matters is the clarity that arises out of the moment, and the power that comes from this. The Roshi herself is not in charge of anything. Her practice has taken her, of course, to a place of great clarity, but she understands as well as any of us that she is merely a vehicle for that clarity: should it arise in another form, as is frequently does through someone else's insight, then she must give over to that clarity as any other monk would. I believed that I had clarity. I understood that my actions were soaked in the most humiliating disobedience, but I still believed in the power of the perception that drove me to them. And I was right, in a way: I had seen something so fundamental to my transformation that it rocked all of my world. It was the assumptions I made and the conclusions I drew in response that were not clear. Not seeing this distinction, and feeling the power of the change happening inside of me, I thought that I could carry my desires past my teacher, appeal to the monks, and win.

I could not assemble the monks without the Roshi's approval, however, and so I asked for it. She would not say yea or nay. "Let's see where you are when you return from the retreat in a few weeks," she said. I was scheduled to staff a retreat on the East Coast, you see. The thought of waiting that long with this issue burning inside appalled me. I could not rest; I could barely eat. Instinctively I challenged her. "You think there is nothing to this but conditioning," I said.

"No," she replied. "I cannot know these things. I can only require people to pay attention. I will need to decide if I will permit you to go to the other monks in this way. In the meantime you must look to see where all of this is coming from in you."

I cannot say that I resolved to look because I felt sure that I was right. I did resolve to wait, however, as I had no choice. The frustration and suspense I endured was indescribable, but somehow I survived it and the time slowly passed.

I am astonished now that I was permitted to leave the monastery at this time, in such a chaotic state of mind. The faith that this suggests the Roshi still retained in me moves me even now. In support of her faith and to my credit, I was able to set my confusion aside for the week that I was away, and I worked well. In fact, the need I felt to give over my struggles so that I might fully serve; the reality, which could not escape me, that I accomplished this; and the experience of myself suddenly released from the anguish that had enthralled me those many weeks, is likely what saved me in the decisive moment soon to follow.

I flew back to California on a Sunday and spent the night at our center in the Bay Area. On the way, as I waited to board a plane in Washington, I left a voice message for the Roshi saying that the time she had asked me to wait had passed, and that I humbly requested a decision about how we might proceed. The next morning after I awoke I found a reply waiting for me.

"You will have to do as you think best, Dave," she said. "I do not have the right to interfere, even as much as I would like to. If I could have my way, you would sit still with this until the confusion in it is gone—until you had seen through it all and followed each piece of it back to its source within conditioned mind. I am afraid for you. But I give you my permission to do as you must, trusting in Life to show you the way, and in your willingness to follow."

I put down the phone and made my way outside. Nearly insensible, I stumbled across the road to the same park where the Roshi and I had spoken some weeks before. It was done. I could not have said how I understood this at that moment but I did: the game I played was finished. I can see now that through this whole time conditioned mind had staked its hopes in its expectation that the Roshi would ultimately fail to meet the challenge that I presented to her. In alignment with conditioned mind, I projected that her compassion was not true, that it would falter, and when it did, a way would open up for me to escape the awful, wonderful destiny my life had put before me: to walk the way of the Buddha and to devote my life to service and the end of suffering. If only she could have made me wrong, or assumed she knew what she could not know, or have acted out of conditioned mind just one time, even for just a moment, then I could have broken my relationship with her forever and thrown myself back into a life of suffering, as I believed I wished to do. Her compassion, however, was true. She opened the door herself to that old, unhappy world and said, "I believe in you even now." In the reflection of the wisdom of that act and of the deep practice that her clarity arose out of, I could not help but see finally for myself how confused I was and to glimpse the possibility that she held out for me. All she wanted was my freedom. Seeing this, I realized that I could not continue with my resistance. I must, at last, do the work that I am here on this earth to do, and set aside conditioned mind so that I may be free.

Looking back upon those tumultuous days, I am moved, as I have been so often before, by the compassion inherent in the Life that animates us all, and how rarely it is embodied by a human being. Few understand what true compassion is. What we do in the name of compassion often is but more conditioned mind, thinly disguised. To give ourselves or others what "I" wants, for example, or to assist ourselves or others to avoid pain, is generally considered to be good and helpful, but there is nothing compassionate in these. Compassion is that which supports true happiness in freedom from conditioned mind. The tricky distinction here is that what is kind to conditioned mind is unkind to the being trapped in its delusions. Not knowing the difference, we offer "sympathy", or "help", or "support", or any of a host of other things instead of compassion. Without a ton of spiritual practice people will overwhelmingly choose to protect ego and unconsciously allow it to go on ruining lives without impediment. This is what makes the clarity of the Roshi so powerful and so threatening. She requires our freedom without consideration for conditioned mind; this unyielding stand is her compassion.

Over the years I have watched in awe as the power of compassion has transformed the lives of those around me. When Life dumps people onto the monastery grounds they are broken in most cases by their suffering. You have to be in pretty rugged shape before you will consider monastic training as a way to get help; most who do exhaust themselves first trying to find some other alternative. People arrive here as abandoned children, and for a long while, as they learn to trust the compassion of the Roshi and their own capacity to endure it, as children they remain. But slowly, as they learn to live in present time, and as the moment revives their discarded hopes, the shoot of happiness that conditioned mind had crushed underfoot raises itself to the sunlight again, and gradually it begins to flower. One of the most moving things in the world is to witness this miracle as it happens in the heart of someone who had lost the hope of it. Some of these people have become my fellow-monks, and I have seen them as I have seen myself grow to become the beautiful and strong and compassionate people that we are. Day after day we train with whatever the suffering is that troubles us, day after day we see through it more and more, and we let go, and suffering ends.

The day that followed the collapse of my hopes was the longest of my life so far. I wish I could adequately convey the horror of the fact that stood in front of me, that there was no escape from my destiny, and that there likely would never be. It was as if this were my last day in the open air before a lifetime of imprisonment. I often wished again to die during that interminable day, so destitute had I become. I had gambled my life upon a desire that was not true; when I lost, as was inevitable, what remained seemed not worth living for.

A retreat was to begin that evening at the monastery. For this reason, I was told, there were not the resources to pick me up in the Bay Area. I would need to take a train to Stockton instead. This journey would require several stages and an entire day to accomplish. I did not mind: solitude was the only thing I craved.

I ate my breakfast in tears, then walked to the train station, dragging my baggage behind me. I changed trains in a nearby town and headed east. It was late morning before I arrived at the half-way point of my journey, in a city just west of the foothills. Here I learned that the next train to Stockton would not depart for several hours. I left my bags at the station, found something to eat, and then wandered aimlessly through the streets for a while. Never before had life seemed so dreamlike to me. I felt myself to be an alien in this world. I watched jealously as the people around me smiled and laughed and rushed busily here and there. They did not share my hard future, as it seemed to me, where I must work to give up all that they enjoyed, all that humanity as a mass holds dear, for the sake of a promise of freedom that I could not access as I watched them and that I believed, at that moment, I did not want. After a time I found a park and lay down in a patch of deep, green grass, but the shouts of children playing nearby tortured me, and so I returned to the train station. There, for the next two hours, I walked slowly from one end of the platform to the other, over and over. It was the most sorrowful two hours of my life.

As I walked I found a discarded playing-card on the platform. Turning it over, I saw that it had come with a new deck of cards. Written on the face were instructions for an elaborate poker game. I wish I had kept it and had it now as a memorial to this strange time in my life. At the bottom of the card, after outlining the sequences of dealing and betting that were a part of the game, the text described the last step like this:

"Finally, the player to the left of the dealer becomes the new dealer. The cards are shuffled, the top card is discarded, and then the dealer deals a new hand."

I stared at that card for a long time, wondering at its appearance on that day. The voices of conditioned mind called it a sign. "The game is not over!" they said. I knew that this was not true, however. In my heart I understood that it was done. You might say that this was the accomplishment I achieved during those weeks of turmoil: I had bet my ego, laid my hand on the table, and lost. I now knew the answer to the question that I had set out to find at the beginning: would Life support me in what I believed I wanted? The answer, it was clear now, was "no". Life wants something other than suffering for me; I am here for some other purpose. Even as devastating as this knowledge was at the time, it brought the one gift with it that I needed in order to survive what followed: I knew what I had to do. I must accept the opportunity I was given, discover the true life that it led me to, and find the joy that must, somehow, be awaiting me there.

With this thought I heard the train approaching in the distance. I tore the card in half, tossed the pieces down over the tracks, and prepared to board.

25

A Gradual Recovery

I wish I had the space to describe in detail the nearly two years that followed that fateful day. It took me that long to find myself again. Out of kindness for me as I made that long journey back from despair, the monastery took away all of my responsibilities and spread them out amongst the other monks. For the first time in years I just performed the simple daily tasks required by our communal life, pulling my work assignments from the message board each day, as I had when I first arrived. I lived for ages during that span, it seemed. I will detail just a few of the memories that stand out from that time.

I remember sitting on the ground in the pouring rain outside of the hermitage along the lower road. I had been sent there to repair one of the windows. It started sprinkling as I headed for the hermitage with my tools, and as I worked the rain began to come down in earnest. I was only just alive and able to function. This was in the early times soon after my disappointment, when each day seemed an eternal ordeal I must survive. How unhappy I was! That afternoon I attempted to steel myself against despair as usual, but failed. I honestly could not see how I could go on. I no longer fantasized about life beyond the monastery gates. The illusion that I could be happy there had been exploded. I had no place to go, and I lacked the strength, it seemed, to live where I was. At last the tools fell from my hands and I collapsed into a heap beside them. I leaned back against one of the posts that supports the building, rested my head there, and closed my eyes while the rain fell down over my face and torso and legs. I sat there like that for an hour, maybe more, breathing, still as death.

I remember driving to town in a 1968 Dodge pick-up that we called "George," on some errand or other. I had fallen out of integrity again, as happened several times during those two years, and had attempted to get myself expelled. I can recall exactly the state of my mind and heart as I followed our dirt driveway up and out of the monastery, towards the world outside. "This is it," I told myself. "When I return I will be asked to go." Hope that this might actually happen drowned out the shame that lay beneath it. I did not care about ending suffering. I only cared about finding some way to live that would involve less pain. On the way to town George blew a hose and started spewing steam everywhere. To my credit, I laughed out loud at the irony of this. I remember standing beside the road, leaning against George, waiting for the tow truck I had called, and understanding, once again, that there was no hope for me in forsaking the life that I am here to live. There is no life without pain. I cannot describe what remained as "determination", as this implies an intentionality that I did not possess. I simply had no choice but to go on, and so that is what I did.

I remember exiting the meditation hall one evening at the deepest point of my desperation and finding Rhea waiting for me in the archway, as she often did. As I crouched to pet her and kiss her on the nose, which was the reward she always waited for, I saw suddenly how much she had aged. My heart filled with love and gratitude—her devotion and constant acceptance had supported me more than I can say during those silent years, and especially through the dark times of my confusion—and as I looked into her bottomless eyes I realized that she could no longer leave the monastery, her home for two-thirds of her life. She was too old to travel now in the way we had once done. "Who would have thought it would be you, dear Rhea," I said to her, "who would ask me to stay?"

I remember most of all the sickness that plagued me during that time. After the loss of the wild energy that had carried me so recklessly through the first months after my return from

213

Africa, my health abandoned me. One sickness followed another: I simply could not get well. How many days did I spend lying in bed in my hermitage, staring out of the window at the rain or at the light of the sun as it crossed the sky, my mind full of sorrow and my body full of disease? The trouble was, of course, that I had so little will to live. I can remember saying to the Roshi once, in the middle of yet another episode, "I'm afraid that I will die."

"If you do not decide that you want to live, you will," she replied, then smiled kindly. She knew me better than I did myself. I was put on this earth for some good purpose; in the end, when I finally had let go of what I believed I wanted instead, I would choose, she knew, what would heal me.

Once I became very sick indeed, with pneumonia. Ignoring my protests, a monk dragged me off to the local clinic for assistance. Gradually I recovered, but before I did the most amazing thing happened.

For three or four days, at the point where I was the most unwell, I dropped into a state of peace and ease such as I had rarely experienced before. In my delirium my confusion dropped away. It was as if I had been reborn into a new life where nothing concerned me anymore: the illness so overpowered my habitual patterns of thought and assumption that it erased all of my past and all of my imagined future. During the long hours of those days I realized the profound truth that nothing important in the universe exists, not even my own life.

All I did, all that I could do, was lie in bed, breathing, and watch the movement of light and shadow outside the window. I did not even eat that I can remember. Everything became perfectly simple: it was just me, my body, my illness, and my breath. My fellow-monks, bless them, brought me what little I needed when I needed it, but otherwise I was alone all that time, with none of the conditioned urgency that usually kept me company. There just wasn't room for it. As I lay there, and as I breathed, the most wonderful experience of acceptance washed over me—sometimes, as far as I could tell, for hours on end.

Everything seemed completely okay, including the pain of my sickness and the life that awaited me when I finally recovered, if I did. I did not have the strength to resist it. Both life and death felt near—so close that it was as if I could experience them both in contrast. For the first time ever, I think, I accepted the two extremes: both the death of my physical body, and, much more difficult, the life that remained within it, which would carry me as soon as I was well back into the world of angst and trouble. I glimpsed the stillness and the peace that lay beyond the illusion I had suffered within those past months. Everything seemed so clear, so simple, and so easy—it was amazing.

As the antibiotics pulled me back to health and my strength returned, all of my suffering revived with it. Unimportant things became important again, and the struggle with conditioned mind resumed. Still, I could not easily forget the experience of acceptance that I had over those days. It was a most moving gift.

Many times I did not believe that I would complete that dark journey. Once, during a guidance session under the oak tree, I expressed this to the Roshi. "I just cannot do it," I said.

"Yes, you can."

"I would rather die."

"No, you would not."

I went on as if she had not spoken. "I would not kill myself in the way people usually do," I said, as if musing about something insignificant. "I couldn't do that. Instead, I would just throw some things into a backpack and disappear. Sooner or later something would take me out." I said this half-humorously in order to take the edge off of the fact that I was in earnest and had considered this many times.

The Roshi matched my tone in her reply, and said half-jokingly, but with the same veiled seriousness, "We would go for you and bring you back."

I dropped all pretense of humor. "I would be impossible to find," I said in defiance.

The Roshi frowned. "You know how things are," she said. "We would have Life behind us. We would find you."

I nodded and lowered my eyes, moved by that promise. It was futile for me to resist the path my life was taking. There was not even a way out in death. My life, I understood, was not my own.

What Life wanted for me was to grow into the person who I am without conditioned mind; to grow up to become the compassion that is my inherent nature. This is the one choice we have as human beings, and the one that almost no one will make. Almost nobody wants to grow up. Instead, everyone wants to remain children and have Life just give them what they want. This is a very appealing notion, I will admit (I belong to this club myself, obviously), but it will never work. We must learn to provide for ourselves the life that we dream of. It is one of the unavoidable realities of life that nobody can do this for us: we are ourselves our own true parents, and nobody else is. This leaves a lot of room to complain, but this reality, even as hard as it may seem sometimes, is actually the foremost gift of Life. If we are willing (and this is a gigantic if), it will ultimately lead us to the discovery of our power to take real care of ourselves.

Never be confused that people who engage in adult things are actually adults: most are not. In general people are identified in childhood survival strategies most or all of the time. An adult is one who can truly meet her or his own needs. Because we are not taught how to take care of ourselves in this way, because it was seldom modeled by the people who raised us, and because we have so much practice surviving instead, tremendous dedication and courage is required to take the necessary steps towards real adulthood. This piece of work is made especially difficult by the fact that it is not possible to grow up, even now, without parenting. We cannot do it as the abandoned children who we are when we begin. It can only be done by giving ourselves over to the Life that inhabits our bodies and everything else that exists. As we give our lives to Life, we end the illusion of separation that has prevented us from seeing that who we actually are is this Life. Every time we let go of conditioned mind and say yes to the Life that animates, we move a little closer to becoming not the child we were trained to be, but the parent we were born to experience as ourselves.

I can see now that this was the transition I was attempting to make during that long time of trouble. I see also that a lifetime of rejected pain stood in the way, pain that needed to be seen, embraced, and let go. Like we all do, I identified with conditioned mind because I did not know how to care for the hurt that had happened to me and that still remained inside, longing to be healed. To be who we are in each moment requires such strength and clarity because of the necessity of facing and feeling that hurt. As I fought conditioned mind for the power to be present once again, I gradually found the willingness to put my attention on the actual experiences occurring within my heart and mind rather than ego's interpretations of them. As I did I discovered within myself the compassion needed to address the ancient pain that lay beneath it all. I perceived that my work was to embrace all of those rejected experiences. If I could feel the pain I had avoided—feel the pain, not be the pain—from a place of compassion and acceptance, I could heal it for good.

All I needed—all we all need—was to have my own attention. This is the entire truth. I dreamed I wanted many outside things, but all I truly wanted was to be held within my own awareness with love. This is all that had ever been missing. Over time, as I began to understand this, as I recovered from my delusions, as I let go of my misery and began to trust myself to be what I was looking for, I was able to go to the work of my healing with joy.

The months passed slowly and the intensity of my unhappiness faded away. Gradually I began to recover my lost willingness, and began to remember the man that I am and the sweet delight I had known before in simply being alive.

I remember working one cold winter morning out at the west end of the property. I was repairing the barn, as I recall. Suddenly I looked up from my hands and tools and became aware of the frosty leaves on the trees around me, the grey sky, and the damp earth beneath my feet. My life moved within me, joy sprang up and danced a little jig in my heart, and I laughed aloud with pleasure. I realized that I felt strong and well, as I had not for a long time. "Check it out!" I exclaimed to Rhea, who stood nearby and rooted for me as usual from the sidelines, "I'm back!"

I remember sitting in the meditation hall late one summer evening after the other monks had retired for the night. During my recovery I made it a habit to sit when our evenings were free in order to outfox conditioned mind, which needed only a bit of space to concoct the unhappiness that I worked to transcend. Normally during those days meditation was little more than a wrestling match with ego, but for some reason that evening I let go and dropped into a most beautiful state of serenity and confidence. I felt cherished and adored; I felt myself united with the force that carried me day by day through my suffering to the other side. "This is what I practice for," I said to myself as I departed. "If I will not give up then Life will save me."

I remember joking with the Roshi one morning outside of a retreat center in North Carolina. I had gone with her to staff an event there. Anyone who knows the Roshi will tell you that she is a born comic. Her specialty is making herself ridiculous by way of mimicking conditioned mind. I can't recall what it was that she taunted that morning—most likely it was my own drama and perplexity—but I remember the two of us dissolving into giggles at the hilarity of her antics. How good it was to laugh! Especially, how good it was to laugh at conditioned mind! How good it was to love my teacher once again, who had rescued me from a life of suffering, in recent times and from the moment I met her, and who accepted me and loved me in spite of all that had occurred.

Small awakenings like this began to occur more and more as time went by. Each time that I apprehended once again the compassion within the strange life I lived, the perfection of that life, and the longing of my heart to live it, I was guided towards the end of that time of trouble. Bit by bit I found gladness in the fact that I lived and sensed the old excitement growing within me. My ancient eagerness returned to explore the tender mystery of myself, and I slowly began to live again. I became certain at last that I would make it through.

26

Sangha

It is because the path of awakening is so tremendously difficult, I suspect, that the Buddha encouraged us to practice in community. "Sangha" is the word he used for this. A Sangha is a group of people who practice together to end suffering. My own particular Sangha includes the monks I live with, all of the hundreds of people who practice with us regularly in various places, all of the thousands with whom I have practiced at one time or another, and even, I dare to say, the dedicated reader of this book. On a larger scale, my sangha includes all who have practiced to end suffering since the beginning of that possibility, and all who ever will. We practice in Sangha to support each other along the way, and to experience our interdependence through our collective dedication to the end of suffering.

I heard an interview on the radio once with an older gentleman who, as I recall, had spent nearly his entire adult life as a monk in the Christian tradition. Over the course of the conversation he was asked any number of questions about the life he had led. His answers all intrigued me, but one of them I feel sure I will never forget. He was asked:

"What has been the hardest thing for you about being a monk?"

The monk thought about it for a while, then he replied, "Well, the other monks, I suppose."

That's sangha for you. We practice together because we are our own best teachers and our own best "opportunities". We inspire each other, we spur one another on, and we mirror for each other the suffering that we each have dedicated this present moment of our lives to transcend. We share a commitment that unites us and that makes a lie out of the deception of our individuality.

I have lived side-by-side every day with some of the monks for many years without knowing where they came from before they entered the monastery, how they spent their lives up until that point, or anything else that in other places would be the first order of business to learn. I only know their last names by accident. As monks we do not maintain personal relationships with each other; because of this a connection exists between us that transcends personality. As a group we are a part of something larger than ourselves as individuals; this something larger brings us together in a way that most people experience in their lives but rarely, if at all. Together we experience true intimacy. Together we observe the movement between the illusion that there is a self and an other, and the awareness that there is not; we go in and out of separation, and as we do we see the difference. And just in case we should become confused, every once in a while Life in its great wisdom and mercy throws something in our way that pulls us together so completely that doubt becomes impossible. I could give you many examples of events that accomplished this, but my favorite is the one that has come to be known as "The Well Project." Here is what happened.

On a Friday afternoon about a year and a quarter after the trip to Africa I described, in August, as I worked to dodge the story of my deprivation as usual, a monk walked up to me and handed me a note. I opened it and read these words:

Something is wrong with the well.
Gassho

With that, seeing that she had delivered her message to the appropriate person (I had recently been re-appointed as the monk in charge of our physical infrastructure), the monk bowed and departed. Rhea happened to be sitting nearby. "Why me?" I asked her. "What do I know about wells?"

Let me tell you something about being a monk. Someone who is a monk always has in front of her or him two fundamental choices. Actually, someone who is anything always has in front of her or him two fundamental choices: to resist the circumstances that Life offers, and within this to complain, to drag your feet, to distract yourself in any number of ways, to be a victim, and all sorts of other unpleasant things; or to accept the circumstances that Life offers gratefully, to let go of the suffering that arises in response, and to figure that you're about to learn something. I figured I was about to learn something. Very carefully I examined the well. After applying all of my genius I ascertained that the monk who had handed me the note was correct: there was indeed something wrong. I deduced this fact from all of the water that wasn't coming out.

As this reality sank in I became aware of the gravity of the situation. The thermometer on the tool shed read a hundred and five degrees when I checked it. That in itself presented us with no emergency, but imagine my horror when I thought of our gardens full of thirsty growing plants, and of our buildings and grounds full of thirsty growing monks, all baking in that heat, and all depending upon that well to survive. In that moment I had two insights simultaneously: that we were in trouble and that I had no idea what to do.

In a panic I called the Roshi. Her response, as always, was profound. "Curses!" she said.

"Any ideas?" I asked her.

"Hmmm…. We'd better find somebody who knows something about wells."

"Right!" I said. You'll never meet anybody with better sense than the Roshi. "I'll call you when I know something."

So I got on the horn to every well-drilling outfit in the county, but with no success. It being the late Friday afternoon that it was, they were already home drinking beer. I gathered, however, from the few tired people I did manage to talk to, that all the well-drillers in these parts are kin to one another, descended from the same man, now deceased, who had dug our well originally.

Armed with this information and incredible persistence, I finally tracked down the matriarch of the clan, who promised to send somebody out Monday morning. I pleaded for the morrow, but she stood firm. "They are drinking beer," she said.

There was absolutely nothing more I could do, but in my anxiety my helplessness was unacceptable to me, so I decided to walk up and down and fret. As I fretted I made a horrible discovery. The building that houses the kitchen and dining hall, which had been constructed after the well was first drilled, had been placed in such a way that it obstructed any possible access to the well from the road. "Holy miscalculation!" I exclaimed to Rhea, who never left my side once during this entire adventure. "There ain't no way to get a truck in here!" All weekend I worried over this while I watched the water drain from our storage tank, hoping somehow I was wrong, but Monday morning the well guy confirmed my apprehensions.

"There ain't no way to get a truck in here." he said. "Without a truck we can't pull out the pipes." When I asked him what we should do he just shrugged and drove off.

Again in a panic I called the Roshi. "Looks like we'll have to do it ourselves," she said. A long pause ensued as I let that sink in. Was that even possible?

There is nothing so motivating as having no way out other than your own resources. All of monastic practice profits from this fact—you will hear it called sometimes "the wisdom of no escape." So long as we have a way out we will take it, but as soon as we do not we discover within ourselves the wherewithal to rise up in whatever way the occasion demands and create out of ourselves the thing that makes the difference. This is what happened to me that Monday, and soon what happened to all of us as we worked together for a solution to our common difficulty. "Right!" I said to the Roshi, and then I got back on the horn to find out what in the world that would entail.

I called every well driller in the book. They all said the same thing: "You're crazy." Then, at last, after nearly every possibility had been exhausted, I found Marvin. "That's very interesting," said Marvin.

Marvin was one of the sweetest and gentlest men I had ever met. He told me later that as a boy nobody ever taught him how to do anything; that is where his willingness to help us came from, that he never wanted anyone to feel the way he felt then. All he said was this: "What do you need from me?"

"For starters, just tell me what's down there," I replied, and he did. We had a length of pipe, he said—one hundred eighty feet of it, as it turned out—a pump at the bottom, and electrical wire following the pipe all the way down. "It's going to be awful heavy," said Marvin, "because the pipe will be filled with water. How heavy depends upon where the rupture is." As I discussed the situation with Marvin, and as I began to understand exactly what we needed to do, a plan slowly began to form in my mind.

This is the point at which it became a "we" rather than a "me" situation. No, that's not right: it was a "we" experience from the very beginning, even while I worked on it alone. This is the point at which "we" embraced the entire community. After the conversation with Marvin I recognized that it would take all of our joint resources to pull off this experiment, so I collected all the monks together and told them what we were going to have to do. We all put on our grubbies, and then, in a little speech before we went to work, I invited all the monks to set everything aside but their willingness and our need for water. To my delight, and as I had expected, they did.

First, we agreed as a community to stop bathing and washing clothes. Next, we put together all of our garden hoses and ran a line from our neighbor's house through the woods to our big storage tank up on the hill—that way at least we could save our trees. After that we sent somebody out to rent a chunky block and tackle from the local rental outfit. With great cunning we built a tower above the well out of long four-by-fours all strapped together, with a crossbeam at the top, to hang the tackle on. We made a vice out of some bar-clamps to grab hold of the pipe with. Then we stopped because it was dark. We made plans to begin again at first light, then we went on in to meditate.

This is where the magic started. The next morning it rained. Only if you are from this part of the country will you get the full import of that statement. It never rains here in August—never. Until that day it had not rained since May, and it did not rain again until October. For an entire hour as the day broke water poured impossibly out of the sky onto the thirsty ground while we watched in disbelief. I cannot describe the profound impact this had. We are religious people, you know, and a bit inclined towards superstition. I am not prepared to make what happened mean anything (that just wouldn't be Buddhist), but let's just say the magic of that impossible morning rain erased any thoughts that we might have had of failure. By the time we had breakfasted and were ready for work the rain had stopped and even the clouds were gone. Nothing could have been more perfect.

The block and tackle was a spectacular idea except for one thing: it didn't work. Even with the tower we could only pull three feet of pipe out of the ground at one time. "We'll be old people before we're done at this rate," I complained to Rhea. "What are we going to do?" Then came a pregnant fifteen minutes of silence while we all stood around the well and waited for inspiration to hit. Finally, it did. One of the monks walked up to me, bowed, and whispered in my ear. I thought about it for a while, and then I said to them all: "Okay. Let's see if we can jerk that rascal out of the ground with just monk-power."

Here is what we did: all the monks but two climbed on the tower we had built, and readied themselves for action. The two stayed on the ground. In this way we created a vertical line of muscle three tiers high above the well. We tied a stout rope to the fitting at the top of the first piece of pipe, and then, after everyone perfectly understood what we had to do, together we all gave it a heave and found to our joy that we could lift it, the eight of us, just barely. Groaning and sweating we strained together to hoist that pipe out of the ground foot by foot. Finally, after the first twenty-foot section was out, we set the joint on a plywood stopper we had cut for that purpose, and let go to rest. As we stepped back we beamed with wonder and delight at what we had done.

The job required two days to complete. Suffice it to say there was not a dull instant that whole time. How could there have been, what with the discovery of the break in the pipe that had caused the problem; the glorious moment when the pump at last emerged from that dark hole; the morning I spent with Marvin as he collected the pipe and fittings that we needed and taught me everything there is to know about wells; how we used the wrong pipe dope and had to pull a hundred forty feet of pipe back out of the ground after we were nearly finished; and—this was the big one—how as we lowered the new pump and new pipe back into the hole, we dropped it (don't tell the Roshi), and how the safety-line after the three interminable seconds while it fell saved us from losing it all forever.

Thursday morning around ten we wired the new pump to our power system—everything else was finished. We took a few moments of silence to do our letting go in, then one of the monks flipped the switch. It worked. The water came pouring out of the pipe just as it was supposed to do, and we all cheered. Never have you seen a dirtier, wetter, more tired or happier group of people in your whole life. Tears come to my eyes even now as I remember it. Anyone who was there will understand. It wasn't about the well—that was just the content of the miracle that happened. It was about us; it was about what we together became. We became during those days one thing.

27

Humility

I emerged from my time of trouble with a deeper understanding of Life and my place within it. I accessed the simple truth that if I could renounce my dependence upon conditioned mind and center myself instead in conscious, compassionate awareness, this would remove egocentricity as the center and focus of my life. What seems obvious now was a revelation then, that this planet we live on does not revolve around my needs and desires. I discovered that I am not the author of my destiny, as I had imagined, but only its hero. I am merely an open heart that receives the bounty that pours into the life of anyone who desires it.

For the first time, I think, I experienced true humility. Humility, as I see it, is the realization of our relationship to life as a part of the whole. Who I am is not the center of the universe, no matter how ego will argue otherwise. From center, from the place where we experience our emptiness of self, we may perceive how we are, in fact, the center of nothing. We each participate in something so huge that it is impossible to imagine. We are infinitesimal: each human life is but an idea, you might say, within the limitless consciousness that animates it.

Beside true humility the arrogance of conditioned mind is appalling. What we do or say in our lives matters not a fig. Time will erase even our greatest achievements and our most stinging disasters. No matter what we do—even if we achieve the impossible, becoming the most perfect person who has ever lived—soon after we die nobody will remember we even existed. This is why conditioning appears so ridiculous from center: the only intelligent response to anything that could ever possibly concern us is, "Who cares?"

The freedom of our authentic being to emerge upon this earth demands that we cease to take our own lives personally. I began to understand as I recovered that it is possible to attain an impersonal relationship even to the most intimate content of my mind. Whenever I escaped conditioned mind, which happened more and more as time passed and my willingness returned, I no longer felt the need to cling to any private relationship to the content of my experience; I no longer needed to claim any of it as "mine." There is no "my" in compassionate awareness. From the point of view outside of ego, whenever I found myself there during those days, it was obviously absurd that I could own this existence that we participate in: life is just too huge for that. Freedom and joy began to return with the realization that if this life that I witness from my own unique perspective is not mine, not me, then nothing it contains could have anything to do with me. I need not suffer over any of it.

Grasping this profound fact, I watched with awe the infinite intelligence of Life manifesting through my form. I fell in love with practice once again, remembering how to relate to life as if it all is a gigantic workshop in which I might study the creation of misery and woe, of harmony and love. I recognized that the pain I felt through my recovery was not mine: it was just pain. It did not matter what variation that pain took—whether it was loneliness, frustration, anger, the horrible wanting, or anything else—none of it belonged to me. It only occurred within my awareness. I saw that I need not do anything about any of it. I need only to relax into the moment and be, and through the gift of awareness to see what it is to live a human life at this time, in this place, with this conditioning, in this form.

Gradually, as I practiced my new-found humility, I became available to serve Life once again. This both thrilled and appalled me, because to serve Life is what I most intimately desire and what ego most fears. And no wonder: when we sacrifice our suffering for freedom, when we discard the illusion of our individuality, and when we open ourselves to serve the presence that animates us, Life naturally accepts everything we have to offer. In fact, Life asks for everything from us; it asks for our whole lives, completely and absolutely. This had always been the case—Life had asked me for this from the beginning— but I had refused, claiming my life as my own. That is why I was unhappy. The reality, I saw, is that our lives are not our own. They belong to Life.

Luckily, it just so happens that in giving up ego in order to serve Life, we receive exactly what we have been looking for. This is one of the many miracles of human existence. All the saints from the beginning of our collective memory have said it: in order to receive you must give. If we live to give rather than to get, then we will receive everything we could hope for, but if we live this life for "I," then we will get only "I," which is worse than nothing.

Through all of this I tapped into the mysterious truth that it is only when we give our lives to Life in this way that we find our own unique place in the inscrutable scheme of things. I began to discover the vast world that is just mine, carved out by the incredible generosity of Life for just me to live in. This place is mine alone, but I am not alone when I am there, because in that place there is no separation between me and everything that is. Peace and safety live in that place, as do confidence and an understanding of my own adequacy. To my surprise, in that place I did not find myself to be important or necessary or anything else that had seemed essential before. I did not even find myself to be special, except insofar as everyone and everything are special as unique manifestations of being. Much better, I found myself to be essentially no different from anyone or anything else. Who wants to be the center of the universe, anyway? There is nothing worse! Being the center of the universe requires separation from everyone and everything. No wonder I had been so lonesome! I had lived alone on my own little planet where nothing mattered but me.

Life began to excite me once again. Little daily miracles began to occur as they once had, confirming the path that I traveled on. The one I remember best happened during the attack of pneumonia I described earlier. When I met the doctor who treated me—a big, sweet man with a round face and a caring smile—I explained to him that I am a full-time religious volunteer with no income. I told him also that the monastery would support me if necessary to bring me back to health, but that the monastery's money was dedicated to ending suffering in the world and would be better spent on that than on things my body did not need. And so I requested of him that he consider this as he made his decisions, then I placed my health in his hands, trusting him to do for me what was best.

"You know what?" the doctor said. "We hold some money back for cases like yours. No guarantees, but I'll get you a form to fill out, and maybe we can cover you." With this he went and got the form for me and then left me alone with it.

"This is very good," I said to myself, and, even though I had not actually asked for this sort of help, I willingly began to answer the questions on the form.

Everything went smoothly until the final one. Here is what it asked me to consider: "Will paying for the services offered by this clinic constitute a financial hardship for you?" I stared at those words for a long, long time. I wanted so much to answer that yes, it would, but I was aware at the same time that this was not true. To pay for my treatment would not be a hardship for me or for the monastery. We have little, but enough, and the monks are cared for perfectly without extravagance. The universe provides most beautifully for us: I eat better than almost anyone else on the planet; I have comfortable and functional clothes to wear, and good shoes, and I feel confident I always will. And yet, it was difficult indeed not to say yes to that question and the free money. "It would be so easy," the voices said to me.... But I did not listen. Luckily, I was too sick to take them seriously.

When the doctor returned I told him that I could not both answer yes to that question and keep my integrity. He attempted to argue, but the effort of my honesty had moved me, and when he saw my tears, the doctor, bless him, was moved himself.

"Okay," he said, and went about doctoring me, and I figured that was the end of it.

It wasn't. Instead, a most amazing thing happened. From that point on, over several visits to the clinic, the doctor did everything in his power to wash my pneumonia through the system without it costing me a dime. When he saw me in the waiting room he called me back right then to avoid the computers at the front desk; he talked all of the technicians into performing services for me under the table, he gave me lots of free stuff, and he refused to charge me for his own time. I couldn't believe it. The doctor's generosity caught on, and everyone in the clinic acted with the greatest of kindness towards me. I found that when I called in if I gave my name nobody knew who I was, but if I told them I was the monk with pneumonia, everyone recognized me immediately and got me exactly what I needed. I could not have received better service if I had been the king of some large country somewhere.

When it was all over I shook the doctor's hand to thank him for his compassion. "You are a very kind man," I told him.

"Think nothing of it," he replied. "Just keep up the good work."

Finally, two years after that fateful hour high over the west coast of Africa, after all the toil and trouble I have described and much, much more, I arrived where I began: as a monk, having dedicated my life to service once again, and to whatever that life might bring. I returned to a place of trust within the community. The time rolled on and my responsibilities increased beyond what they had been before the whole trial began. The events of those two years moved into the past and I moved on into the life that was offered me—often, though not always, with my whole heart.

Meanwhile, things had changed within the monastery itself. After over three decades of dedicated service, during which the Roshi's attention never wavered from the countless daily details involved in running the monastery and overseeing the practice, she began to feel the need to free her attention for even larger things. Ever since I had known the Roshi, I had watched with awe as she stepped out over and over into the largest possibility that she could see. More than ever during the time of my trouble she pushed beyond what she had done before and into newer, greater possibilities. For much of her life, I think, the monastery had served as a needed vehicle for the expression of her genius. At some point it began to hold her back. The practice itself needed for her to pass that opportunity and that responsibility on to people who needed it as she no longer did, so that the Roshi might expand as her own practice demanded. To this end, one summer afternoon she called the four senior monks together in the meditation hall.

"I have a great deal yet I wish to accomplish with my life," she told us. "I have a lot I want to give. This place," she continued, gesturing to indicate the beautiful building that enclosed us, the grounds that surrounded it outside, and the monks striding here and there, working and practicing in silence, "and this practice that we do here together are the core of my life's work. I would like to see them continue long after I am gone as a refuge from self-hatred and a sanctuary for the work of ending suffering."

The Roshi paused here to give us time to take in the significance of her words. After some moments of silence, she continued: "At the same time, I no longer feel the need to create and maintain the practice here. I am willing if that is what my life calls me to do, but everything that I can see suggests that this is your work now, and that I am called to other things."

My heart beat loudly as I understood where she was taking us. Along with the others I hung on every word.

"You people," the Roshi said, "are the ones in the position to pick up what I would put down. You have the necessary training, and you all have proven that you have the willingness to do it. None of us can know, of course, what Life will set before us, but the time has come to see. We must look to see where our practice will take us next, how we will carry it to the next generation, and how the monastery will or will not be a part of that."

Just then Franklin, one of the monastery cats, walked by outside the hall. He stopped and peered inside as if he, too, wondered what would happen to all of us and to the physical place where all of us had suffered so much and found so much joy.

"Now, it is important to me and essential for the integrity of what follows, whatever that may be, that each person chooses to accept this opportunity from a clear place and a genuine desire to take the next steps with this practice. Each person must fully commit to the process of discovering where we might go from here, and to truly walk the path towards the end of suffering. It may be that some or all of you have other ideas about how you would like to spend your life and what you yourselves feel called to give. If so, that is completely fine. I wish you the best. I will just need you to say that now so I will know who will be a part of this experiment as we go forward. And so I am asking for you to take some time for deep discrimination. I want you to look and see what you truly want for yourself, knowing that you are free to follow your own heart, and then to let me know when you feel clear."

A long silence followed the Roshi's words. I felt as if I lived for years in those few profound moments. Finally, one of the monks raised her hands in prayer position, as we do when we wish to speak. The Roshi nodded. "I do not need any time," the monk said. "I already know the answer. I can think of nothing I would rather do, no way that I would rather spend whatever time remains to me, than to serve this practice in this place in whatever way would be best."

The Roshi nodded again to accept the monk's commitment. The two other monks followed with similar expressions of their willingness and devotion. Then came the time for me to speak.

A wave of energy rushed through my body as the words rose to my mouth. I felt the sick thrill that came with the understanding that I was about to do what I had so often believed was no longer possible for me. Here it was at last, the opening I had waited for during all that time of trouble. Here was an invitation to make an honorable exit from the hard life I had chosen—that had chosen me—those past years. At last I was free to go.

As so often happens, however, the opening was given me at exactly the point when I no longer wished to take it. How kind Life is! I had longed for this moment so often, and so feverishly; now it was here and I only wanted for it to pass me by. The audacity of this decision dizzied me even as I made it. I perceived that the time had come to set uncertainty behind me and to freely choose the life at last that I am here to live.

"That leaves me," I said, and smiled. "I'm in."

28

An End and a Beginning

I cannot say, alas, that my battles with doubt and all the many forms of desire ended during that meeting with the Roshi. The struggle went on and continues to this day. What departed during that afternoon was the fear that I would succumb to the voices in some way that was fatal to my practice; that I would throw my life away upon a dream that could never obtain reality and miss the opportunity I have to end suffering in this lifetime. I ceased to question my integrity, and so could go on with the confidence that whatever arose in the course of each day would soon pass; that I am adequate to any amount of pain, and that each day I would see more deeply how I cause myself to suffer. I gave myself again to my life as a monk. Day by day I practiced, and the time gently passed.

I recall the next several years of my life and practice with gratitude and joy. For a long while I enjoyed the grace and ease that come with an undivided mind. It was a good, beautiful, simple time.

I remember the several journeys I made back to Africa. Over time the community we created there grew from a mere idea to a thriving center of life and hope amidst a world of suffering and despair. We started out feeding 25 children twice a day. During the years I traveled to Zambia that number grew to 800. I helped out mostly with the physical aspects of the project, in particular with the buildings we constructed to house the school and health clinic, and with the well we dug to provide clean drinking water. The day the well was finished was one of the best and most inspired of my life. It had been a major accomplishment just to get a well driller out to the property, as there were only three or four in the whole country. While the drillers worked the community gathered around, hundreds of them, with their black skin and beautifully colored clothes. Many of the children climbed trees and watched the action from there. They were all thirsty for clean water, having been sickened their whole lives by the filthy water the government provided. The people sang and danced while they waited, then the moment came at last when water erupted from the ground and everyone cheered. It was an exquisite, tear-filled moment for all of us.

I remember the great many retreats and workshops I facilitated during those years. I began to mature in my ability to offer practice to others, and this was deeply satisfying to me. I will always be grateful for the experience and understanding I gained through my facilitation practice. It is such an honor and a privilege to work with people in the intimate way a retreat provides, and the learning that resulted for me personally never slackened the whole time. I travelled a couple times a year to offer retreats on the East Coast, and even flew to Maui twice (oh, the jealousy of my fellow monks!) to represent the monastery at a conference there.

Most of all I remember the small daily moments of clarity and insight, of relaxation and peace, that occurred along the way. How often did I stop during some task or other to feel the sun on my skin, or the rain? How often did I suffer in the silence from grief or loneliness, from anger or despair, from all the types of pain that come with being human, and yet hold myself in compassion in the midst of it, as the practice had taught me to do? It is an awful, wonderful thing to live in the monastic environment, and often the smallest things that happen there are the most profound. I am thankful to have had so much time to experience myself and the Life that guides me in stillness and silence.

One morning about two years after the completion of my time of trouble, I awoke early and rolled over onto the floor to hug Rhea and to give her some kisses, as I usually did. To my surprise I noticed that her bed was wet. I sat up in alarm. "My goodness, Rhea!" I exclaimed. "Are you okay?" She looked at me happily and wagged her tail, a picture of unconditional love and devotion.

With a full heart I looked down upon her face. She had become so old! Her face was now white where it had once been black, and her body, once round and full with health and energy, was now angular and stiff. She could no longer accompany me on my Sunday walks; the most she could do was totter around here and there, from sunlight to shade and back again. I stroked her face and thought back to the day I had found her, some fifteen years before. She had been my constant companion ever since, the best friend I ever had, and had trained with me for twelve years at the monastery, keeping me company and soothing my heart each day in the silence. "Oh, Rhea!" I whispered, hugging her. "Where did the time go?"

The next morning her bed was wet again. After consulting with the Roshi I decided to take her to a veterinarian. The vet did some tests and learned that Rhea was in the early stages of kidney disease. "It is not reversible," the vet said softly. "You can help her to be more comfortable with appropriate care, but I'm afraid there is nothing beyond this that we can do. I'm sorry," she added when she saw my tears. "This is hard news, I know. Rhea has some months still to live, maybe more—but probably not a lot more."

I looked down at Rhea, who was gazing up at me as she so often did, with absolute trust in my ability to care for her. I petted her gently. "We have been through so much together!" I said, partly to the vet, but more to Rhea. "It looks like we have just one more thing left to do."

Gradually, Rhea declined between that day in early March and the beginning of July. I did everything in my power to help her, but that was little. I bought her special food to eat that would cause her body less pain to digest. Even then I could only persuade her to eat a small bit each day. Then I began to cook her food, following recipes that the vet had given me. For a time, this revived Rhea's appetite, but only for a time. Then she refused to eat altogether. After two days of this I drove to town to buy her a package of treats—the sort that she had delighted in when she was well. I opened the package and poured the entire contents in front of her nose where she was resting in the shade on the west porch. "Rhea, sweetheart—please eat," I said, but Rhea did not move. She could only stand on her own with great effort at this point. She just looked at me and weakly wagged her tail. She seemed happy—even serene—but it became clear to me in that moment that she was finished living. Her eyes, it seemed to me, were full of the deep wisdom that inhabits Life in all forms, and of perfect love for me. "This is it, isn't it, Rhea?" I cried softly, then hugged her little furry body in my arms. "It's time for you to go."

Rhea did not eat for twenty-six days. The vet advised me to give her fluids under the skin to prevent the pain of dehydration, but, otherwise, there was nothing I could do but love her while she died.

"Do you think we need to help her go?" I asked the Roshi.

"I think we need to let her tell us that," she replied. "If that is required at some point I feel sure you will know. In the meantime we need to attend to her carefully so that she can communicate what she needs. And we need to honor her for all she has given us in her life and hold her in compassionate awareness while she waits for her time."

That is what we did, for twenty-six days. I made a place for her to rest and wait where the other monks would see and visit her often so that they could participate in her dying process as I did. Much of the time during those days someone attended to her, stroking her body while she breathed. She seemed quite comfortable and content—as happy as ever, perhaps. Day after day she walked the line between life and death. In the evenings I loaded her into a monastery car and drove her to my hermitage, where I could sleep beside her all night long. It was a most beautiful time. I felt profoundly grateful for the opportunity to fully say good-bye to her, and I thanked her every night before we went to sleep for the gift of another day. I also thanked her for going on ahead of me and showing me so bravely how to die.

Every morning when I awoke I looked to see if Rhea was still living. When I reached over to touch her body she would wag her tail as if to say, "I'm still here!" It seemed that we went on in this way for lifetimes. Then one night I awoke to a horrible sound she had not made before—Rhea was struggling to breathe. I sat up and turned on the light. Rhea looked at me with the most serious eyes imaginable. Something, I could see, had changed—she was suffering now. I sat and stroked her the rest of the night and listened to her labored breath. By morning I knew what I had to do.

In the morning, with the Roshi's approval, I sent another monk to town to see the veterinarian. We had arranged for a tranquilizer to be provided, if needed, that would put Rhea to sleep before we took her in to the clinic for the fatal shot. That way she could experience her last conscious moments at the monastery, where she had spent most of her life, among people who loved and cared for her. The monk returned some time later with a vial and a syringe. I took them from her and set them near Rhea's bed.

Next I gathered the monks together and asked them to say their good-byes if they wished. One by one they did. The Roshi was the last. Then all the monks departed and left Rhea and I alone together.

"This is it, sweetheart," I said to her. "Thank you so much for all that you have given me. You did a wonderful job—more wonderful than words can say. Thank you most of all for teaching me how to love. I will miss you tremendously, little one. Don't worry about me, though. I will be okay. Go quickly and gently to the next place, wherever that may be. If it is good and right that we see each other there some day, help me to recognize you, will you? Take good care, my friend. I love you."

Rhea watched while I punctured the vial with the syringe and drew up the liquid that would put her to sleep. Then I gave her the dose and held her while she went away.

I sat still with her for some time, then I carried her to the car and drove to town. The people in the veterinarian's office gawked at me as I came through the door. I can only imagine how I appeared to them, with the limp form of Rhea's body cradled in my arms and tears streaming down my face. The vet was wonderfully kind. "You are being very brave," she said to me, as if I were a child—which I suppose I was in many ways. I held Rhea's head in my hands while the vet administered the fatal dose. Suddenly it was over, and my time with Rhea was done.

On the way back home with Rhea's body I bought a large metal tub and several blocks of ice. Back at the monastery I put the ice in the tub, covered it with towels, and then laid Rhea's body on top. I set a mat and a meditation cushion beside the body so that people could meditate beside her if they wished. It is our tradition to sit with the body for three days while the spirit moves on. The Roshi had advised me that I would know when Rhea's spirit finally passed. "You will feel it go," she said. She was right. On the morning of the third day, as I meditated by Rhea's body, suddenly I felt something lift inside of me and I knew that she was gone. A few moments later I stood up, then left to dig the grave.

That afternoon we held Rhea's funeral. After the monks gathered together I picked up her body and held it in my arms while the monks formed a line behind me, single file. Slowly we walked in unison around the property, visiting all the places Rhea had enjoyed, until our journey finally ended at the grave. I laid the body down before the deep hole I had dug, and for a time we exchanged stories about Rhea and expressed our appreciation for her life and all she had given. I told the story of our time together before Rhea and I had entered the monastery, which none of the monks had heard before. Then I lowered the body into the hole, wrapped in the blanket Rhea had used for years. Before I covered her, I took my beads from around my neck, bowed deeply, and draped them over Rhea's body. The Roshi nodded her approval—Rhea was a monk as much as I. I tossed the first shovel-full of earth into the hole, then passed the shovel on to the next monk in line. For the next fifteen minutes we passed the shovel around the circle, burying Rhea one shovel-full at a time. Next we piled some stones on the grave to mark it and bowed deeply as a group. Then we dispersed.

My heart opened as wide as heaven as the others departed. "I will follow you soon, sweetheart," I whispered. By most standards, I was and still am a young man, but it was clearer in that moment than ever before that death would find me one day as well, and soon. As I turned away from the grave, with my own death in my eyes and my love for Rhea and for life itself breaking my full heart, I vowed to live the remainder of my life as deeply and as fully as I am able. I vowed to remain true to my calling, whatever that may prove to be as it unfolds; to be as present as I am able to each moment as it arises; and to embrace all that Life brings my way. Above everything else, I realized, I wish to practice. I want to wake up and end suffering, and I want to give what I can from what I have. As I walked away from Rhea's grave with the shovel on my shoulder, I looked back over all that had passed—all that I had been through before and since I became a monk—and knew that I was blessed. "My life is yours," I said to Life. "Do with me what you will." With that I returned the shovel to its proper place, made a deep bow of appreciation for its service, then mindfully went back to work.

Afterword

So ends the text that I wrote at the monastery. My assumption when I finished it was that I would remain, training in the silence until my final day. I intended that the book be published without the story of my departure from the monastery, as I did not expect for there to be one. As it turns out, there was in fact a departure. This leaves me with one more story to tell.

I have debated with myself for some time over the wisdom of offering this final tale. The events that occurred, and particularly the role of the Roshi in my departure, are surrounded by an ambiguity that was violently unsettling to me at the time and could be confusing to the reader, who is used to seeing her in a clear light. I worry that the story will be misunderstood and cast a shadow of doubt over what has come before. In the end I have decided to share it, however, for the good I imagine it will do me. The telling of it, I believe, will wash away whatever residue remains of those final years of my training, so that I may move cleanly into the new life as has appeared before me since I left the monastery. I would ask the reader to avoid making assumptions about what follows. The bond between student and teacher in a Zen monastery is unlike any other; the rules and expectations involved are radically different from those that guide more usual relationships, as is the intended outcome. My interconnection with the Roshi had just one purpose: to end suffering through whatever means were necessary. It would be best to keep this in mind as you read what follows.

A change began to occur towards the beginning of my sixteenth year of training. I began to play a sort of game with the Roshi that we had not played before. It was a deep, intricate game that had my future and possibly the state of my "immortal soul" (a favorite expression of the Roshi's) at stake. The game was ever-present; we played it through every aspect of my monastic life, and yet we never spoke of it. I understood even then that to acknowledge the game was to spoil it and lose the opportunity that it presented me. This is because the nature of the game was to teach me to find my own clarity. Though I played it overtly in relationship with the Roshi, in reality I played it within my own mind. It was there, in my own intimate relationship with myself, and on my own, that the work needed to be done. The Roshi orchestrated the game and maintained the structures that made it possible; she prodded me when needed and gave me a kick in the pants when prodding was not enough, but in such a way that her attention to my training was disguised. It seemed as if I was, in fact, without the support of her compassion, and I was always left wondering what she was really up to.

The central question of this time was never answered. Before this I always had the Roshi's authority to assist me in sorting out what occurred along my wandering spiritual journey. There was a sense of safety in this arrangement that I leaned on: I emerged from every scrape and tussle with a clear understanding of the skirmish that had happened and a sense of the places where I had acted skillfully and those where I had not. If I could not see these things on my own, the Roshi would assist and then guide me towards the next steps in my spiritual work. During those final monastic years, as the decision gradually matured within me to leave the monastery and head out into the world on my own, I acted apart from her guidance, as I never had before. Naturally, I wondered if I were deluded or inspired. Or somehow both? Many things were said and done through that difficult time, and I wonder what actually happened: did I continue to tread faithfully along the path I had followed from the beginning, only under my own impetus, or did I lose my way? There is no way to know for sure. I will offer the interpretation that seems true to my heart, as this is all I have, with the understanding that I may have been deceived at the crucial moment.

You likely recall that I struggled from the beginning against my commitment to monastic life. Most of this, I know, was simply the resistance of conditioned mind against the transformation that occurred. It always seemed to me, however, that there was something in it that could not be explained away as resistance; that there was a backbone of real intuition within the reluctance I felt to give myself over to my life as a monk without question. Something through all those years was working itself out in the depths of my mind, sensed but unknown. During the time of trouble that followed my first trip to Africa this something came closest to the surface, but it was not ready then to manifest—it had too much desire and confusion in it—and so it plunged back down beneath awareness to be purified. Six years of relative quiet passed after the trouble until the time came for it to rise again—this time, perhaps, to be resolved.

I began to be aware that I no longer felt called to be a monk. I would have said so at various times from the beginning, of course, but this appeared differently to me: it seemed to come from a place of acceptance rather than resistance. It felt like a moving towards rather than a running away. I felt called towards something else, something new, with different challenges and forgotten opportunities. I did not know what that was, or why it was given to me, but I began to feel that there was some other life that had waited all the previous years of training for me to become ready for it, and the time was now at hand.

At the crossroads of this possibility lay my relationship to the Roshi. In many ways she and I were as a parent to a child. It seems natural that at some point I would need to leave the nest in order to fully mature as a human; otherwise it would be too easy to remain the child and to hold the Roshi responsible for my life and for my choices. There was often talk of the need to grow up within the monastic structure and change the dependent nature of our relationship to the Roshi, but I was not able to do it while remaining under her tutelage. I did not see others accomplish this, either. The power of her authority was just too great. Gradually I began to accept that I must turn towards the Guidance within myself, and that I must act from that Guidance as best I could in order to free myself from dependence upon the Roshi and fully accept responsibility for my life.

There was a problem with this plan, however: conditioned mind did not agree. From its point of view, the correct and noble choice was to remain a monk forever. Conditioned mind will always object to the guidance of Life, of course, no matter what position this requires it to take. The moment I began to actually consider choosing another way, conditioned mind labelled this possibility as bad and wrong. I believed the voices—the choice was terrifying, after all—and so I fought against it with all my might. I believed that my integrity lay with the choice to stay, that my heart demanded it, that all my future happiness depended on it, and so I worked to close the door that had begun to open. I imagined I must save myself from the disaster of abandoning my training before it had flourished, and the life of suffering and unhappiness that it seemed would inevitably follow. I just wanted to peacefully pursue what had become the easier way, but I could no longer do it. Self-hatred bludgeoned me whenever thoughts arose of having real choice, but the beatings were not enough to drive them from my mind.

From the beginning of my monastic journey my dream had been that one day, when the Roshi and I were both prepared, I would take her place in some capacity. For many years this seemed likely, even certain. Even during the time of trouble I described earlier this remained a possibility. To depart was to give that up and sink down to some much humbler destiny. What would become of me, I wondered, if I left the monastery without having accessed the clarity I had gone there to achieve? It seemed there would be nothing left but a life centered upon that catastrophe. Conditioning had me in a bind, you see: it set things up such that there was no way out except through the door that was no longer open to me. I can see now that it was not open—I was not called to be a monk the rest of my days—but not so then, and so it seemed to be my failure that the door was closed.

I sought assistance from the Roshi many times as the struggle continued, of course. She remained neutral on the content, as she must, and would not advise me what to do. She pushed me on the process level with painful incisiveness, however. We had the same conversation over and over again. It went something like this:

"I feel trapped!" I would say, or something similar.

"You are trapped," she would reply. Sometimes she would smile and laugh with mock wickedness. Other times she would frown, but her message was clear either way: there was something I could not see that all my confusion rested upon, and it was critical that I see through this something and be free.

"What is the trap?"

"You are tangled in identity," she invariably said. "You believe in a self that is separate from Life, and there isn't one."

"You mean I still believe in 'Dave'?"

"Yes, indeed. And bigger than that: you believe in the reality of conditioned mind."

"I get that, but I can't manage to shake it loose. How can I see through the illusion of separation?"

"This is the point in the conversation where I always bring up the Einstein quote. 'You can't solve a problem,' he said, 'with the same mind that created it.' Conditioned mind, ego, is a fiction, a mirage. It is what you are attempting to go beyond, not the means to get there. Dave is not real and so cannot truly see. When you cease to believe in the reality of a separate identity, then you will truly see him, and you will see as well what else you truly are. As long as you believe in conditioning, believe that you are ego, you are lost and can accomplish nothing."

I understood what she meant intellectually, as I had for many years at this point, but I was unable to see my way out of the bind in terms of my actual life. I sensed the blindness I suffered from, and I acutely experienced the misery of it, but I still felt powerless to escape. I even understood that the failure I felt was ego's failure, not mine. There is no such thing as failure in the present moment, when we are in touch with our true nature. This understanding was not enough, however, to open up a way to a larger awareness that included identity, and so I doubly suffered, believing in an illusion and knowing it to be an illusion at the same time.

The Roshi took pity upon my desperation at one point and offered me a potential way out. It happened during a meeting in the meditation hall, with the Roshi sitting at the front of the room and the monks forming a circle around her on their cushions, as was the custom. Immediately after a conversation such as the one outlined above, the Roshi paused for a moment and looked intently at me, as if making up her mind about something. "Dave," she said finally, "I have an idea. What if we were to start calling you by your middle name? That may be just enough to push you outside of the identity, where you can see it. What do you think?"

"Sure!" I said, without any hesitation. I sensed instantly what a good idea it was. The Roshi then asked the other monks if they were willing to assist me in this way. They said yes, and just like that it was done. From that moment onwards I was called "Justin" as if I had never worn any other name.

The effect of this little trick was imperceptible at first, but over time it worked: identifying as "Justin" gave me permission to recreate myself, in a way, and it helped me to see the "me" I had believed in for so long. I lived as both, actually, in parallel: the false me, with all his dysfunction and unhappiness, and the natural, happy possibility that the practice uncovered within me. It felt good to have a name for my authentic nature, and more power to choose to be who I wanted rather than who I had to be out of habit and unconsciousness.

Gradually, as I worked through my confusion, my relationship with the Roshi began to change. This is, for me, the most fascinating aspect of my entire monastic adventure and the one I feel the most curious about now. Gradually the Roshi began to harden towards me. There were still flashes of kindness here and there, and occasionally I felt connected with her in the same way I had before, but more and more I began to receive what felt like disapproval. Her feedback went from honest, to hard, to harsh, in my perception. There were occasions where she just clobbered me for things I had done or said. The Roshi had always been tough—this is a part of the teacher's job description, going back to the beginnings of Zen—but never unfair. Over time it seemed to me that she lost the calm good humor that had been her calling card before. I had always feared her because of her awareness and her honesty; now I began to fear her because she seemed volatile and unreasonable. The summer of my seventeenth year I almost up and left after some particularly harsh feedback. She began to exhibit an impatience with me that I had never seen before, and what appeared to be dislike.

Towards the end the Roshi appeared to resent my presence at the monastery and the time I required of her. A couple of months before my departure she told me that she regretted the time she had put into me over the years. She said that I had not taken advantage of her teaching, that I had chosen to remain safe and defend ego instead of doing the work I had come to the monastery to do. She said, essentially, that I had indeed failed; that I had chosen conditioned mind over freedom and so had missed the opportunity she and Life had offered me.

The change was hideous to bear. I loved the Roshi as I had loved no other before. I loved her for the compassionate being that she had created herself to be. She had given my life back to me through her teachings; she had taught me how to love myself and others, and how to enjoy this human life, which had seemed so worthless and confusing before. It hurt more than I can express to lose her approval and her trust. I felt like an outcast, even at the monastery, where I interacted with her almost every day. I could not but accept what she said—she was my teacher— and the shame and guilt with which I received her final assessment cut deep. I tried everything to regain her approval, but with no success. I would work hard for weeks, even months, to accomplish what she set out for me to do, and generally would feel pleased with myself as a result, but sooner or later the Roshi would stride in and strike it all down, dismissing my work as more failure. I suffered a great deal as a monk over the years, but this was the worst. It seemed I had lost everything.

Looking back, I wonder what all of that was about. It would be simple to take everything at face value and leave it there—and perhaps that is the correct place to leave it. Perhaps all that happened is that I failed and lost the trust of my teacher because of it. It would be easy and convenient to assume the opposite, that it was the compassion of the Roshi that failed, that she failed to see and understand what it was I went through and what I needed, and that she judged instead of accepting at a critical moment. I do not expect to ever know what really happened, but my heart says it was neither of those. I now believe that all of this was a part of the game she played with me, a masterful game that led me finally to act for myself and take responsibility for my life as I needed to in order to mature as a person.

She must have seen that it was time for me to go. She could not simply tell me to go, however, because then it would have been her decision, not mine. This would violate the independence I needed, and, in addition, would set things up such that I could blame her if things did not go well. Her hands were tied, she could not act in any overt way; her only option was to push me covertly to do for myself what I needed to do. So she cut the ties that bound us together. At first she tried just removing the supports she had provided for so long. This was not enough to overcome my stubborn dependence upon her, so she began to employ more direct means. In the end she had to reject me entirely in order to break the bonds and force me to choose my own way, through my own clarity and compassion. If this was indeed the game she played, then I bow down to her as a true master.

This possibility did not occur to me at the time; mostly I just thought she was a witch. Gradually the situation became unbearable. As it did, the beginning of my seventeenth year rolled around. Seventeen years is a long time to live in silence, to practice every day all day, and to do without all the pleasures and distractions of a worldly life. It seemed I should have finished by now: that I should have succeeded and stepped into a larger life. This obviously had not happened, and it appeared would never happen. Eight more months passed with no improvement, and I despaired. Every day it seemed I could not sink deeper into failure, and every day I found a still more abject state of failure to fall into. My state of mind went from desperate to hopeless. Finally I admitted to myself that what I desired in my heart would never happen: that I would never be free and truly happy. And so I gave up. I ceased to strive. It was done.

It was then, naturally, that the miracle happened. One Sunday afternoon I headed down the path towards the creek and beyond, as usual. It was late summer. The wildflowers had come and gone already; the creek was dry; and the gentle slopes of the hills all around were covered by knee-high, brown grass that waved serenely in the breeze. It was blazing hot, as I recall. My plan was to walk off my despair all afternoon and return late in the evening. I relished my Sunday walk as the one time when I could escape, at least in outward form, from all the trouble and angst that besieged me the rest of the week. For a time, I could forget that I was a monk, that I had failed as a monk, and just walk down a country road. Ordinarily as I returned to the monastery property I retrieved my unhappiness to carry like a sack of stones for another week, but not this time. This time, at last, Life in its infinite goodness and mercy saved me from myself.

It was the simplest thing in the world. I just let it all go—all the struggle, all the guilt and shame, all the humiliation, all the self-blame and self-hatred—or it let go of me, and I stepped free into a place of tremendous grace. This was the same movement that had happened ten thousand times since I first entered the monastery, only bigger. It always goes the same way, for me and probably for everyone: first a new possibility arises, then conditioned mind resists. Conditioning tends to have all or most of the power in a person's life, and so identification happens as soon as a new possibility occurs as a way to shut it down. With the identification inevitably comes suffering. We suffer and suffer and suffer until we just can't suffer any more. The pressure of our unhappiness becomes unbearable, and then, finally, just at the point where we give up, the letting go happens.

Suddenly the suffering disappears, the heart opens, we are in touch again with Life rather than only with conditioning, and we can see how we have been deceived. As I broke free I realized that I had wanted freedom as "Dave", not real freedom. I wanted a freedom in which "I" could be "myself" and be rewarded for it. "I" wanted to be looked up to and admired; "I" wanted to maintain selfishness and autonomy; "I" wanted to be, in the Roshi's phrase, "an enlightened ego". Real freedom includes a deep and transcendent humility which "I" does not desire. The entire existence of ego is built upon the arrogant assumption that it exists, and, in its existence, should be as mighty as a god, with the power to force Life to go where it wills. Seeing this, I finally gave up trying to succeed as "Dave". Instead, I stepped back into a much larger sense of myself which did not include a "self". I remembered who I truly am, and as I did, a tremendous flood of compassion and acceptance washed over me.

I laughed out loud, right there in the middle of that dusty road in California, to see how I had been fooled, and for so long. There is nothing to accomplish, I saw, nothing to become, no such thing as failure. Those were just the bars of my cage. I could just be myself, whatever that might be in each moment, with no need for self-consciousness. There was nothing wrong with me, and there never had been. Who I intrinsically am is beautiful, perfect, exquisite, as is everything else that exists in this amazing world. There was no need for me to be anything particular any more: I could just be, and live in the joy of that being.

I look at that experience now as the fulfillment of my monastic training. It was tiny and sweet, just as I might have wished for, I shed a few tears, but that was all. And yet it was everything I had worked for and hoped for during all the years that preceded it. I received finally what I had entered the monastery to gain: that compassion, that beautiful acceptance, was my reward for all the hard work and determination I had put into my spiritual life. I saw that the voices had convinced me of the opposite of the truth, as they always attempt to do. I had not failed at all. Ego had failed, it is true, and it would never get what it wanted, but that is a happy thing. I cannot say that I succeeded, because there is no "I" to succeed any more than there is a "Dave"; no such thing as "success" any more than "failure", but I felt in my heart that what needed to happen had happened at last. In the days that followed many new insights flooded through the opening this letting go had created, adding detail to my understanding of what had occurred, but the basis of it remained fundamentally the same. There is no "I" to suffer: there is only the peace of pure being.

Suddenly I knew what I needed to do. I did not reason it, just as in the time when I first realized I needed to go to the monastery. Suddenly it was there, the understanding and acceptance that it was time to seek new challenges on my own. I had no idea what form this would take, but I imagined that Life was inviting me to leave the silence to be with people in a more normal way, to take my practice into the world and test it there, to learn from new sorts of relationships, to see Life from other points of view. At long last it was time to go, and I felt no doubt or hesitation.

The next day I told the Roshi. She remained perfectly enigmatic. "Okay," was all she said.

She and I arranged that I would take a month to get my things in order, to make a plan for myself, and to pass off my responsibilities to the other monks. I set about those tasks with great excitement, wonder, and happiness. I enjoyed the great blessing of having no regrets. Over and over I marveled at the perfection of my life, and that I departed at exactly the moment when I was ready. Before this would have been too soon: I would have left something unfinished behind to wonder over during the years to come. I knew I had accomplished what I had set out to do, that it was completely done, so there was no reason to look backwards. I could just look forward to whatever awaited me in the world beyond the monastery gates.

My unknown future scared me at times. I had no idea what would become of me. I had not worked for money for eighteen years, had not been free to decide on my own how I would spend my time, how I would pursue my practice, what I would eat and wear. I had not loved a woman in all that time. I wondered how I would support myself, where I would go, what I would do with the remaining years of my life. I trusted I would be taken care of, however: that the force of compassion that had brought me to the monastery, that had supported me through all the years of my training, and that now asked for me to go, would provide whatever I needed. And this has proven to be the case. Since I departed I have been most fortunate.

I was scheduled to depart on a Monday. That Sunday afternoon, instead of my usual long romp in the country, I spent my free time packing up and cleaning out my hermitage. This task seemed perfectly natural and absolutely surreal at the same time. It felt absolutely correct that I should go, and yet it was nearly impossible to believe that the sometimes joyful and often painful journey I had embarked upon nearly eighteen years before had come to an end. I felt a pang of regret as I began carrying boxes of my belongings outside my hermitage. That tiny building with its bare walls and mismatched windows, with its woodstove and its rocking chair, had been a great friend to me through tremendous stress and trouble. It was hard to say goodbye. And yet say goodbye I must, and hope that Life would provide me with another home, just as safe and comfortable as this one.

Towards the end of the afternoon I loaded a monastery truck with some trash to take to the dump. As I drove past the monastery gates I spied the Roshi. She was walking along the road, almost as if she were expecting me. I felt surprised and nervous to see her: I had interacted with her but a few times since my decision to depart, and only on matters of business. It frightened me to imagine how she might respond to this, our final meeting as monk and teacher and possibly our last conversation in this life. To my relief, as I pulled up beside her and rolled down the window, she smiled and laughed contentedly.

"Ah! We might have guessed this would happen, don't you think?" she said, and laughed again. Gone was the dreaded tension of the previous two years. I perceived at once that the game we had played was finished, that her work with me was done, whatever that was from her perspective, and that we were free to just enjoy the moment together as in days gone by.

"I'm grateful for the chance," I replied. "I had hoped to speak with you again before tomorrow."

"Chance?" she said, as if wondering aloud at the word. "Perhaps…. Did you have something in particular you wanted to say?"

"Only thank-you," I replied softly, my voice choked unexpectedly with emotion. Tears sprang up in my eyes and began to roll down my face. I had loved and feared this person so much, had suffered and received so much under her guidance, had lost and gained more that I could ever express, more that I could ever know. She had taught me how to love, and how to live. "You have given my life to me," I continued. "I would have lost it without your help. You have given me the greatest thing one human may offer to another… Thank you."

"Think nothing of it," she responded. "This is what you and I both are here to do." Time stood still as I received her words. That moment was so simple—there we were, just two people talking on a dirt road on a sunny afternoon—and yet so profound. We both smiled at the awesome implications of that moment, with all that had come before, and all the unknown adventure that was yet to be.

"I also want to acknowledge what a huge pain in the ass I have been for you all these years," I said finally. The Roshi laughed heartily at this but allowed me to continue. "I hate to think of all the trouble I have put you through. Will you forgive me?"

The Roshi became suddenly serious, and peered intently at my face through the window. "It is not a question of forgiveness," she said. "The question for me is this: how will you use the gift? My teacher often said that the gift of the teachings is one that can only be repaid with the same coin. Will you repay it in whatever way Life offers to you, or will you hoard it for yourself?"

The Roshi gave me a moment to consider this, then continued, "Will you accept one final bit of coaching?"

"Of course."

"Justin," she said, "nothing begins or ends tomorrow. I trust you are aware of that. Your practice continues unless you choose to abandon it. If anything, you must work even more diligently to maintain your practice out there..." She waved her hand down the road, indicating the vast world that it led to. "Where there is little support for it. I predict that your practice will be tested in ways you cannot even imagine now. I need nothing from you in this—our time together is done, at least for now—but I do have a hope for you, that you will not squander the opportunity you have been given; that you will not spend it maintaining a separate self but will continue to work to realize your true nature and to be open to Life for its guidance. If you close that door you will be lost, but if you keep it open, well…. who knows the good you could do?" With this the Roshi smiled deeply to me. It was, I believe, her final blessing.

I thanked her and drove off with tears in my eyes. I have not spoken with her since.

I had arranged with my brother to drive down the next morning to his apartment in San Francisco. To that end I had rented a truck from a local company to carry my things. The next morning I left a little after dawn to walk to town to pick it up—a four-hour journey. The monastery would have assigned one of the monks to take me, I'm sure, if I had asked for the favor, but I wanted one last romp along the creek road before I departed. And what a glorious romp it was! How many hundreds of times had I walked that way in years past, and in how many different states of mind and heart? I knew every bump in it, every twist and turn of the creek that flowed along its dusty edge. Many of the great pines and buckeyes along the way were ancient acquaintances of mine; many of the half-hidden stones beneath my feet had witnessed both my triumphs and my despair. The sun rose early over the road. I began to sweat before I was half-way to my destination and took a last, unplanned dip in my favorite swimming-hole. My heart was light as a butterfly, and my mind soared. I had dreamt of this day so many times before and it had come at last, with all of the happiness and excitement that I had anticipated. The leaves of the trees waved good-bye to me as I walked past, and the stream sang to me of hope and the great love for Life that filled my heart.

I emerged into town as if onto an alien planet and arrived at the rental place as they opened. A few minutes later I pulled the truck out onto the street and turned it towards the monastery. The gate was closed when I arrived. As I got out to open it, I paused for a few moments to breathe and take in what was happening. Driving past the main buildings, I thought of my fellow monks. They would be busy about their tasks, I knew. I imagined them looking up to determine the source of the noise I made coming down the road. Other than the Roshi and the acting head monk, none of them knew I was leaving that day, or that I planned to depart at all. I drove to my hermitage, then spent a couple of hours packing my belongings into the truck and doing a final cleaning. I started the truck, but before I left I made a deep bow to my hermitage and to the monastery property, which had sheltered me for so long and had taught me so much. On the way out I passed the buildings again. There was no farewell offered to me—not a wave, or even a glance—and I had expected none. I left as I had arrived: in silence, a lone seeker after truth and happiness.

With my heart full and tears in my eyes I followed the familiar roads to town. Once in town I chose the highway that lead down into the valley. I felt proud and happy as I drove. "I did it!" I shouted to the sky, to the compassionate intelligence that had guided me so truly along my way. I had stayed until it was time to go, despite the hell I was required to endure to get there, and I left without regret. It was a tremendous accomplishment. I looked down the road towards my unknown destiny with hope and joy; I raised my eyes to the unseen author of that destiny with deeply felt gratitude and murmured a little prayer of thanks. All that had happened, I saw, was good.

For more information concerning the author's current work, which includes spiritual counselling, remote and in-person workshops, and a blog, please visit:
www.theoneopendoor.org

To contact the author directly, use this email address:
djmckay429@gmail.com

Made in the USA
Las Vegas, NV
18 January 2024

84553536R00152